CARE TO REMEMBER

Nursing and Midwifery in Ireland

edited by
Gerard M. Fealy

MERCIER PRESS

Mercier Press
Douglas Village, Cork
Email: books@mercierpress.ie
Website: www.mercierpress.ie

Trade enquiries to CMD Distribution
55A Spruce Avenue, Stillorgan Industrial Park
Blackrock, County Dublin
Tel: (01) 294 2560; Fax: (01) 294 2564
E-mail: cmd@columba.ie

ISBN 185635 456 3
10 9 8 7 6 5 4 3 2 1

A CIP record for this title is available
from the British Library

Mercier Press receives financial assistance from
the Arts Council/An Chomhairle Ealaíon

Printed in England by J. H. Haynes

CARE TO REMEMBER

CONTENTS

LIST OF CONTRIBUTORS

MARIE CARNEY is Head of School at the School of Nursing and Midwifery, University College Dublin (UCD). She is a registered general nurse, registered midwife and a registered nurse tutor. She holds an MBA from UCD and in 2003 was awarded a PhD in Health Service Strategic Management from the Michael Smurfit Business School, UCD. She is currently writing a book on strategic management in the health services.

DECLAN DEVANE is a registered general nurse, registered midwife and a registered nurse tutor. He holds a BSc from the University of the West of England and an MSc in Midwifery (Education) from UCD. He is a lecturer in midwifery at the School of Nursing and Midwifery Studies, Trinity College Dublin (TCD) and is currently undertaking a PhD, researching the implementation and evaluation of pilot midwifery-led services in the North Eastern Health Board.

GERARD M. FEALY is Director of Undergraduate Studies and Assistant Head of School at the School of Nursing and Midwifery, UCD. He is a registered general nurse, a registered psychiatric nurse and a registered nurse tutor. He holds a BNS and an MEd, and in 2003 obtained a PhD from UCD for a study of the history of apprenticeship nurse training in Ireland. He is currently preparing a book on the history of apprenticeship nurse training in Ireland for Routledge.

SIOBHAN HORGAN-RYAN is a registered general nurse and holds the Orthopaedic Nursing Certificate and the Intensive Therapy Nursing Certificate. Her clinical background is in adult and paediatric intensive care nursing, and she has worked in the intensive care units of the Royal City of Dublin Hospital, the Mater Misericordiae Hospital and Our Lady's Hospital for Sick Children. In 2005, she was awarded a PhD from the Department of History at UCC, for research into the career of nursing in Ireland between 1890 and 1920.

ANNE McMAHON is a midwife teacher at the National Maternity Hospital, Dublin. Following a period of teaching at second level and raising her children, she entered nurse training, qualifying as a general and sick children's nurse in 1986 and later as a midwife in 1990. She holds a postgraduate diploma in Adult Education, a diploma in Professional Studies in Midwifery and was awarded an MA in Women's Studies from UCD in 2000.

MARTIN McNAMARA is a lecturer at the School of Nursing and Midwifery, UCD. He is a registered general nurse, a registered psychiatric nurse and a registered nurse tutor. He holds degrees of MA (SocSci), MEd and BSc from The Open University and a degree of MSc (Nursing) from UCD. He is a course writer and tutor for the Open University and is currently pursuing a Doctorate in Education (EdD) with The Open University.

THERESE MEEHAN is a lecturer at the School of Nursing and Midwifery, UCD. She is a registered general nurse, a registered nurse tutor and holds an MA and PhD. She has published extensively on nursing policy, practice and history. She is a founding member of the Irish Society for Nursing and Midwifery History and is a member of the American Association for the History of Nursing.

JO MURPHY-LAWLESS is a sociologist and author of *Reading Birth and Death: a History of Obstetric Thinking* (Cork University Press, 1998). She has worked extensively on the issues of women and childbirth for over two decades. She is currently completing a research project on young women's fertility decision-making in the School of Nursing and Midwifery Studies, TCD for the Crisis Pregnancy Agency.

MALCOLM NEWBY is a freelance researcher/lecturer living in Lincolnshire. He holds a degree in History from King's College London, a postgraduate certificate in Education from Exeter University, and a diploma in the History of Medicine. He is a founding member of the Royal College of Nursing Society of Nursing History and served on its first executive committee. In the late 1980s, he moved into teaching film and media production and has co-produced a number of videos.

PETER NOLAN is currently Professor of Mental Health Nursing in a joint post between Staffordshire University and the South Staffordshire Healthcare Trust. His clinical nursing experience has ranged from working with substance abusers at St Thomas' Hospital, to working in various healthcare facilities in Libya, Egypt and the UK. His PhD, completed at Bath University, examined the evolution of psychiatric nursing in Britain.

MARY O'DOHERTY is archivist at the Mercer Library, Royal College of Surgeons in Ireland and is a leading authority on the archives of the history of medicine in Ireland. She has published a number of papers on the topic of medical historiography and, along with Davis Coakley, has co-edited *Borderlands: Essays on Literature and Medicine in Honour of JB Lyons*. With A. D. H. Browne she is also co-author of *The Art of Obstetrics*.

ANN SHERIDAN is a lecturer at the School of Nursing and Midwifery, UCD and was formerly Assistant Director to the Nursing and Midwifery Planning and Development Unit in the Eastern Regional Health Authority. She is a registered psychiatric nurse, a registered general nurse and a registered nurse tutor and is a former principal nurse tutor at St John of God Hospital, Stillorgan. Her PhD research analysed the activity patterns of psychiatric nurses practising in Ireland in the period 1950–2000.

MARGARET (PEARL) TREACY is Professor of Nursing and Director of Postgraduate Research at the School of Nursing and Midwifery, UCD and is Associate Dean of the Faculty of Medicine, UCD. She was awarded a PhD from the University of London in 1987 for research into the socialisation process in nursing education. As former Head of School at the School of Nursing and Midwifery UCD, she has led much of the developments in nursing education in Ireland, including the introduction of new undergraduate and postgraduate courses for nurses and midwives.

ANN WICKHAM is a historian and is currently lecturer and coordinator of the Bachelor of Nursing Studies programme at the National Distance Education Centre (Oscail) at DCU. She holds a PhD and her research interests include the development of women's occupations in the nineteenth century, nursing history and social policy. She is the author of *Women and Training* (Milton Keynes: Open University Press, 1986) and is a founding member of the Irish Society for Nursing and Midwifery History.

INTRODUCTION

Reflecting international interest in Irish social history, this collection of essays examines aspects of the history of Irish healthcare from the perspective of nurses and midwives.

A vibrant and scholarly collection that brings together for the first time in a single volume the work of some of the leading scholars writing in the field, the book reveals many previously hidden aspects of the social and professional histories of Irish nurses and midwives. It documents and analyses a range of diverse topics, including Irish military nursing in the Great War, early district nursing services in the west of Ireland, the work of psychiatric nurses in the 1950s, midwifery and childbirth in the early modern period, midwifery regulation, and the work of some of the first Irish and English hospital matrons.

The book also explores wider issues of concern to nurses and midwives, including the public image of Irish nurses in cinema and television, the quest for admission to the ranks of the learned professions through entry to the academy, and the role of caring in the new millennium.

The twelve essays draw together the fruits of recent scholarship and reflect a range of perspectives in the western European and American tradition of sociological and academic analyses. The aim is to present an authoritative collection of essays for scholars of Irish social history, Irish healthcare history and for a professional and lay readership. This book is a significant milestone in the international project of writing the history of nursing and midwifery.

Dr Gerard M. Fealy
School of Nursing and Midwifery
University College Dublin
September 2004

CHAPTER 1

Lessons from History

Gerard Fealy and Mary O'Doherty

For social practices like nursing and midwifery, knowledge of the past informs understandings of historical developments and establishes contexts for current developments. In common with the wider discipline of history, the writing of nursing and midwifery history has changed over time, such that distinct trends in subject matter and in the interpretation and narration of that history are evident.

How does the writing of nursing and midwifery history in Ireland compare with international developments and trends, in terms of its quality and its contribution to scholarship within and beyond the disciplines? Who writes the history of Irish nursing and midwifery and what are the themes and trends in the body of published work? In the accounts of the history of the Irish health services, how visible is the nurse and/or the midwife? For the would-be historian of nursing and midwifery in Ireland, where is the historical evidence to be found and how may that evidence be interpreted and presented?

Archives of Nursing and Midwifery in Ireland

Existence

The evidence of nursing and midwifery in the past is contained in published and unpublished documents and artefacts and in the *voices* of those who provide testimony, either through oral history or through letters and diaries. Much of the documentary evidence is located in historical archives. An archive is a collection of records, in whatever medium, brought together as a result of the private or professional activities of an individual or organisation and retained by the generating body or its successors, or transferred to the custody of an approved repository. Three broad aspects of archives relating to nursing and midwifery in Ireland may be considered, *viz.* their survival, their preservation and their retrieval. The historical record of nursing and midwifery in Ireland lies buried in archives belonging to other professions and institutions and, in the main, has to be gleaned by trawling these archives to recover details which were often incidental to the original recording purpose.

The archives of the medical profession, of Irish hospitals and of religious congregations record not only their own histories, but are also the principal and variable sources for nursing and midwifery history. For the most part, these archives remain in their establishment of origin where that establishment is stable and substantial. Others have been removed to secure repositories such as the National Archives, to newly built hospitals and to medical libraries, such as at the library and archives of the Royal College of Physicians of Ireland and the Mercer Library at the Royal College of Surgeons in Ireland. Some archives remain in situ in their place of origin and, while they have been surveyed, are in jeopardy of being lost.[1] Others are already lost.

Keeping track of archives of all types within Ireland has been fraught with difficulty. The *Directory of Irish Archives*, now in its fourth edition, starkly illustrates this both in its development and its standing.[2] The *Directory of Irish Archives* is an indispensable reference tool that has grown in its coverage and content from an initial 155 entries, detailing archives held in 1988, to 262 in 2003. A thorough perusal of this directory is a prerequisite for any study of Irish nursing and midwifery history and for any exploration of archives. Seamus Helferty and Raymond Refaussé's introduction to the fourth edition of the directory provides an invaluable and authoritative overview and explanation of this expansion in Irish archives over the previous fifteen years. It is as if the records of centuries are just recently being brought to light. While the documentation of the archives of medicine, nursing, and midwifery is increasingly covered in the *Directory of Irish Archives*, it nonetheless remains seriously deficient. The closure of unprecedented numbers of Dublin hospitals in the 1980s and 1990s clearly demonstrates the need for a list detailing where these various records ended up and what they comprise.[3] Records in long-standing institutions tend to be relegated to out-of-the-way stores, where they at least endure. In the event of any upheaval though, they are at risk of dispersal, although the risk of destruction is *theoretically* less possible since the enactment of the *National Archives Act* in 1986.

An example of the neglect and destruction referred to above appeared in the *Irish Journal of Medical Science* in 2004; Dr B. D. Kelly, when describing the research method of his paper on the topic of mental illness in nineteenth-century Ireland, a qualitative study based on workhouse records, remarked:

> Original workhouse records and minutes *recently uncovered* from the Ballinrobe Poor Law Union, County Mayo, were examined so as to extract all information relevant to the provision of healthcare and accommodation to the mentally ill in Ireland between 1845 and 1900 [my emphasis].[4]

Meanwhile, records that one might reasonably expect would be retained have been destroyed. The headline 'Destroying records was shortsighted' appeared in *The Irish Times* on 29 June 2004.[5] Written by the newspaper's health correspondent, Eithne Donnellan, the article in question referred to the annual report of the information commissioner, wherein a case had been referred to the commissioner where access had been sought to records of a procedure carried out at a Dublin maternity hospital in 1959. Responding to the information commissioner's enquiry, Donnellan reported that 'the Hospital produced extracts from Hospital Board meetings outlining the policy of retaining records dating back to 1968 on microfilm and stated that all records prior to 1968, apart from Labour Ward Register records, had been shredded.'[6] The article went on to state that 'the Hospital was unable to pinpoint the exact time period when the requester's records had been shredded or provide any certainty that the requester's records were among those shredded.' Affirming the position of the hospital that no further records existed, the information commissioner commented:

> The decision to destroy a vast body of medical records, personal to a large number of individuals, was at best lacking in foresight and would not today be considered good administrative or record management practice.[7]

The 'Annual Report of the Information Commissioner 2003', especially the part headed 'Records Management', makes for most interesting reading. In highlighting the practical application of archives theory and the implications of recent legislation in this regard, it relates very closely to the themes under consideration here.

The publication for the first time in 1997 of 'Standards for the Development of Archives Services in Ireland' reveals the level of neglect and the lack of care for archives in Ireland.[8] Since the Local Government Act of 1994 (Section 65), the statutory responsibility of local authorities to manage and preserve their archives has implications for the archives of nursing and midwifery. Present-day managers of institutions formerly associated with the Poor Relief (Ireland) Act of 1838 (i.e. the former workhouses) can at least nowadays be expected to recognise the nature of historical archives and their importance as a national resource. The 'Standards for the Development of Archives Services in Ireland' elucidates the nature of archives and how they should be treated, and includes information necessary for the understanding and use of archival material in historical studies.

Published as a booklet by the Local Authority Archivists' Group and launched by the Minister for the Environment in June 2004, *Local Authority Archives in Ireland* provides essential information on the nature and use of the archives held by local authorities in Ireland.[9] The archives of the Poor Law Unions and the boards of Health and Public Assistance are listed and briefly treated. Whatever possibilities these records hold for researching the history of Irish nursing and midwifery, the article by the historian Raymond Gillespie on 'the significance of local authority archives' contained in this publication is essential reading for anyone contemplating such research. Also essential reading for the would-be historian is an article by Margaret Ó hÓgartaigh entitled 'Archival sources for the history of professional women in late-nineteenth and early-twentieth century Ireland'.[10] Published in 1999, the article discusses archival sources in the areas of education, health, and the higher professions, and points to numerous sources for the history of nursing and midwifery.

Much that remains in archives exists as much by default as by design. As long as records were left alone, their very neglect assured their survival. It is hard to estimate the percentage of loss for the whole country. However, it is safe to suggest that it is greater than in other countries, such as England or France, the country of origin of archival science, where the written record was traditionally more highly valued.[11] At least since the passage of the *National Archives Act* in 1986 and other legislation in subsequent years, the future of extant archives is more assured. Bodies such as the National Archives of Ireland and the Society of Archivists Irish Region as well as the section of the History of Medicine of the Royal Academy of Medicine in Ireland (RAMI) exist, at the very least, as pressure groups with watchdog and advisory roles. In the case of nursing and midwifery, the Irish Society for Nursing and Midwifery History, a non-statutory voluntary group based in Dublin, is perhaps the closest analogue of these groups. However, An Bord Altranais (the Nursing Board), the regulatory authority for nursing, in meeting its statutory obligation to regulate nursing and midwifery, preserves important historical records and may act in an advisory role in the matter of archival materials that it holds.

By their very nature, archives tend to be secreted away in the recesses of institutions and organisations. Consequently, discovering the state of archival collections or the plans for their collection and preservation is a very real difficulty, and success in discovery can depend often on serendipity and diplomacy. Hospital closures and the re-organisation of health and local authorities represent hazards for the survival and transfer of archival collections. A survey of archives in the hospitals throughout Ireland undertaken in the mid 1990s by the ministerial-appointed Steering Group on Local Authority Records and Archives led to the recovery of much material in abject conditions.[12]

Preserving the Archives and Gaining Access

Numerous standards exist to ensure the preservation of various forms of archival material; all aspects of their physical care are documented and a helpful list of these standards provided in 'Standards for the Development of Archives Services in Ireland'. The real difficulty in Ireland is not in knowing how best to care for such collections, but in eliciting and securing the appropriate attitudes and necessary resources from those in charge of organisations. While legislation enacted since 1986 has undoubtedly brought a changed response in improved provision for archives, by their very nature, archives are far from being a priority for organisations whose primary objective is more likely to be the provision of some social service in the here-and-now. The appropriate keeping, housing and preservation of archives requires investment in essential related resources, including qualified staff and properly appointed repositories, all of which presuppose commitment on the part of an organisation to its archives and the concomitant financial investment.

Helferty and Refaussé refer to 'a more leisured and informed research clientele and one, it must be said, with ever higher expectations'.[13] This is borne out in the numbers engaged in research and the high standard of this work in nursing and midwifery in Ireland. A transformation has been taking place from an amateurish to a more scholarly and rigorous approach. As Eric Freeman remarked:

> ... the history of nursing was cursed with dull narrative and anecdotal accounts. Recently, there has been something of a minor renaissance in this blighted corner of medical history.[14]

While Freeman clearly, if erroneously, holds nursing history to be a part of medical history rather than a discipline in its own right, the point remains that nursing history was indeed a 'blighted corner'. In this regard, the absence of any reference to archival material in the bibliography of Pauline Scanlan's *The Irish Nurse* (1991) is telling.[15] Accounts of the history of Irish nursing prior to its publication were, according to Mary O'Doherty, 'mere scraps'.[16] An indication of the veritable renaissance that the writing of nursing and midwifery history now enjoys in Ireland can be seen by the greater usage of primary sources by scholars.

The organisation of archives entails setting up the means for their retrieval. Retrieval aids exist at a number of levels, from guides to an entire repository, to indexes to the collections, and lists of the items in a collection. There is much variation in the provision of retrieval aids from one repository to the next. Likewise, the publicising of archival holdings is also patchy. The more one considers the developments in Irish archives, the more obvious becomes the significance of the *Directory of Irish Archives*, which gives myriad points of entry to a wide variety of archival holdings. When used imaginatively, the directory opens up even more possibilities.

The nature of Irish nursing and midwifery archives is such that the historical researcher needs considerable ingenuity to track down the variety of primary sources. It is by exploring the links between individuals and organisations and between two or more organisations that one comes upon archives and private papers. Often there is no documentation or citation of such material in the lists or guides that repositories make available. Such lists rarely include every item of material in a repository. Due to the sensitive and confidential nature of hospital and medical records, access is usually restricted or often closed. Applications for access must be made in writing by *bona fide* researchers, who must sign forms of undertaking to comply with the conditions that apply if access is to be permitted.

The world-wide-web is an increasingly important means of finding out about aspects of nursing and midwifery history, especially in the way that it can present search results from diverse sources. In this connection, the 'links' option is often most helpful in directing the researcher to relevant websites. For example, the 'links' option on the website of the National Archives of Ireland[17] leads to a range of other websites, including *Irish Archives, Manuscript Libraries and Related Resources*.[18] This site, in turn, leads to Irish local authorities' websites. By selecting Donegal, for example, it is possible to turn up a treasure trove for the history of nursing and midwifery, such as 'Monthly Report of District Nurses, including Patient Visits at Home and in Dispensaries'. A wealth of primary sources for the history of nursing and midwifery in Ireland can be unearthed in this way.

One application of the web that is helpful for midwifery historians has been the posting of the *Catalogue Raisonné of Antiquarian Obstetric Books*, held in the libraries of the Royal College of Physicians of Ireland and the Royal College of Surgeons in Ireland. The former master of the Rotunda Hospital, Professor Alan Browne, has provided a catalogue of these works and a valuable commentary from the viewpoint of an obstetrician.[19] While this catalogue is of published works, searching various fields may yield information that points to original sources.

A variety of historical records is available in a range of locations, including university and municipal libraries and institutions. These include manuscripts and printed documents, such as the minute books and annual reports of institutions, hospitals and agencies.[20] Parliamentary papers, including reports of House of Commons select committees and parliamentary commissions, and reports of the debates of Dáil Éireann and Seanad Éireann constitute a major historical source.[21] These official publications include documentary evidence relating to policy and practice in healthcare, hospital management, medicine, nursing and midwifery, and professional education and training. The archives of An Bord Altranais contain important records for historians of nursing and midwifery. These include the minute books of the General Nursing Council for Ireland and An Bord Altranais as well as a wide range of official documents emanating from both.[22] Letters and early printed textbooks located in libraries, such as the library of the University of Dublin, also provide important source materials. Early nursing journals represent yet another source, since they contain evidence on what nurses were doing at the time the journal was written, evidence of the social conditions and aspirations of nurses, and evidence concerning the political and professional arguments that influenced the profession and its policy-makers.[23] Early professional journals contain records of appointments, retirements and obituaries while newspapers and periodicals are also important primary sources in that they provide reportage of past events as well as being a window on public opinion and lay interpretation and projection of nursing and midwifery.[24]

The establishment of the UK Centre for the History of Nursing, now located at the University of Manchester, means that internationally important archival collections will be widely accessible.[25] The centre has developed a website, which provides free access to the complete run of *Nursing Record*, one of the UK's first nursing journals. An invaluable resource for researchers of nursing and midwifery history, the site offers access to each page of the journal, giving insight into all aspects of nursing as a profession. It includes articles, photographs, illustrations and advertisements, with numerous references to nursing and midwifery in Ireland.[26]

Interpreting and Framing the Evidence

Since the functions of historical inquiry are to uncover evidence about the past and to interpret and present that evidence, then good history relies on good sources and good historians. In the debate concerning the functions and processes of historical enquiry, two divergent philosophical perspectives are evident. One perspective holds history to be concerned with the pursuit of objective truth concerning the past, while the other holds history to be concerned with interpreting the past based on the best available evidence.[27] These opposing perspectives are respectively represented in the writings of Geoffrey Elton and Edward Carr, and this 'history debate' places Elton and Carr on opposite ends of a science–art spectrum.[28] The locus of concern thus lies in the issue of *truth*: whether knowledge of history can ever be gained objectively or whether it is intersubjective and interpretive, whether history 'is innocent or ideological, unbiased or biased, fact or fancy'.[29] Beyond this art–science distinction is the post modern perspective; with its emphasis on language and discourse and its sceptical view of the historian's expert knowledge, post-modernism calls into question the possibility that objective historical truth can ever exist.[30] On this view, there may be multiple meanings when interpreting historical evidence.[31]

While interpretations should be made on the basis of the evidence to hand, they may also be informed by other scholarship in the field and by perspectives that best fit as explanatory frameworks. For example, the perspective of the sociologist or the anthropologist can inform the ways that historical evidence is interpreted and represented in the historical narrative. In the western European and American traditions of analyses, neo-Marxist, neo-Weberian, Foucaultian, and feminist perspectives can be used as modes of analysis and interpretation.[32] In the way that they challenge taken-for-granted assumptions about social history, these various perspectives permit historical interpretations that uncover the implicit and expose the less obvious aspects of social history.[33]

The discipline of history exhibits discernible trends in the subject matter that historians choose to deal with, and in the way that they write up that subject matter, that history. In this way, new subject matter and new interpretations can come to represent particular traditions of historical scholarship. For much of the twentieth century, 'political history' was the dominant tradition within the discipline; using politics and the state as a vehicle for understanding society, the tradition exhibited a consensus and linear view of history and it focused on great people and great events.[34] Thus, history took as its subject matter the major events and activities in the political macrocosm and historical narratives were framed from the perspective of the state and politics.

After the 1960s, political history began to be replaced by a more critical approach that took as its subject matter the lives and experiences of ordinary people in the events of history.[35] In the 1990s, the boundaries between political and social history began to be blurred, such that a new synthesis of social and political history was emerging.[36]

These wider trends in the practice of history tended to get replicated in the way that the history of healthcare, including the history of nursing, midwifery and medicine, was written.

International Trends in the Writing of Nursing History

The earliest nursing histories mirrored the wider consensus approach of medical historiography and, according to Connolly, differed from medical histories only in their greater focus on institutions, professional organisation and 'great women', as opposed to great men.[37] Early histories, such as the four-volume *A History of Nursing* by Lavinia Dock and Adelaide Nutting published in 1907, represented the history of nursing as a linear development towards ever-increasing progress and the general tone tended to be self-congratulatory.[38] These early progress-oriented accounts were typical of, what Christopher Maggs terms, the 'old historiographies', in the way they presented a 'cosy profession-centred celebration of [nursing's] past' and in the way that they represented nursing as a profession that emerged from the 'dark ages' into today's age of 'enlightenment'.[39] Reflecting professional agendas, they were written by nursing scholars whose principal concerns included women's suffrage, the pursuit of professional organisation, and international co-operation, and their writing represented an intrinsic part of the reform campaigns being pursued by their authors.[40]

The celebratory, progress-oriented, leadership-dominated trend in nursing historiography continued well into the twentieth century, until

Brian Abel-Smith's *A History of the Nursing Profession*.[41] Published in 1960, this seminal work focused on the development of the nursing profession within the context of changing patterns of medical care and the dominant role of the hospital.[42] Also representing the new idiom was Monica Baly's *Nursing and Social Change*, which examined the history of nursing within its wider social and economic contexts.[43] As one of the most prominent and prolific writers on nursing history, Baly also revised some of the popular beliefs surrounding the achievements of the Nightingale experiment at St Thomas' Hospital in her study *Florence Nightingale and the Nursing Legacy*.[44]

Rewriting Nursing History, a volume of essays edited by Celia Davies, has been characterised as 'the forerunner of a new historiography of nursing'.[45] Also described as 'mould-breaking', the book was published in 1980 and it addressed nursing history from perspectives of politics, class, gender, and nursing as an occupation; it examined issues such as recruitment and employment, patterns and characteristics of the nursing workforce, education and training patterns, and trade unionism.[46] Maggs' *The Origins of General Nursing*, an account of the experiences of nurses as workers, complemented the work of both Abel-Smith and Davies.[47] Written as social anthropology and couched in contemporary sociological argumentation, edited volumes such as *Anthropology and Nursing*, *An Introduction to the Social History of Nursing*, and *Nursing History and the Politics of Welfare*, added to the output of high quality scholarship in the social history of nursing and midwifery.[48] These 'critical' histories were complemented by new social histories of nurse training, including Anne-Marie Rafferty's *The Politics of Nursing Knowledge* and Ann Bradshaw's *The Nurse Apprentice*, both of which challenged earlier explanations and interpretations of that history.[49]

Retrieving Nursing History from Medical History

According to Edward Carr, when history is written, it is written from the perspective of the historian who is 'imbued with a particular view'.[50] This holds true for the writing of medical and nursing history. Thus while early medical historians attributed the advancement of nursing to the advancement of medical science, their nursing counterparts represented nursing as a discipline that had evolved from the sphere of private nursing and from the Nightingale experiment.[51] Like the approach of political history, the writing of the history of healthcare has exhibited a consensual, taken-for-granted determinism that was devoid of critical analysis or social context, representing a 'celebratory linearity', which Connolly depicts in the following terms:

> Traditional histories of healthcare were usually physician-driven enterprises, that romanticized heroic doctors, scientific discoveries, and technological innovations. These linear narratives … exalted Western medical knowledge, and presented science as offering unfettered, value-neutral gifts to humanity.[52]

This trend has been especially evident in the writing of Irish medical history; referring to this trend, Elizabeth Malcolm and Greta Jones observe:

> Developments [in Irish medicine] are praised uncritically and are portrayed as part of the inevitable progressive advance of modern medicine … many [publications on Irish medical history] are limited in scope and antiquarian in approach.[53]

Institutional histories and biographies have exhibited this same representational style and medical historians tend to adopt the approach of recording and praising the achievements of their predecessors in medical practice.[54] By focusing on the lives and achievements of past great medical men, traditional medical history has been narrated at the expense of the telling of histories of the other important participants in healthcare.[55] Despite a general trend towards a more critical social history of medicine in international scholarship, much contemporary medical history in Ireland continues to exhibit this traditional consensual style of narration.[56]

A considerable part of the history of nursing and midwifery in Ireland has been related within the genre of amateur medical historiography.[57] For this reason, it is largely imbued with the perspective of the doctor-historian. When describing the less enlightened past of nursing practice and the modern nurse's uneducated predecessor, many doctor-historians treat of the subject in a non-judgemental, light-hearted way.

They also tend to portray nurses as larger-than-life individuals or as caricatures and the nurse is frequently represented through the use of stereotypes, which variously invoke the drunk and incompetent untrained nurse, the oppressed probationer, the powerful ward sister, the loyal and devoted nurse, and the matron as firm-but-fair matriarch. Where great medical men get portrayed with reference to their achievements in medical science, nursing leaders get portrayed with reference to their personal characteristics and/or their style of leadership. Kirkpatrick's description of Miss Kelly, lady superintendent at Dr Steevens' Hospital, is typical of the manner in which many doctor-historians depict nurses in medical histories. Miss Kelly is the archetypal firm-but-fair matriarch:

> With her nurses, Miss Kelly was a strict disciplinarian. Thorough and energetic herself, she expected similar qualities in those who worked under her ... Gifted as she was with a wonderful command of language, a scolding by her was an experience that few nurses wished to repeat. Though strict and sometimes severe in her judgements, she was always ready to forgive and to forget when faults were atoned for; and her nurses never turned in vain to her for help when they were in trouble.[58]

With a few exceptions, the majority of hospital histories has been published in the late twentieth century.[59] Most are written by doctor-historians as either commemorative histories or as scholarly treatise in the amateur tradition; large differences in the quality of scholarship between and amongst these two categories is discernible.[60] Published to coincide with a significant anniversary or event in the life of a hospital, commemorative histories generally aim to celebrate rather than analyse and, in their general tone, they tend to be nostalgic and celebratory. Commemorative hospital histories include Freeman's *Mater Misericordiae Hospital Centenary 1861–1961*, Widdess' *The Charitable Infirmary, Jervis Street, Dublin, 1718–1968*, O'Brien's *The Charitable Infirmary, Jervis Street, 1781–1987: A Farewell Tribute* and O'Brien, Browne and O'Malley's *The House of Industry Hospitals: 1772–1987: the Richmond, Whitworth and Hardwicke (St Laurence's Hospital): a Closing Memoir*.[61]

In these commemorative histories, nursing tends to receive cursory mention only. For example, in O'Brien's history of the Charitable Infirmary, Brigid Walsh, a former principal nurse tutor at that hospital, contributes a chapter that includes passages on the appointment of the Sisters of Mercy, the establishment of the nurse training school and the achievements of former matrons Brigid Kelly and Anne Young.[62] O'Brien, Browne and O'Malley's history of the Richmond, Whitworth and Hardwicke hospitals contains a chapter on 'nursing in the Richmond'. Written by three former nurses of the hospital, the chapter includes anecdotes and 'reminiscences' on the past experiences of former nurses and it includes portraits of some former nurses, such as the larger-than-life Miss Ita Byrne, who 'ruled Theatre two with an arm of steel'.[63] Commemorating the 150th anniversary of the founding of the Adelaide Hospital, Mitchell's *A 'Peculiar' Place* includes a chapter on the School of Nursing.[64] Based on oral testimonies, what the author terms 'nurses' memories', the chapter includes a series of passages in which individual nurses relate their past experiences while working at the Adelaide. Sister M. Eugene Nolan's centenary history of Dublin's Mater Misericordiae Hospital is the only commemorative history of a Dublin hospital written by a nurse.[65] Ostensibly a history of the hospital's school of nursing and developments in nurse training, the work is interspersed with a chronology of the development of the hospital and its medical and surgical services, and it contains accounts of individual nurses and significant events in the life of the hospital.

Scholarly treatise in the amateur tradition of medical historiography include Lyons' *The Quality of Mercer's: the Story of Mercer's Hospital, 1734–1991*, Coakley's *Baggot Street: a Short History of the Royal City of Dublin Hospital*, Meenan's *St Vincent's Hospital 1834–1994: an Historical and Social Portrait* and Gatenby's *Dublin's Meath Hospital 1753–1996*.[66] Unlike commemorative histories, these publications adhere more strictly to the standards of historical scholarship, in terms of their use of primary sources. Like commemorative histories, however, they are essentially *medical* histories which contain mention of aspects of nursing history. They variously include passages on nurses' conditions of employment, nursing reform, details of misdemeanours and breaches of rules by nurses, commentary on the quality of nursing care, and short biographical accounts of former matrons. The experiences of probationers, the strictness of the regime of work and discipline, and the praiseworthy achievements of former matrons are common themes.

A history of the Royal Hospital Donnybrook by the social historian Helen Burke is an exception among the various hospital histories, in that it is not of the nature of a medical history.[67] Rather, it is a synthesis of social, medical, nursing and paramedical histories presented against the background of social and political change in Ireland. The work contains numerous references to nurses and the development of nursing services at the hospital. As a social history, Burke's account offers a more balanced portrayal of the history of a hospital, in the way that it implicitly recognises that a hospital's history is a function of the activities and ideas of many individuals and groups and that its development does not exist in isolation of wider social developments.

Nurses and Midwives in Social History

Aspects of the history of nursing and/or midwifery in Ireland are also found in social histories and include a number of studies of social policy and labour history that deal with the subject in a more critical way than do medical histories. Margaret Preston explores the role of upper-class women philanthropists in bringing about nursing and sanitary reform in Dublin, while Ann Wickham examines the role of the Dublin Hospital Sunday Fund in nursing reform during the late nineteenth century.[68] Margaret Ó hÓgartaigh explores a range of topics concerned with nurses and midwives as workers in Ireland, including their quest for professional identity, their conditions of employment, and the tensions and conflicts between religious and secular nurses.[69] The role of nuns in workhouse reform is explored in Maria Luddy's essay contained in Malcolm and Jones' edited collection *Medicine Disease and the State* and also in Burke's history of the Irish poor law system.[70] In her study of the professional lives of eight prominent leaders of modern nursing, Susan McGann includes a portrait of Margaret Huxley, Ireland's most influential nursing leader, and this work includes a discussion on the pursuit of state registration from the perspective of Irish nursing.[71] Ruth Barrington's political and social history of the Irish health services includes some mention of the development of nursing services, including references to the Jubilee and Lady Dudley nursing schemes.[72]

While doctor-historians and social historians have traditionally been the main wellspring for the writing of nursing and midwifery history in Ireland, there is an increasing output from nurse historians. Although limited in number, published works includes Scanlan's *The Irish Nurse: A Study of Nursing in Ireland, History and Education, 1718–1981*, a sprawling and diffuse history of nursing and midwifery in Ireland.[73] While not a definitive history, *The Irish Nurse* represents the seminal and most comprehensive work in the field. Covering a period of some 250 years, the book was researched in the early 1960s. Since the work was ostensibly concerned with the system of nurse training at that time, it did not aim to be a historical study *per se*. Nevertheless, a substantial part of the book deals with the history of nursing and midwifery; the author explores the origins of modern nursing and midwifery in Ireland, the growth of the Irish hospital, and the development of nurse training. Scanlan's narrative is more descriptive than critical. The work lacks an overall theme, thereby militating against a coherent narrative, and its broad scope is to the detriment of in-depth analysis, such that it lacks the perspective of contemporary critical scholarship.[74]

The Crimean War is viewed as an event of immense importance in the development of modern nursing and given the existence of official records and preserved diaries from the period, the history of military nursing in the Crimea has been the subject of numerous studies. The body of published scholarship on the topic includes Mary Ellen Doona's work, which examines the role of the Irish mission to the Crimea, and Therese Meehan's exposition and exploration of 'careful nursing', the system of sick nursing proffered by the Sisters of Mercy in the nineteenth century.[75] Sioban Nelson's examination of the influence of Irish denominational care on the emergence of modern secular nursing also points to the important role that the Irish Sisters of Mercy played in the development of modern nursing.[76] Other published works by nurse-historians include Meehan's short biographical portrait of Mary Quain, a district nurse-midwife practising in West Galway during the 1930s and 1940s, and Hanora Henry's commemorative history of the Irish Guild of Catholic Nurses.[77] Published in 2000 to commemorate the fiftieth anniversary of the founding of An Bord Altranais (the Nursing Board), Joseph Robins' book contains a collection of essays on the development of nursing and midwifery education, policy and practice from the period 1950 to 2000. Aside from the book's editor, the contributing authors are nurses and midwives.[78] The book examines the development of the various branches of nursing in Ireland and it includes chapters on general nursing, sick children's nursing, psychiatric nursing, mental handicap nursing, midwifery, and nurse training. As a collection of essays on a diverse range of topics, the book is authoritative, but it does not constitute a project in critical scholarship.

Conclusions

There is a sparse but growing body of knowledge concerning the history of nursing and midwifery in Ireland, and while doctor historians have written much of it, a small number of nursing and midwifery scholars have entered the field with authoritative accounts of their respective histories. The potential subject matter for the history of these disciplines is enormous and the available archival sources provide a gateway to a range of possibilities for the would-be historian of this much-neglected area of Irish social and labour history.

CHAPTER 2

Caring, Past and Present

Peter Nolan

Despite progress in many fields of human endeavour, such as science, technology and healthcare, human beings are probably as fearful as they have ever been about what life holds in store for them. As Roy Porter remarked, westerners are now living longer but, for many, longevity means having more time to be ill, or suffering anxiety about having sufficient resources to keep well.[1] Bertrand Russell questioned whether, despite the great strides that have been made in some areas of life, we have made any progress at all in understanding ourselves.

Robert Putnam argues that the fall-off in social participation over the past three decades in the US in areas like voting, voluntary work, membership of clubs and so forth, is now spreading across the western world.[2] Despite higher incomes, many Americans are experiencing a markedly reduced quality of life. Philanthropy and reciprocity are less evident than they were a hundred or even fifty years ago. Frank Furedi contends that people are struggling to find meaning in their lives and this struggle is reflected in 'an expansion of therapeutic language and practices in everyday life'.[3] He observes:

> Terms like stress, anxiety, depression, compulsion, negative emotions, counselling and trauma are now widely used and reported in the news. Therapies that address low self-esteem, poor self-image, low motivation and poor social integration are now proving popular …[4]

Tom Tiede describes a cultural epidemic sweeping the US, characterised by people investing millions of dollars in books and courses that promise to 'fix' their problems.[5] Greedy and unscrupulous self-publicists are eagerly exploiting this vulnerability. Tiede calls for a return to informed self-reliance and the recognition of interdependence as a way of living.[6] John O'Donohue sees similar trends emerging in Ireland, where an increase in personal wealth, the diminishing place of religion in people's lives and greater openness to pluralistic values have caused some people to rethink many aspects of their lives.[7]

The beginning of the twenty-first century is therefore witnessing an unprecedented interest in how people should be cared for and what are the responsibilities of individuals, communities and states. At the centre of this interest lie a number of vexed questions, such as: how much care should a state provide to its citizens? Who should the care providers be? What should individuals provide for themselves and each other? and How much should be spent on healthcare?

The UK for example is a country with a history of more than half a century of providing care free at the point of delivery. Today, a 'modernisation' project is being implemented. Some interpret this as the imposition of a market economy model on social services, while others see it as a commitment to interventions that have been proven to be effective; others defend it as a mechanism for directing resources to those most in need. Yet 'need' is becoming increasingly difficult to define. Health economists describe it as the 'ability to benefit'. According to this definition, an individual cannot be said to be in need of something if it will not increase his/her wellbeing. A sick person cannot be in need of healthcare if there is no effective treatment that will improve his/her condition. Such a definition of 'need' is clearly unsatisfactory, since the sick person remains in need of compassion and sympathy, even when the medical condition is a terminal illness. However, in a harsh, cost-conscious climate of healthcare, strategists may conclude that there is no point in devoting scarce resources to someone who will not benefit from them.

What then is care? How has it changed over the centuries? What are the challenges to caring in today's society?

Definitions of Care

Karen Armstrong notes that definitions of 'care', 'compassion' and 'altruism' have changed over time, and so trying to make comparisons between caring in the past and the present requires a linguistic analysis in order to understand which concepts and beliefs have driven care over the centuries.[8] For example, the term 'patient', generally used until fairly recently to describe those in receipt of healthcare, is often now replaced with 'client', 'service user', 'customer' and 'consumer'. Although these terms are often used interchangeably, they in fact signify different relationships between the person providing and the person receiving the care, and they signify different underpinning philosophies and approaches to healthcare provision. Changes are inevitable in the way that those involved in the healthcare transaction are described, given the radical changes in the ways of recognising and defining illness and the types of interventions used to treat and care for patients.[9]

Change in nursing has been driven, in part, by advances in medicine, but more especially by the need to contain costs, improve services and find ways of coping with the shortage of nurses. Florence Nightingale's observation that 'the elements of nursing are all but unknown' is no longer considered a statement about the 'art' of caring.[10] Rather, it is seen as a dangerous abrogation of responsibility when purchasers and commissioners of nursing services may be non-professionals, who, in the absence of a widely accepted definition of nursing, may base their assessments on ignorance or misunderstanding of the nature of nursing, nursing costs and nursing productivity.[11]

Yet there is no legal definition of nursing in the UK, the home of the most extensive healthcare system in the world. The recent Health and Social Care Act 2001 stopped short of a definition of nursing, making instead a distinction between health and social care, presumably for the benefit of the purchaser and the provider of services.[12] In 2000, the World Health Organisation sought to locate nursing within the context of community rather than organised services:

> The mission of nursing in society is to help individuals, families and groups to determine and achieve their physical, mental and social potential, and to do so within the challenging context of the environment in which they live and work. This requires nurses to develop and perform functions that relate to the promotion and maintenance of health as well as to the prevention of ill health.[13]

This WHO definition resonates strongly with the attempt by many of today's advanced health services to empower people to take responsibility for their own health rather than merely turning to services when they become ill.

At a time of such radical philosophical, legal, organisational and technological change in healthcare, members of the caring professions must ground themselves in the history of caring, of caring institutions and of caring people, so that they are aware of the traditions and values that they have inherited. With this grounding, they can also make judgements about which aspects of the change should be incorporated into the new world order. A nation, a profession or an organisation that does not make time to recall the past and reflect on it runs the risk of impoverishing itself and of diminishing the quality of the service it seeks to provide. The values and beliefs that underpin caring practices and caring behaviour must be kept constantly under surveillance; if they are not, they can easily become devalued. Shimón Peres highlighted the importance of knowing one's history, when he warned:

> If we find the burden of history too heavy to carry, let us abandon it, but in doing so, let us recognise that we are abandoning our finest teacher.[14]

Reflecting on the History of Caring

The twenty-first century presents us with increasingly complex choices in healthcare where there is so much evidence to consult, and so much of it conflicting. In a society increasingly focused on self-gratification and individual rights, it is vital that we reflect on the nature of caring and on the provision for the sick, the poor and the socially dispossessed. In this reflection, fundamental questions arise, such as: How can the 'me' generation learn to care for others? Where should caring be put into practice? and Which organisations and professions should be asked to define and promote the characteristics of caring? We must scrutinise the direction in which professional bodies and governments are taking healthcare, in order to ensure that a system which purports to be democratic and compassionate does not instead encourage social divisions and ration out what is available to meet the demands of the powerful and the articulate at the expense of the weak and the voiceless.

The inter-connectedness of ethics and politics has been recognised since the time of Aristotle. Ethics is about excelling at being human. Nobody can excel by keeping him or herself isolated from others, and nobody can excel unless the nation's political institutions allow them to do so. Aristotle described a particular way of living, which aimed to help people to realise their own excellence. This was a life conducted according to the *virtues*. Centuries later, Henry James and George Eliot were still discussing the *virtuous person* and defining him or her according to the way that he/she cared. For these authors and other thinkers of note, caring meant trying to feel one's way into the experience of another, and to share their joys and sorrows without thinking of oneself. James and Eliot showed how human excellence was not possible if women and men removed themselves from society by regulating their engagement with it through rules, prohibitions and obligations. The Judaeo–Christian tradition has defined the virtuous life as one of charity and love, people must strive to achieve a greater awareness of themselves through helping others achieve a greater self-awareness of their own selves. The political form of this ethic is socialism. Karl Marx stated that the free development of each is the condition for the free development of all; this is love politicised, or all-round reciprocity.

St Catherine of Siena

The Middle Ages provides some notable demonstrations of the virtuous life embodied in caring. St Catherine of Siena practised in the hospital of Santa Maria della Scala, founded in the early twelfth century. Situated opposite the magnificent cathedral, it was finally closed in 1997 and its history and functions are illustrated in the magnificent frescos in the Pilgrim's Hall at the entrance to the hospital. Founded by a cobbler, but later winning recognition from popes and emperors, Santa Maria was noted for the quality of care it provided for the sick, the assistance it gave to the poor, the education it offered to abandoned children, and the hospitality that it extended to pilgrims travelling to Rome. Although slight in stature and frail in health, St Catherine was renowned for her ability to put herself in the place of others and do for them what they would wish to do for themselves, were they able. Patients found her nursing inspirational and there were instances where her mere presence caused people's health and sense of wellbeing to improve.

From her writings, it is perhaps not unreasonable to imagine what St Catherine's answer might have been to a question about caring. She might define the caring person as possessing three types of virtues. The first, the theological virtues comprising faith, hope and charity; the second, the cardinal or moral virtues – prudence, justice, temperance and fortitude; and the third being the capital virtues of humility, liberality, brotherly love, meekness, chastity, temperance, and diligence. All are dependent on reflection, meditation and a well-developed conscience. St Catherine stated that life is made meaningful through developing the compassionate side of our nature. Her ideas permeated the monastic hospital system and were central to the practices of the great religious orders for centuries after her death.

The Post-Enlightenment Period

The eighteenth century was the century of the grand, even the theatrical, gesture. Philanthropy flourished on a considerable scale when concern for the old and infirm, the sick and the destitute was guaranteed to meet with social approval. A plethora of hospitals came into being at this time. In England, infirmaries in Manchester, Leeds and Bristol were built in the period. In Dublin, the Charitable Infirmary was founded in 1718, Dr Steevens' Hospital in 1720, and Mercer's Hospital opened in 1734. The Hospital for Incurables was founded in 1744, the Rotunda Lying-in Hospital in 1745, and the Meath Hospital and County Infirmary in 1753. Supported financially by the writer Jonathan Swift, St Patrick's Hospital opened in 1746; today, the hospital is one of the oldest and most distinguished psychiatric hospitals in the world. Swift's comment that his intention was 'to build a house for fools and mad' disguised the commitment he wished to make in response to bitter personal experience of the havoc that mental illness could wreak in individuals, families and countries. All of these 'charity hospitals' were expressions of altruism, beneficence and concern for the sick and were simultaneously expressions of power, wealth, control, and wealthy people's need to establish their place in society. In this connection, Peter Gatenby comments:

> These hospitals were naturally all Protestant institutions. While the Protestants in Ireland then were in a minority of one to six because of the penal laws and land confiscation, they were the only people who had the money and the will to spend it on this type of charity.[15]

Historians place this expansive, philanthropically-driven building programme within the broader context of what was happening in European philosophy and science at the time. This was the post-Enlightenment period and the 'charity hospital' reflected the aspirations, insights and political developments of the age.

The German philosopher Emanuel Kant saw the Enlightenment as mankind's final coming-of-age, when human consciousness was emancipated from immaturity, ignorance and error. It marked the ascendancy of reason and of scientific rationalism, which would enable people to be more fully and happily human. Based on religion and faith, the old order had located power outside the person, in God, the Church and the State. Now order and power were located within the person. This humanism proclaimed that human beings were the creators of their own identities and were masters of their own fate. When reason was harnessed to the will, there were no boundaries to what people could achieve.

The elevation of reason and science nonetheless tended to encourage an absolutist cast of mind and to discourage respect for plurality of values. As science became the dominant force, it allowed people to assume an 'absolute' distinction between true and false, right and wrong, between what counted as evidence and what did not, and thereby gave rise to a raft of repressive social policies. The casualties of an age that believed that reason makes us human and lack of reason reduces us to the level of beasts, were the social outcasts, the confused elderly, the chronically sick, beggars, criminals and the insane. All of these had to be locked up lest they contaminate the rest of rational society. The great psychiatric institutions of the eighteenth and nineteenth centuries represented the means by which society protected itself from those whom it saw as a threat to its order. The notion of the hospital as the repository for those who could not contribute to society led inevitably to the great abuses of the twentieth century. Hitler's hospitals 'took out' the unwanted, the mentally ill, the physically disabled, homosexuals, and Jews.

Caring in the Twenty-first Century: a World in Crisis

In the twentieth-first century, western society would seem to have developed in such a way that we are now seeing an inevitable decline in how we care for each other. How has this situation come to pass?

In his book, *Bowling Alone* (2000), Robert Putnam writes about 'social capital', which he sees as the chief means by which we sustain and enhance our humanity. He argues that where communities are high in social capital, there is less crime, better care of children, improved welfare provision, better educational outcomes, enhanced economic performance, better mental and physical health, greater life satisfaction and, at the macro level, better government. Putnam contends that social isolation is the cause of more illness than either tobacco or alcohol consumption. Social networks are vital because they transmit information, provide support, encourage mutual obligation, and confer identity.

For social capital to thrive, children need to acquire certain skills and values. People need space in which to live, which encourages social capital, and this necessitates creative, community-orientated town planning. People need to be empowered through the decentralisation of authority and given control over resources, in order to enable them to develop their own communities. It is Putnam's conviction that people who are open and democratic, altruistic and compassionate tend to live in societies where there is governance that is transparent and that promotes social justice and opportunities for all. In short, caring people are the product of caring societies and vice versa.

The theologian Gordon Lynch attempts to explain why American society in particular, and some western societies in general, are so low on social capital, by referring to the experience of Generation X, the eighty million Americans who were born between 1961 and 1981.[16] Generation X has the highest divorce rate ever seen; half of its marriages end in divorce. More of its babies have been aborted than those of any other generation. One in four of its children is born to a single mother. For Generation X, the second most common cause of death after road traffic accidents is homicide, followed closely by suicide. Generation X grew up in families where both parents were working and they amused themselves not by playing on the streets, in the parks or joining young people's groups, but by watching television, and listening to aggressive music. The members of Generation X defined themselves according to a culture produced for the masses and they learned to respond to the world as one of a million, not as one of a community. Generation X does not find meaning in churches, political parties or academic learning. It tries to find meaning at the level of the individual and the way in which he or she wishes to engage with other people and with the world. When meaning cannot be found at this level, disappointment and despair ensue. Generation X's spirituality has no means of expression; its limited fulfilment lies in shopping malls and, beyond this, life is given over to 'nothing', to nihilism.[17]

Francis Fukuyama discusses the growing influence of the pharmaceutical industry in helping people to fill the void that they are experiencing in their souls.[18] Drugs such as Zoloft and Prozac attempt to provide self-esteem in a bottle by elevating serotonin levels in the brain, what Peter Kramer, in his book, *Listening to Prozac* (1997), terms 'cosmetic pharmacology'.[19] Tiede examines this spiritual poverty of the most powerful nation on earth:

> There is currently a terrifying cultural epidemic sweeping across America. Every year, we waste millions of dollars on books and courses that promise to fix all our problems. Each tome proves to be a resounding thud, and yet we continue to buy them, hoping for the non-existent magic bullet that will solve all our problems and leave us happy ever after. Self-deception knows no bounds.[20]

Catherine McGeachy also touches on the same theme when she writes:

> Western-type culture, wherever it is found on the globe, is awash with the immediate, the material, the selfish manipulation of things, experiences and others. Our spiritually dumbed-down culture is a victim culture.[21]

In a world where the quick fix is mandatory and outcome measures must be clearly defined, there is a grave danger that real human needs will be misunderstood, dumbed down or ignored. Yet it would be hard to imagine a time when caring was more called for in a world tormented by the effects of violence at all levels. Today, the concept of virtue may seem foreign and perhaps difficult to apply in the context of caring. Yet the need for some kind of philosophy to underpin our approach to the vulnerable, a clear formulation of what it is health professionals are trying to do and how they might achieve it, has perhaps never been so urgent.

In the last twenty years, fifty of the poorest countries in the world have been involved in wars. In thirty of these, more than fifteen per cent of the population have been displaced. Approximately ninety per cent of casualties have been civilians. In 2002, it was estimated that over twenty million combatants and ex-combatants were to be found in these poorest countries. Between 1992 and 1996, 16,000 people were killed in Bosnia, 650,000 fled the country, 42,000 were internally displaced, and over thirty per cent of healthcare facilities were destroyed. In countries where torture is the principal means of controlling dissent, post-traumatic stress disorder and major depression affect individuals, families and whole communities. The offspring of parents who have been traumatised have an increased risk of major depression, phobias, panic disorder and alcohol dependence. Over fifty per cent of the world's population has less than one dollar per annum spent on their healthcare, in contrast with countries such as Canada, which spends over two thousand dollars per annum on each of its citizens.

These are disquieting figures and would seem to depict a world in crisis. 'Domestic terrorism' has also increased enormously; every week in the UK, two children and two women die as a result of domestic violence. Countless numbers of children and older people are assaulted in their own homes on a regular basis. Such is the destructive nature of parent–parent and parent–child relationships that many children live in a state of perpetual fear. Dysfunctional families are the training ground for the future bullies in the playground and the workplace and for the future victims of domestic violence. As a result of living in violent households, children grow up with anger and resentment in their hearts, have low self-esteem and, in adult life, may demonstrate a pattern of rejecting friendship and love for fear of being rejected themselves. The effects of poor parenting are often cyclical; children grow into adults who are vulnerable to physical and mental ill health and who are likely to become the kind of parents they themselves had.

In the UK, thousands of people are turning to alternative therapies, 'new age' spiritualities and outlandish health fads, because they are so dissatisfied with orthodox social and healthcare services. They want to be listened to, talked *with* rather than talked *at*, and held emotionally. Disasters, such as the terrorist attacks on the United States on 11 September 2001, confront humanity with its own vulnerability and provoke a search for explanations among people, who frequently turn to journalists, politicians, psychologists and academics to provide the explanations. Writing in *The Daily Telegraph* shortly after the events of September 2001, Philip Broughton observed how good the business of the New York yoga teachers and other alternative practitioners was and how brisk trade was in the city's restaurants. He questioned whether the kinds of comforts that people were seeking after the events were a means of confronting or sidestepping terrifying issues of impermanence and helplessness:

> There is certainly an appetite for emotional comfort in New York. Churches are fuller than they have been in years. Masseurs are knuckle-weary from kneading all those caffeine-booze-and-stress-knotted backs. Shrinks are cancelling their Christmas holidays, business is so brisk. Behind Mayor Giuliani's up-and-at-'em façade, New York is scared and anxious, with every Woody Allenish neurosis coming to the surface.[22]

Nursing and Caring Today

What is the state of nursing in the face of such apparent crises? In the UK, Janet Magnet argues that the prevailing ideologies are impacting on nursing care to bring about a crisis of quantity and quality.[23] While large numbers of people enter nurse training, drop-out is considerable and it is even more difficult to retain staff once qualified. Britain and Ireland are being forced to sustain their nursing workforce by recruiting nurses from overseas, often from countries that can least afford to lose them. Many nurses experience dissatisfaction with the way in which nursing is structured and managed. They do not like being labelled as F, G or H grades and they equally dislike seeing their patients labelled as 'problems', 'symptoms' and 'outcomes'. They may find themselves bullied by managers and forced to provide services that are driven by budgets and targets rather than patient needs. As a consequence, many become disenchanted and experience burnout.

In the UK, doctors, nurses and many other healthcare professionals now prefer to be employed through agencies rather than be employed directly within the National Health Service. As a consequence, governments find it difficult to implement policies because of a shortage of regular, committed healthcare workers.[24] Perhaps the real crisis, however, is to do with caring, and it is this that we see reflected in the recruitment and retention crisis. Magnet considers that nursing has tried to 'stamp out' the notion of 'calling'.[25] Theory, bureaucracy and status have replaced charitable work and service to the sick, which were once the impulsions that drove the caring person. Reflecting on her own experience of being in hospital, Magnet comments:

> Many modern nurses work as if in a factory, clocking off the minute their shift is complete. My night nurse usually left at 7.00am bang on without giving me my anti-nausea medicine. The day nurse assumed I had been given it, but didn't bother to check. I stayed in my bed, retching. I have never before felt that the provision of my own care lay in my own hands. What if I were too ill to get out of bed?[26]

The world is now quite different from that which existed at the time of St Catherine of Siena and the monastic foundations. Hospitals were then the expression of a holistic and essentially spiritual concern for those admitted to them. Patients put their *faith* in the people who worked there and appreciated what was done for them. Today, people as patients are increasingly disenchanted with health professionals and many appear to have little trust that the healthcare system is driven by *their* needs. They are looking for other ways of understanding and responding to their illnesses and their unhappiness; they seek out practitioners, institutions and communities where people have time to care and understand.

If the apparent crisis in nursing is to be overcome, healthcare employers and organisations must learn how to care for those who care for others. They must address such issues as the selection and recruitment of appropriate personnel, the creation and support of teams whose members respect and care for each other, and the organisation of working arrangements that enable nurses to maintain a healthy and satisfying balance between home and work. In addition, they must also consider better selection and training of managers, the identification and nurturing of skilled leadership, and the breaking down of barriers that exist between and among the professions. Since nurses' job satisfaction partly stems from a perceived and actual lack of time to relate to their patients, employers and organisations must recognise and address this constraint.

Concomitantly with trying to improve the working lives of nurses and other healthcare professionals, employers and organisations will need to draw on the considerable body of evidence that describes how people want to be cared for. Patients and their families are increasingly demanding to be provided with the kind of services that they want and the way they want to receive them. In this regard, nurses and other health professionals need to provide the sort of physical and emotional safety that those in their care crave and ensure that care is tailored to individual needs. Additionally, they need to build on local community strengths and pass on health knowledge and skills to carers, families and communities, provide continuity of care to individuals and communities, and help patients to reintegrate into their homes and communities as soon as possible after their treatment. Meeting the needs of people also involves giving them accurate, full and accessible information so that they themselves can make the choices about healthcare and the kinds of treatments that are right for them.

Some Closing Reflections

The fast moving world of the twenty-first century seems likely to continue to subject people to myriad changes during the courses of their lives. In the Middle Ages, patients could go to a monastic hospital where they would be known and would feel part of a community that cared about them. Today, healthcare professionals are less likely to *know* their patients and patients are 'guests' on the professionals' territory. When those giving and those receiving care do not know each other, it becomes necessary to place a strong emphasis on investigations and particularly on risk assessment. People may receive only that care which protocols state that they are entitled to and no more. Cost effectiveness and targets for minimum periods of hospitalisation and early discharge are as likely to determine the experience of being in receipt of healthcare.

John O'Donohue suggests that there is much to be learned about caring from Celtic spirituality and that the care-full person is one who has discovered the beauty of what it is to be human within themselves and within those whom they encounter.[27] Being able to care is not a position that we arrive at; it is a direction in which we are travelling. Jonathan Swift ridiculed those who believed in absolutism, in utopias, to solve all of mankind's problems. Striving for the best in the imperfect world of healthcare means minimising human suffering and maximising human dignity.

Ironically, while we have never been more individualistic in our outlook, we have never been more dependent on each other, in terms of the global economy.[28] Victor Griffin remarks that in the modern world we must be able to relate to others who are different from ourselves and that it is in accepting and celebrating difference that we manifest our ability to care.[29] He reminds us that the caring person is open-minded and open-hearted, is open to other lifestyles, to other religions, to other ways of seeing things and, above all, is open to the myriad ways in which caring must respond to people's needs. Alaister Campbell calls on healthcare professionals to condemn 'the cold, distant and professional approach … engendered by reductionist, scientific medicine'.[30] He denounces the abuses of medical power, sexism, racism, and the disguised self-interest that are more prevalent within healthcare than is often acknowledged. Instead, he argues for a 'moderated love', one that takes into account individual values, the socio-political context in which people live, and the aspirations that they have for themselves and those close to them.

CHAPTER 3

'Invisible' Nursing[1]

Margaret Pearl Treacy

The contribution of nursing in Irish healthcare has, for the most part, remained invisible. This is not to claim that nursing and the work of nurses is not recognised, but rather that nurses and much of their knowledge and practice can remain unseen in both public debate and in the articulation of health and social policy.

The Legacy of Irish Military Nurses in the Nineteenth Century

Nursing in Ireland has a long and distinguished history. However, until recently, the contribution of nineteenth-century nursing was largely understated and went largely unrecorded and unrecognised. The early development of nursing in Ireland occurred within a wider European context of pastoral care of the sick. Sioban Nelson remarks that, 'as a serious and skilled activity', the care of the sick appeared in seventeenth-century France with the work of St Vincent de Paul's Daughters of Charity.[2] She points out that French Catholic nuns were part of the social landscape in the nineteenth century, but according to their rule, they said little and did much.[3]

Women in nineteenth-century Ireland emulated their continental counterparts; they found scope for their Christian charity and expressed their talents in founding and leading religious congregations for the express purposes of teaching and caring for the sick.[4] In particular, the work of Mary Aikenhead, who founded the Irish Sisters of Charity in 1813, and that of Catherine McAuley, who founded the Sisters of Mercy in 1831, extended the tradition of pastoral care in Ireland. Evelyn Bolster's study of the Sisters of Mercy in the Crimean War of 1854–56 has described the contribution of the Irish contingent of military nurses in that war and has drawn attention to their role in the development of sick nursing alongside Florence Nightingale.[5] Bolster's work describes a group of brave and intelligent women who provided nursing care for the wounded British and Irish soldiers in the field hospitals of the Crimea. More recently, other scholars including Doona, Meehan and Nelson have provided further analysis and new interpretations of the historical evidence and, in so doing, have succeeded in making the contribution of the Irish military sisters more visible.[6]

Shortly after the outbreak of the Crimean War, a contingent of nurses travelled from England under the leadership of Nightingale. They were recruited from a number of sources and included among their numbers were Mary Clare Moore and other members of the congregation of the Sisters of Mercy from Bermondsey in London. Almost immediately after their arrival in the Crimea in October 1854, it became clear that there was a need for more nurses than the Nightingale contingent could supply. In responding to the call for nurses, Sister Vincent Whitty, the superioress at the Mercy Convent at Baggot Street in Dublin, remarked:

> Attendance on the sick … is part of our Institute; and sad experience among the poor has convinced us that … many lives are lost for want of careful nursing.[7]

This positive response resulted in the departure of a contingent of Irish Sisters of Mercy under the leadership of Mother Francis (Joanna) Bridgeman of the Kinsale Convent. The group of fifteen women gave a total of sixteen months of service as military nurses living under the most appalling conditions; they ate and slept in the close company of the many rats that infested the hospitals. In accordance with the Irish bishops' contract with the British War Office, the group had a distinct organisation and 'a good deal of freedom' under Mother Bridgeman's leadership.[8] Aside from Mother Bridgeman, the company of fifteen Irish sisters included Mary Joseph Isabella Croke, Aloysius Doyle, Clare Keane and Elizabeth Hersey.

For ten months from December 1854 to October 1855, ten of the Irish sisters worked under Bridgeman at the Koulali hospital in Constantinople, and their nursing system was said to have made Koulali the 'model hospital in the East'.[9] Carol Helmstadter writes of Mother Bridgeman's work at Koulali, noting that she 'had years of experience ... and possessed a skill and judgement in nursing that few could match'. At Balaclava hospital under Bridgeman, the sisters had sole charge of nursing from October 1855 to March 1856, during which time they were noted for their efficiency and their caring approach. Doona contends that the Irish Sisters of Mercy were the best prepared nurses in the nineteenth century, and by the time of their service in the Crimea, they had accumulated twenty-seven years of corporate knowledge of sick nursing through visiting the sick poor in their own homes.[10] While receiving no formal training in sick nursing, they had built up their considerable nursing expertise in that period. They had much experience in nursing starving people dying from scurvy, typhoid and typhus, and during the Asiatic cholera epidemic of 1832, Catherine McAuley and her sisters had organised and provided a nursing service in the temporary hospitals that were set up in Dublin at that time to deal with the situation.[11]

Visiting the sick poor was a central part of what it meant to *be* a Sister of Mercy. In the battlefield hospitals, their nursing expertise was put to good use in a range of activities from the provision of comfort and nourishment, to the relief of pain and the treatment of wounds and frostbite. Much of the work of the Sisters of Mercy has been made visible through their diaries, which many of the sisters kept while in the Crimea. One of the sisters, Isabella Croke, recorded in her diary:

> A doctor said to me 'Sister, you must not listen to the patients when they ask you for anything. It will be impossible to get them out of the Hospital, they will be so petted.' [I replied] 'Oh Doctor, Sisters of Mercy always listen to their patients.'[12]

Further evidence from the historical record comes from contemporaneous studies of the different systems of nursing operated by Nightingale and by the Irish sisters. In a confidential report presented to the War Office at the end of 1855, the deputy purveyor-in-chief to the forces in the Crimea, Davis Fitzgerald, wrote on the nursing system at the Balaclava hospital:

> The superiority of an ordered system is beautifully illustrated in the Sisters of Mercy ... the Medical Officer can safely consign his most critical cases

> to their hands … stimulants – or opiates – ordered every five minutes, will be faithfully administered, though the five minute labour were repeated uninterruptedly for a week.[13]

Silent Knowledge and Practice

Much is written about Florence Nightingale as the founder of modern nursing and, without doubt, Nightingale did contribute in a significant way to the development of modern nursing techniques and practices, including modern hospital management. However, the flow of ideas and expertise in sick nursing did not come from Nightingale's direction alone. In this connection, Nelson writes that long before Nightingale came to prominence, 'professional and capable nursing [by Irish nursing sisters] had begun to transform the care of the sick poor and to demonstrate [nursing's] … importance to the success of medical/surgical innovation'.[14] Nelson contends that the expertise of the Irish sisters, in both the spiritual and material domains, 'fostered imitation' among secular women, such that their model of sick nursing provided the prototype for modern secular nursing, such as that proffered by Nightingale and her contemporaries. Their model of sick nursing also provided the means for addressing governmental concerns in the early nineteenth century in relation to the control of populations and the promotion of welfare and sanitation among the urban poor, particularly the Irish poor. In contrast, nursing in Britain in the middle of the nineteenth century was disorganised and, as Hart notes, was 'cast as work of very low status'.[15]

Thus, despite the effectiveness of the Irish Sisters of Mercy, Nightingale quickly became identified as the leader in the development of modern secular nursing and the Irish sisters were expunged from the celebrations of Crimean War nursing.[16] The reasons why the Irish military sisters' contribution was not visible included the fact that their knowledge and expertise remained intuitive and experiential, and it was passed down among the sisters and transmitted as corporate memory. In addition, few formal records existed of the sisters' contribution. In the immediate aftermath of the Crimean War, other more powerful voices, including the Established Church, proclaimed Nightingale as the heroine of the Crimea. The cult of Nightingale as the 'lady with the lamp' would continue to blind later generations of nurses to the contribution of the Irish Sisters of Mercy, who were not given to singing their own praises.[17]

Thus, the first period in the development of modern nursing knowledge and practice is characterised by an intuitive, experiential, silent knowledge; knowledge was embedded in the practical experience that women brought to sick nursing and it was transmitted as a corporate memory. Invisibility of the nursing contribution may not simply be a feature of nineteenth-century Irish nursing. Even today, aspects of modern nursing knowledge and practice can remain silent. Clarke suggests that nurses' clinical decision-making processes and aspects of their interpersonal care are not recognised and can remain invisible.[18] In an examination of 'secret nursing', McWilliam and Wong alert us to nursing's hidden work in such areas as the discharging of hospital patients, and they note that nursing plays an important role in co-ordinating the work of other health professionals to the benefit of patient care.[19]

Developments in Nurse Training in Ireland

An examination of the developments in nurse training in Ireland suggests that until fairly recently the system of training served to perpetuate the invisibility of the Irish nursing contribution in the nineteenth century. While important steps in the development of modern nursing occurred in Ireland following the Crimean War, aspects of the legacy of invisibility remained.

In his doctoral research which examined the history of apprenticeship nurse training in Ireland, Gerard Fealy notes that while medical knowledge and practice within the voluntary hospitals was extremely well developed by the late nineteenth century, nursing care was still being provided by mostly uneducated lay women who had received no formal training in sick nursing.[20] Official reports into the state of nursing in the Dublin hospitals in the 1870s and 1880s, most notably the *Report on Nursing Arrangements in the Dublin Hospitals* by the Dublin Hospital Sunday Fund in 1879 and the *Dublin Hospitals Commission Report* of 1887, highlighted major deficiencies in the nursing arrangements in those hospitals that did not employ properly trained nurses.[21] Calling for the introduction of probationership training and the employment of a 'better class' of nurse, these reports paved the way for the reform of hospital nursing and the widespread acceptance of formal training for nurses. The reforms that followed the publication of these reports also altered the class basis of nursing and rendered sick nursing as an acceptable area of professional work for middle-class women.[22]

After 1880, most of the larger voluntary hospitals in Dublin were required to provide a probationary training period for nurses; by 1892, all of the Dublin hospitals and those in the other major cities had embraced the need to provide proper training of nurses. However, the training was largely of the nature of 'on the job' experience with a smattering of theoretical instruction, given during the probationers' off-duty periods. Thus, as learners, probationers were all but invisible; the knowledge that they used in their practice was frequently gleaned as experiential and it too was largely invisible.

From the late nineteenth century onwards, nurse training in Ireland developed and evolved along similar lines to that in the United Kingdom. In the beginning, hospital structures and nurse training changed little, and hospitals continued to operate a system of in-house training of nurses to support hospital nursing service needs. Young women were recruited to 'fit-in' to the institutions that employed them and recruitment to nurse training was undertaken on the basis of meeting the day-to-day needs of the particular institution.[23] With some notable international exceptions, change in the system of nurse training was piecemeal, and it included expansion of syllabi and the addition of protected and increased study time, such as the preliminary training school system and the block system. Change occurred in an incremental manner up to the mid-1980s in the United Kingdom, Europe and Australia. Up until the mid-1990s in Ireland, nurse training and nursing service remained inextricably linked. However, since the mid-1990s, nurse training in Ireland has experienced a period of enormous change and this change culminated in the full integration of basic nurse training into the higher education sector in 2002.

While it might appear that change in the training system in Ireland took place over a short period of time, debate about the best system for nurse training had been taking place and the case for change has been argued since the 1940s.[24] The impetus for change came from three main sources. Firstly, it was recognised internationally that linking the training of nurses to the service needs of just a single institution was not the best way to prepare nurses for their role in healthcare and there was ample research evidence to support this position. It was also recognised that nursing was the largest resource in healthcare and that its full potential in the health services was not being fully realised within the hospital-based apprenticeship system. The health services needed nurses who could function as flexible, independent, yet collaborative contributors to healthcare, in line with the developing vision and need for skilled and knowledgeable practitioners of nursing. However, one of the major obstacles to change in the system of nurse training had long remained the status of the student nurse as a paid service employee; in Ireland it was accepted that Irish hospitals could not function without student nurses as part of the labour force.[25]

A second impetus for change came when nurses' own professional aspirations for educational developments intensified throughout the 1970s and 1980s in a number of countries. In Ireland this was represented in a number of publications, discussion documents and reports, including the *Working Party Report on General Nursing* of 1980 and the *Report on the Future of Nurse Education and Training* in 1994.[26] Within the profession in Ireland, there was concern that nurses should be better prepared for their increasingly complex role in patient care. With developments in knowledge and practice in other countries, there was an increasing awareness among the profession in Ireland of the need not just for good clinical practice, but also of the need to develop up-to-date research-based knowledge for that practice. It was becoming increasingly understood that a change in the system of nurse training was a necessary prerequisite in bringing this about.

A third factor in the impetus for change in basic nurse training was economic. In this regard, Fealy contends that while professional concerns regarding the need to develop nurses' knowledge and skills were important, the most significant factor driving the change was economic.[27] Ireland's entry to the European Economic Community in 1973 had a significant impact on the training of nurses in Ireland. In implementing a number of European directives on the training of nurses in 1979 and again in 1991, the Nursing Board (An Bord Altranais) required training hospitals to provide student nurses with minimum hours of theoretical and clinical instruction in the training period. This resulted in a greatly expanded syllabus and an expansion in the range of students' clinical experiences, such that by the early 1990s, training hospitals were now deprived of their (paid) student workforce for half of their training period. Fealy notes that, as the students' training needs increasingly encroached on their service role, the apprenticeship training system had become economically unsustainable.[28] The foundations of the system were ostensibly dismantled when a new three-year diploma in nursing course was introduced in 1994 to replace the traditional system of training. The system was finally ended in 2002, when a new four-year degree in nursing was introduced on foot of a recommendation of the Commission on Nursing in 1998. Officialdom, as represented by the Commission on Nursing, had finally created the conditions to make nursing education – and indirectly the contribution that nursing could make to healthcare – visible.

Creating the Foundations for Making Nursing Visible

The changes in basic nurse training were matched by a range of developments in postgraduate and continuing education, which included the introduction of a range of clinically-focused higher diploma programmes and masters programmes in both nursing and midwifery. Prior to these developments, much of the continuing professional education that qualified nurses undertook was invisible, in the sense that nurses pursued their academic studies without the financial support of their employers and without formal recognition of their enhanced knowledge and skills for grading and promotions purposes. Notwithstanding this lack of recognition, nurses continued to provide for their own professional development and were carving out new and important clinical roles as a result. Sarah Condell notes that while many of the roles were closely associated with medical specialities and were complementary to the medical role, others were forged into specialist nursing roles that incorporated educational, research and administrative aspects.[29]

Today, in collaboration with nurses' employers, the higher education sector plays a critical role in the provision of continuing professional education and training for nurses. Through academic recognition of specialist clinical nursing qualifications and through the development of new clinical grades, such as clinical nurse specialist and advanced nurse practitioner, the knowledge and skills that nurses develop beyond their initial nursing qualification have become more visible. While some have expressed concern at the move to the academy, the contribution of graduate and postgraduate education for nurses is best illustrated in the empirical research evidence, which demonstrates that better educated and more skilled nurses provide better patient care which leads to improved patient outcomes.[30] In this way, the contribution of the educated nurse to patient care has become more visible.

These educational changes to date represent a shift from a vocational to a professional mode in nursing in Ireland and they should serve to contribute to enhanced patient care. The changes provide opportunities for the further development of nurses' critical thinking and enhanced decision-making capabilities, lifelong learning, flexibility in clinical roles and delivery of enhanced patient care. They are a prerequisite to the achievement of these goals and for making nursing visible. However these developments will be wasted unless nurses, as learned professionals, can progress scholarship in nursing.

The Role of Scholarship in Making Nursing Visible

Kim Lutzen, a Swedish nursing scholar writing in 2000, remarked that nursing is in danger if it continues to be defined by 'doing' and argues that the theory must first be generated which can then be used to build knowledge for practical use.[31] Parker similarly contends that 'the relationship between nursing scholarship and health improvement, between academics and the social mandate of nursing' must always be kept in mind.[32] Internationally, there is clear acknowledgement of the importance of scholarly pursuits, most notably empirical research, for quality nursing care. In Ireland, recent affirmation of this position is seen in the publication of the *Research Strategy for Nursing and Midwifery in Ireland*.[33]

By examining countries with established higher education programmes for nurses, it is evident that research activity in nursing is directly associated with nursing developments within higher education. For example, it is noteworthy that the first professor of nursing was appointed in the United States in the 1920s. This early development is reflected today in the fact that the United States is highly productive in terms of nursing research output.[34] In Ireland, there are a total of six chairs in nursing, all established between the late 1990s and 2004, and the contribution of nursing scholarship in Ireland is at an early stage of development, as nurses in the academy clarify and develop their role.

What then is the role of scholarship in making nursing visible? This question is perhaps best answered by reference to a position statement on 'Defining Scholarship for the Discipline of Nursing', published by the American Association of Colleges of Nursing (AACN) in 1999.[35] Drawing on Ernest Boyer's work, the AACN proposed that scholarship in nursing relates to activities of rigorous enquiry that systematically advance the teaching, research and the practice of nursing.[36] This work must be documented, replicable and subject to peer review.[37]

Four standards for scholarship are suggested. The 'scholarship of discovery' refers to inquiry that produces disciplinary knowledge in nursing, reflecting the unique perspective of nursing that focuses on the person and that 'takes an expanded view of health by emphasising health promotion, restoration and rehabilitation, as well as commitment to caring and comfort.'[38] It incorporates empirical and historical research, philosophical inquiry, theory development and testing, and methodological studies; it is increasingly collaborative within nursing and across other professional groups.

The 'scholarship of teaching' produces knowledge that facilitates the transfer of nursing knowledge and skill from the expert to the novice and it builds bridges between teacher and student understanding.[39] Such scholarship supports the creation of educational environments and is conducted through the application of disciplinary knowledge, innovative teaching methods or programme development and learning outcome evaluation.

The 'scholarship of practice' is the scholarship of application; it includes all elements in the delivery of nursing service and the evidence of effectiveness in addressing healthcare problems or in understanding community health problems. Components of the scholarship of practice include development and application of clinical knowledge and professional self-development in practice, and it includes research beyond the basic competency level. In this way, practice roles for nurses in academic settings may include direct caregiver, educator, consultant, and administrator.[40]

The 'scholarship of integration' emphasises 'the interconnectedness of ideas'; through critical analysis, it draws on insights from the work of nursing or other disciplines to arrive at enhanced or new understandings.[41] It can also be achieved by engaging in collaborative research with other disciplinary groups and, increasingly, it can be achieved and reflected through the scholarship of discovery, teaching or practice.

In all its expressions, nursing scholarship is critical if the nursing contribution to care is to be made visible. In this connection, the three principal areas that need to be addressed are practice, research and teaching; the fourth area, the scholarship of integration, is possible in the course of achieving the other three. Each of the three areas has, in varying degrees, relevance for nurses, whether in the academic, research or clinical spheres. Nurses need to reflect and identify an appropriate level of engagement in scholarly activity, depending on their primary role. For example, nurse practitioners in clinical settings must pass on their expertise to learners and, likewise, nursing academics need to identify their own engagement with practice.

Within the academy in Ireland, nursing academics face the issue of what their role is, both as nurses and as academics. There is a need (real and perceived) for clarification of these roles and how they relate to the practice of nursing.

Nurses, many of whom are new to the academy, are taking on new challenges as they start on their own personal and professional journey, especially in relation to the scholarship of discovery. Their research draws on theories and methods from a range of academic and professional disciplines, including psychology, sociology, education, and medicine.[42] Diversity is reflected in the wide range of topics that Irish nursing scholars have researched to date; topics have included discharge planning, coping with breast cancer, pain management, strategic management in nursing, student learning, midwifery education and the history of nurse training. This is research that may impact directly or indirectly on practice, education or management in healthcare.

Until relatively recently, nurses in Ireland had spent many fruitful years promoting research awareness among their colleagues and many had engaged in individual ad hoc research studies, but often with little financial support.[43] In the absence of publications, much of this scholarship had remained invisible. With nursing more firmly established in the academy and with the increasing output of research and publications, the contribution of nursing to professional knowledge and practice is becoming ever more visible.

Conclusions

Recent developments in the area of nursing education in Ireland have brought the nursing profession and the academy together in a spirit of partnership. In highlighting these developments, it is possible to see that the contribution of better educated and more skilled nurses can provide better patient care, thereby leading to improved patient outcomes. In this way, the contribution of the educated nurse to patient care becomes more visible. By examining the nature of scholarship in nursing, it is also possible to see that scholarship can also contribute to nursing knowledge and practice and thereby render more visible the nursing contribution to care.

CHAPTER 4

'Dr Nightingale, I Presume?': Irish Nursing Education Enters the Academy

Martin McNamara

The entry of nursing into higher education institutions has been described as 'a massive social experiment'.[1] In Ireland this experiment began in September 2002 when a four-year bachelor of science degree in nursing became the sole route of entry to practice, following recommendations made by a commission on nursing four years previously.[2] Moving nursing education into the third-level sector has long been a source of controversy and continues to generate considerable debate in nursing circles and beyond. An analysis of the language in and through which this debate has been conducted reveals a set of recurring images, metaphors and other rhetorical devices which recall those used in the early decades of the twentieth century. These linguistic features have constructed and sustained a remarkably enduring set of myths which represent and position nurses and nursing in particular ways.

This chapter critically analyses texts concerning the entry of nursing education to the higher education sector. The analysis has two principal aims: first, to determine the extent to which the language in and through which contemporary debate is conducted bears the traces of nursing education's historical struggle for recognition and autonomy; and second, to consider how this language constructs the discursive context within which nurses' attempts to legitimate nursing as an academic discipline continue to take place.[3]

The Right Type of Nurse: Early Debate

The analysis of the debate begins with one of the earliest references to nursing and higher education in Ireland:

> Everywhere we read of ... Preliminary Training Schools with Lecture Rooms, Laboratories with up-to-date equipment and high qualified Sister Tutors ... Still we see the headlines 'Where are we Drifting?' 'What is the cause of the shortage of probationers?' The right type of nurse ...[4]

This extract, taken from a lecture by A. E. Musson, published in *Irish Nursing and Hospital World* in 1931, demonstrates that the training and education required to produce the 'right type of nurse' has long been a matter of public concern and debate. Musson was writing of the 'storms of praise and abuse' accompanying a British Labour MP's proposed bill to regulate nurses' pay and hours of work. Remarking on the diversity of views expressed to the Lancet Commission – established in 1930 to enquire into the extent of the shortage of probationers and their conditions of training and service – Musson observed that 'some consider the [educational] standard might be raised, others that the theoretical training is too severe'.[5] Musson herself considered that there was 'a great deal of unnecessary talk about aching feet and stretched nerves of probationers', which came mostly from those who 'shuffle through their hospital career a trial to the authorities, and of little use to themselves, the public, or the nursing profession'.[6] These 'grumblers' were most likely to be those who took up nursing for the wrong reasons:

> Failure to pass examinations for other posts, or parents think it is a respectable calling ... or a suitable occupation for the fool of the family.[7]

Musson believed these unsuitable and unsuccessful candidates to be the source of much 'hostile and unreliable correspondence from time to time in the press', which gave an 'erroneous impression', and which deterred educated women from entering the nursing profession.[8] While it was a 'fundamental truth' that 'learning comes from actual doing', for Musson the practice of nursing had grown more complex and practical skill was useless 'unless it lead to the development of the powers of observation and judgment in the nurse'.[9] Realising that universities were 'not yet impressed with their Nursing Schools from an educational standpoint', hospitals had raised educational standards, resulting in a 'more intellectual nursing service' but – and here the dilemma is manifest – 'increased theoretical instruction is one of the bones of contention'.[10]

The Practical and the Intellectual

In debates about nursing education, the practical/technical and the academic or intellectual/theoretical are regularly represented as being diametrically opposed and mutually exclusive. There is also a tendency to locate nursing and medicine at opposite poles of this constructed dichotomy, as the following extract from an address to the Irish Nurses' Union in 1936 given by Dr R. Davitt exemplifies:

> However great may have been the benefit conferred upon suffering humanity by the increase in skill accruing to the medical profession, as a result of scientific research and academic learning, it was nevertheless, equalled if not exceeded by the self-sacrifice and devotion shown in the practical carrying out of treatment by the members of the nursing profession.[11]

Within nursing, perceived tensions between the practical and theoretical aspects of education have long preoccupied members of the profession with the often implicit assumption that increases in theoretical instruction were at the expense of and would displace practical training. The fact that students were unavailable to nursing service while in receipt of theoretical instruction suggests an economic basis for much of this concern. In any case, the most valued instruction was said to take place on the wards, with the ward sister presumed to occupy a pivotal role in this regard:

> The importance of the Ward Sisters cannot be overestimated ... On them devolves the duty of giving intensive bedside teaching to the student nurse, and the value of this teaching can never be sufficiently emphasised for a nurse with sound theoretical knowledge is valueless unless she is able to carry out her practical nursing duties deftly and efficiently.[12]

Writing in 1938 about the training of nurse teachers, the writer of this passage was clear that responsibility for skills teaching lay with the ward sisters 'to whose lot it falls to instruct the Nurse in bed-side nursing and make her practically efficient'.[13] However, in an examination of accounts of the amount and quality of skills teaching from the mid-nineteenth to the late-twentieth century, Michael Pfeil shows how ward sisters and other clinical staff were consistently reported to have neglected to engage in the teaching of practical skills and argues that the notion that a golden age of skills teaching ever existed is a myth.[14]

From the earliest days of the debate concerning nursing and higher education, the Irish Nurses' Organisation (INO) was a strong advocate of university education for qualified nurses and accounts of its efforts to establish a university diploma in nursing and a diploma for sister tutors regularly appeared in its journal, *The Irish Nurses' Magazine*, from the 1940s. Communications with the universities began as early as 1942:

> Another project we have in mind is a Diploma in Nursing and also a Diploma for Sister Tutors. We have communicated with the Universities in this matter ... We have been told that this will not be easy but we have also been told by a very eminent Professor that these difficulties ... are not insurmountable. So we will carry on in spite of any discouragement.[15]

The 'eminent Professor' referred to was most probably Michael Tierney who, in a contribution to the *Studies* symposium on 'the nursing profession and its needs', stated that 'the extension of training to include some system of university courses ending in a diploma' would help address some of the 'difficulties and disabilities of the nursing profession'.[16] He recognised that financial difficulties posed an obstacle 'but the means to surmount it certainly exist' and regarded such a development as desirable solely as a means of acknowledging the importance of the nursing profession rather than as a reflection of any 'imperfections' in the then 'admirable' standard of professional nursing.[17] In her contribution to the symposium, Annie Smithson also saw education and qualifications as a route to increased prestige and pay, observing:

> The better educated the nurse is, the higher her qualifications, so much the better should be her status and rate of remuneration.[18]

Justifying higher education for nurses solely in these terms has exposed nursing to the accusation that its educational aspirations are related to a desire for recognition, status and improved pay and conditions rather than arising from a need to enhance the teaching and learning of knowledge and skills in the interests of improving standards of patient care. Opponents of higher education for nurses continue to draw on arguments of this sort, not only to attribute a self-serving or cynical motivation to nursing leaders and educators but also to deny nursing any legitimate claim to be an academic discipline. In this regard, the nurse historian Anne Marie Rafferty notes that the assimilation of new fields of study into the university was and remains a contested process:

> Nursing studies has found a relatively new home in the academy but it should claim squatter rights against eviction. No *prima facie* case exists for placing a particular subject within a university. We have cultural studies, tourism and leisure, medicine, law and divinity; why not nursing? Such practices are the product of history, politics, economics, culture, custom, pressure groups and a good deal of political horse-trading.[19]

Links with Higher Education

In 1945, the then general secretary of the Irish Nurses' Organisation (INO), Eleanor Grogan, articulated a more altruistic reason for establishing 'University Courses for Graduate Nurses'.[20] Recognising that nursing was usually associated with 'the sphere of action rather than of thought', she argued that a university education would result not just in increased 'technical knowledge' and 'mechanical efficiency' but would also offer the nurse 'the possibility that her capabilities of ministering to her patients with her mind as well as with her hands, will be developed to the full'.[21]

In his contribution to the *Studies* symposium, Dr John P. Shanley observed that nursing was 'essentially a work of self-sacrifice for which the reward cannot be here'.[22] Shanley considered the establishment of links between nurse training schools and the university and pronounced them to be an advance that would 'provide an opportunity for those who desire to do so to proceed to higher qualification by taking out degrees in university faculty of nursing'.[23] Shanley also acknowledged that the nurse's contribution to care was 'often not less important … than … the scientific knowledge and skill of the physician or surgeon'.[24] However, the formulation implied that the nurse herself possessed neither scientific knowledge nor skill. Revealing the dilemmatic nature of his thoughts on nursing education, Shanley continued:

> It can never be lost sight of that the main training of the nurse is at the bedside of the patient – her main work being the practical and sympathetic nursing of the sick.[25]

Six decades later, Dr John Fleetwood would invoke Florence Nightingale in support of a similar point, quoting her view that 'nursing proper can only be taught at the patient's bedside and in the sick room or ward [and] lectures and books are but valuable accessories'.[26] Fleetwood mourned the passing of an idealised era of 'noble' nursing:

> The noble art of nursing has changed ... The good old days of 'caring' are gone, to be replaced with nurse practitioners, nurse specialists, nurse this, and nurse that. Nursing school is now academic and dealing with patients takes up a small amount of time as the nurses strive towards their degrees and honours.[27]

Writing for the *Studies* symposium, Dr John Kay Jamieson recognised the contribution of rhetoric, invoking notions of sacrifice, nobility and vocation to lack of action to improve the lot of nurses:

> The Nightingale influence soused the public mind in a cloying sticky sentimentalism of wordy praise – 'devotion' 'sympathy' 'sacrifice' 'nobility of service'. This hampered all efforts to improve the living conditions of the profession and to free the minds of nurses from anxieties and discomforts inimical to the exercise of the very qualities so much vaunted on platforms and in print ... praise and gratitude were deemed sufficient compensation for overwork, underpay, poor living conditions and the prospect of starvation in old age.[28]

As Professor of Anatomy at the University of Leeds between 1910 and 1936, Jamieson had been involved in setting up a nursing school at Leeds Hospital in which a four-year 'graduated course of training in the same regular course as a medical curriculum' was established.[29] Arising from this 'experiment', the need to prepare 'selected nurses' as nurse tutors by means of 'something of the nature of an F.R.C.S.' was recognised and resulted in the institution in that university of 'the first Diploma in Nursing in the Empire'.[30] Echoing contemporary recognition of the importance of context and contingency in developments in nurse education, Jamieson stressed the contribution of 'favourable circumstances' to the success of these initiatives.[31] These circumstances included the 'unrelaxing energies of the chairman, matron and one of the physicians' and the fact that 'the University, its Medical School and the General Infirmary were in close proximity and co-operation'.[32]

The ideological dilemmas in Jamieson's account are soon apparent, however. Referring to the 'perplexities' of achieving 'the fundamental difficulties in balance' attending such a scheme, he noted:

> Much care was taken to lay stress on practical proficiency in the craft of nursing, business capacity and personality. Holders of the diploma are in the first instance picked for proficiency in nursing and may aspire to reasonable offices ... yet undiverted, by too much stress on scientific attainments, from an adherence to the principle in the training of their probationers pithily expressed by a Victorian surgeon: 'The equipment of a nurse is sympathy and list-slippers.'[33]

Jamieson considered the function of the diploma to be the provision of a 'comparatively elementary knowledge of the fundamental sciences' sufficient only to 'render a person intelligent, not expert' and such courses were best provided in an ad hoc manner in 'institutions devoted to the instruction of women'.[34]

Clever or Caring?: Contemporary Discourse

Musson's comments regarding the desirability of preparing an *intellectual* nurse and the nature and amount of theoretical instruction required to do so anticipated much contemporary commentary generated by the movement of nursing education into higher education. Elizabeth Meerabeau notes how the emergence in contemporary discourse of a new construction, that of the status-conscious nurse who is 'too clever to care' and 'too posh to wash', reveals the enduringly problematic nature of the concept of the educated nurse.[35] Seven decades after Musson's comments we still see the headlines provoked by changes to the structure of nursing education in the United Kingdom and in Ireland. These headlines succinctly capture the tone and content of the dominant discourses: 'Irrelevant academic qualifications an insult to nurses – and useless to their patients: Is it the end for nurses?';[36] 'Should our nurses be clever or caring?';[37] 'How the college girls destroyed nursing';[38] 'What's wrong with nursing?';[39] 'Sickened by the nurses who don't care';[40] 'The truth about NHS hospitals: nurses – I would not trust my dog, let alone my mother, to many nurses'.[41]

Writing in 1996 on Project 2000, the preparatory diploma programme for nurses in the UK, Nigella Lawson considered the programme's aim to make nursing more academic to be 'frankly idiotic', declaring that 'the qualities that make people good nurses are not the same qualities that make people good at passing exams ... student nurses need to be in hospitals, not classrooms'.[42] 'Natural nurses' – in Lawson's terms 'the sort of people who would make the best nurses [but who just] can't cope with the academic expectations made of them'; in Musson's terms, the 'fools of the family' – were discouraged or prevented from entering nursing as a result of new and 'stringent' academic entry requirements. For Lawson, nursing was an 'honorable, worthy job' that did not require academic status to gain respectability, and society's current 'misguided emphasis on academic qualifications' resulted in mediocrity and denuded nursing of the 'large infantry' that the occupation required.

Irish journalists have echoed Lawson's concerns. In 1997, Martina Devlin reported on the introduction of psychometric testing as the means of short-listing applicants for interview for the new Diploma in Nursing programme, introduced in 1994.[43] The introductory paragraphs of Devlin's article evoke a romanticised past which is contrasted with an uncertain future:

> She was the girl who made your week in hospital bearable when you were nine and homesick: the nurse who fed you jelly and ice-cream, helped you with your jigsaw and waved you out of the ward when the time came to leave. She is the girl who might not be able to become a nurse under new recruitment procedures to emphasise the academic side of the profession.[44]

Devlin mourned the fact that not every applicant was to be granted an interview, a situation that 'allowed less scholarly hopefuls to show that what they lacked in honours they substituted with caring qualities'. Also echoing Lawson's sentiment, the journalist Kevin Myers remarked that 'academic "achievement" is not in itself necessary or even desirable for large sections of the population of any country'.[45] Myers used the example of nursing to press home his point about the contemporary drive to 'academicise the non-academic':

> Nurses must now obtain a degree, though I doubt their nursing skills will improve because of it, nor our respect for them increase. Their calling requires patience, care and technical skill, but these qualities do not increase merely because their owners can now put B.Pans (or whatever it is) after their names.[46]

For Myers, nursing was a respectable and worthy 'calling', requiring only patience, care and practical skill. Academic qualifications were at best unnecessary and at worst they diverted nurses from their essentially practical tasks. Julia Magnet, an American writer commenting on the state of nursing in the UK, regards nursing as an occupation that demands nothing less than 'self-abnegation':

> There is something in nursing that runs absolutely counter to the instincts of the modern world. Our age concerns itself with empowerment, personal rights; nursing when it's done properly, is about self-abnegation ... In nursing, ideally you realise yourself through service to others. Modern nursing has tried to stamp out the idea of a 'calling'.[47]

An Irish medical consultant, Bill Tormey, also questioned the role of learning and intelligence in nursing when, in a radio interview in 2003, he referred to 'this BSc business or whatever they call it now for nursing degrees, which came in about 1991'.[48] In Tormey's view, the new degree was 'a recipe for madness', in that it involved 'academicalising our own nurses, making them into kind of one-disease doctors [and] making rocket science out of nursing, which is ridiculous'. This resulted in a 'dichotomy in nursing between the silent previous majority [who] didn't approve of all this new development because in fact it suggests that they were inadequately trained'. Things were better, he ventured, when nurses were 'trained in medicine ... in block release' in hospital schools of nursing. Tormey also advanced the view that 'the type of people doing nursing now are qualitatively different ... and one of the problems is they're exiting nursing after getting the degrees to go into all sorts of other things'. This questioning of the commitment of the well-educated nurse to nursing perpetuated a common myth that graduate nurses fail to remain at bedside nursing, and appeared to demonstrate the speaker's lack of awareness of international evidence regarding the retention patterns of graduate nurses.

Dirty Work

Myers' rhetoric involved equating nurses with street cleaners, bin men or sewerage workers who do not need letters such as 'B.Brush or B.Bin or B.Pong' to dignify them.[49] Myers' juxtaposition of nursing work with socially devalued and unskilled 'dirty work', such as street cleaning and refuse collection, draws on metaphors of pollution and contamination, which literally and metaphorically denigrate nurses and nursing. The dismissal of nursing degrees as 'B.Pans' echoes much contemporary debate in which bedpans appear to be a particular source of humour, perhaps indicating, as Meerabeau has suggested, an underlying anxiety about human vulnerability in situations of dependency.[50] Elsewhere, Meerabeau has noted how bedpans feature prominently in discussions of nursing and higher education in the UK.[51] Referring to the then Health Secretary Frank Dobson's determination to 'turn back the clock and take training for nurses out of the classroom and put it back into hospitals', reportage exemplified this association of nursing with 'dirty work' in newspaper headlines such as 'Back to the bedpans for student nurses'.[52] Deriding the recent developments in the system of nurse training in the UK, Magnet's *Prospect* article on 'what's wrong with nursing' contained three illustrations, *viz.* a bedpan, a stethoscope and a picture of two nurses, one sitting at a computer and the other speaking on the telephone, both apparently ignoring a patient's call for attention.[53] In a report from the (UK) Centre for Policy Studies, one chapter opened with the following passage: 'One porter remarked on the nurses, "Why do you need a degree to wipe bottoms?"'[54]

These associations between nursing and 'dirty work' can be traced to earlier debates concerning nursing work and education, and the recruitment and retention of nurses. Addressing the Irish Nurses' Union in 1936, Michael Davitt remarked that nursing was 'a splendid profession for a girl' despite the 'unpleasantness which is mentally associated with many of the duties … [and] the humdrum work and distasteful tasks she is called upon to perform'.[55] Writing for the *Studies* symposium on 'the nursing profession and its needs', a Roman Catholic priest Father P. J. Gannon referred to the 'hard and often repellent duties' of the nurse. Despite the nature of the nurse's duties, the writer also considered that nursing had 'long passed out of the category of menial employments into that of a highly respected calling – as respected as medicine itself and perhaps more universally esteemed'.[56]

Rafferty remarks how representations of nursing work as polluting and contaminating serve to construct nursing as unworthy of academic study:

> Nursing has a problem in perception as an academic subject since its practice involves close proximity to bodily functions and fluids. Excreta, pain, death, stress and vulnerability are … totemically taboo subjects which hardly lend themselves to high table conversations.[57]

Claire Fagin and Donna Diers, both nurse academics, reflect on the reactions of people that they encounter socially to being told that they are nurses: '"How can you bear handling bedpans (vomit, blood)?" was a typical response.'[58] Fagin and Diers believe that statements such as this reflect the 'disturbing and discomforting' images that nursing evokes and which educated, upwardly mobile, middle-class individuals find difficult to deal with. In their exploration of the social perceptions of nurses, Fagin and Diers propose that nursing is a metaphor for mothering, intimacy, sex, class struggle, equality and conscience, and that it is 'the sum of these images [which] make up the psychological milieu in which nurses live and work'. Nursing as mothering, involves tasks which are 'essentially mundane and hardly worth noticing' but which can precipitate 'regressed feelings' by reminding people of the child within. Nursing is a metaphor for intimacy in the way that nurses are involved in the 'most private aspects of people's lives' and are witness to many secrets 'born of vulnerability' and loss of control which are indelibly identified with those 'terribly personal times'. Nursing as a metaphor for sex arises from the fact that nurses are sanctioned to see and touch the bodies of strangers, and are perceived as knowing and willing, yet they are clean and safe sexual partners. As class struggle, nursing represents 'women's struggle for equality' and the position of nursing as the 'classic underdog, struggling to be heard, approved and recognised'. Finally, nursing is a metaphor for equality, since there is often little social distance between nurses and patients, with nurses perceived as working-class and as having 'simply settled for a job instead of choosing a more prestigious profession'. Nursing as conscience, represents an anxiety-provoking, guilt-inducing reminder of physicians' fallibility.

Threat

A recurrent feature of the debate concerning nursing and higher education, and noted by Rafferty, is the way in which nursing education is made a scapegoat for deficiencies in the healthcare system.[59] A feature of some Irish commentary is the way in which attacks on nursing education appear to be smuggled into the discourse and are at best tangential to the main theme being debated. This is noticeable in the contributions of certain members of the medical profession for whom 'academic nursing' is a source of considerable unease. In an article outlining key aspects of a risk management programme to address an impending 'malpractice crisis' in Irish healthcare, Charles J. Ward, a clinical professor working in the United States, concluded with two paragraphs discussing Irish nursing.[60] In a by now familiar move, Ward first extols the virtues of the Irish nurse who 'exemplifies care, compassion, concern and good listening skills', claiming that Irish nursing 'has long been recognised as some of the finest in the world' before attacking the project to reform nursing education:

> Unfortunately, this is being threatened in Ireland, due to an effort to increase academic skills in nursing.[61]

Ward concedes that nurses working in critical care areas and in education undoubtedly need these unspecified 'academic skills', but argues that 'it is generally not required by the skilled ward nurse'. The writer claims that the emphasis on 'academic excellence and managerial skills' has resulted in a great reduction in and even loss of quality nursing care in the US, where the 'new highly trained nurse' has now lost the personal touch and has delegated direct bedside patient care to technicians and nursing assistants. Without citing any evidence for his claims or considering whether the nature and context of nursing in Ireland and the US are comparable, Ward remarks:

> It is unfortunate to discover that clinical nurse instructors in nursing schools, with advanced degrees, but with very limited clinical bedside experience, are becoming the teachers of future nurses in Ireland. It is difficult, if not impossible, to teach bedside nursing and 'TLC' if the instructor has had very limited experience in this critical area.[62]

For Ward, nursing care in the US is a 'disaster', leading to a situation whereby 'the very noble career of nursing' was being avoided, leading to a nursing shortage. Ward urges 'Ireland' to examine the US experience closely before implementing a new strategy for nursing education, and in his final sentence declaims: 'Ireland MUST AVOID this strategy.'[63]

Ward's article contains a number of noteworthy features. Firstly, and as already observed, the writer cites no empirical evidence in support of his claims about the impact on clinical practice of developments in nursing education. Secondly, the account of nursing does not appear to relate to the foregoing discussion in any meaningful way. Thirdly, nursing is constructed as a noble, caring and compassionate personal service, which is under threat from unnecessary amounts of academic knowledge and skills. Although Ward's remarks on nursing accounted for only about three percent of his paper, they alone were reported in the *Irish Medical News* under the headline 'Academic skills emphasis a threat to standards in Irish nursing'.[64] The report appeared in the same week that the new four-year degree in nursing programme commenced in higher education institutions throughout Ireland.

In November 2002, an article in *The Irish Times* reported a leading transplant surgeon's views on the inadequate facilities at a north Dublin hospital and his opinion that the hospital in question should be closed and replaced with a new one. Towards the end of the article, the journalist reported:

> Dr Hickey was also critical of the current nursing degree, claiming it put too much emphasis on academic achievement and was flooding the healthcare system with nurses who were unsuitable. Many new nurses had no long-term interest in the job and only pursued it as a means to a career in other areas of healthcare such as pharmacy, he said.[65]

In a newspaper article discussing the issues arising out of the death of a two year-old girl following the cancellation of her heart surgery at a

Dublin children's hospital, the journalist Patricia Redlich considered the role of nursing shortages that, she argued, were caused by the nursing profession itself.[66] Nurses, she observed, had 'turned nursing into an academic subject ... for status for themselves, and as a mechanism for demanding more pay'.[67] The writer remarked that 'in fairness, they (nurses) did this partially to serve the patient' but that they failed to recognise that 'a university course pulls nurses off the wards, creating nursing shortages as hospitals are denuded of in-service trainees'.[68]

Redlich's language almost precisely echoed that of Melanie Philips, who four years previously wrote of the 'catastrophe' of nurse training in the UK, consequent upon it being 'taken away from the hospitals and turned into an academic subject taught in universities'.[69] In these claims, there is a denial of any intrinsic claim to academic status for nursing; the profession is depicted as having contrived by some sleight of hand to 'turn' itself into an academic subject because 'its leaders decided it had to gain higher status by becoming more professionalised'. This, it is claimed, resulted in a shortage of nurses because 'women are turning away from nursing in large measure because it has changed ... it has driven away people who would make excellent nurses but have no academic bent'. The image of Musson's 'fool of the family' is again implicitly reprised.

Conclusions

The dominant enduring discourse concerning nursing education is one which constructs and sustains a dichotomy between the practical and the intellectual, an opposition that remains at the heart of the disciplinary politics of nursing.[70] Associated with this dichotomy are other binary oppositions: doing versus thinking, caring versus cleverness, manual versus mental and skill versus theory. Each opposing pole is identified with different sites: the bedside (or hospital/ward) versus the classroom (or academy/school). Nurse educators and leaders are frequently represented as steering nursing away from the practical towards the intellectual in the interest of enhancing status and remuneration, but with consequent negative consequences for nursing practice at the bedside. The abundance of images and metaphors concerning pollution, contamination, invasion and mutation press home the notion that nursing is being contaminated by academic values which threaten to destroy its vocational and practical essence and that academia is, in turn, being invaded by nursing students, nurse educators and vocational values, none of which belong there.

As nursing education strives to carve out a new space for itself in the academy, nurse academics are challenged to legitimate themselves as academics and to legitimate nursing as an academic discipline, in the face of opposition to their endeavours from within and outside the profession. This process of legitimation will involve highlighting how assumptions about gender, class, race, the nature of nursing work and the relationship between nursing and medicine continue to underpin contemporary discourse about nursing and higher education. But it must go further than this; in making the case for higher education for nurses, nurse academics must address themselves to epistemological as well as to sociological issues. This requires them to address the nature of nursing knowledge and the ways in which it is produced and transmitted. The form, content and outcome of this process of legitimation will shape the design and delivery of nursing curricula and will determine the status and trajectory of nursing in higher education.

CHAPTER 5

'Through the Lens': The Irish Nurse in Cinema and Television

Gerard Fealy and Malcolm Newby

In the nineteenth-century reforms of Irish nursing, untrained and uneducated nurses from the poorer class were replaced with educated middle-class women and, following the reforms, nursing was promoted as a respectable career for young educated gentlewomen.[1] Arising out of the reforms, an enduring set of images of the nurse soon became fixed in the public mind. The nurse was a young woman, a uniformed health worker, a doctor's assistant and a virtuous and dedicated healer of the sick. In the public mind, nursing was promoted as 'that highest walk of woman's work'.[2]

In Ireland, the new profession cultivated, confirmed and sustained this idealised image of the 'good nurse'.[3] Popular portrayals of the nurse could be found in women's magazines and in the new visual medium of film. As the representational form of film evolved into its many and varied cinematic genres, and as the nursing profession developed throughout the twentieth century, popular images of the nurse changed accordingly. As the new medium of television emerged with its range of fictional and factual narratives, a range of new public images of the nurse also emerged.

As with medicine, nursing's relationship with the visual media is complex and, given the powerful influence that such media have in shaping popular attitudes and understandings, this relationship is one that is worthy of consideration.[4]

Film, Historians and Historiography

Although a relatively new medium of mass communication, cinema has provided a rich source of archival material for social historians. With the advent of film technology, documentaries and newsreels were quickly seen as useful sources for the historian, although feature films were always deemed more problematic. After all, feature films were and are primarily business enterprises and are only secondarily entertainment. They are often dependent on the star system, on box office demands, studio formulae and genre expectations, and are of course the product of multi-person collaboration. So what can historians expect to learn from such films? At the very least, they learn occupational details, the prevailing ideology and value-system, relationships and possibly audience expectations.[5] However, historians often learn much more of everyday detail from cable or made-for-movie or video films, partly as a result of their lower budgets, but more so because they take less artistic licence.

Following the Second World War, academic historians started to take an interest in film. American historians tended to take the film theory route – usually with a heavy emphasis on representation theory (the relationship between the image and the people, events or ideas that the image refers to) and semiotics, for example – whereas European historians like Pierre Sorlin, K. R. M. Short and Paul Smith in the 1970s and 1980s concentrated on the unique source problems of the feature film, *viz.* the multiple source ownership of a collaborative industry, and studio myth-making.[6] When nursing historians took up this source, there was something of the same dichotomy: Philip Kalisch and Beatrice Kalisch concentrated on representation and later Julia Hallam wrote of nursing films using many more aspects of film theory; while both Michael Shortland and Malcolm Newby emphasised the source difficulties and the need to understand the films in their business setting, particularly studio and genre expectation.[7] From these authors, it is possible to plot a number of feature films which might broadly be termed 'nursing films'. However, to term these a genre or even a subgenre of 'medical' films would be fanciful. A 'nursing film' is a film that portrays nurses in an occupational setting, or is a film in which the fact that the protagonist is a nurse is significant.

A Brief History of Nurses on Film

The relationship between healthcare and the medium of film is as old as the medium itself. Since the earliest days of film, health officials have used the medium as a vehicle for educating the public about health and sanitation; for example the prevention of tuberculosis and venereal disease were common themes.[8] With the advent of talking pictures in the late 1920s, the medical melodrama was quickly established in cinematic film as a popular genre and, as the medical historian Richard Shryock observed, the genre appeared to satisfy a popular taste for the subject matter, in which 'anything in white' was good for box office returns.[9] For much of the twentieth century, the medical melodrama offered the public a variety of narratives, from factually-based films about scientific discoveries and biographies of great medical men – and the occasional woman such as Marie Curie – to romantic fiction that frequently involved the (male) doctor and (female) nurse.

Early examples of the genre on television, such as *Emergency Ward 10* (1956–67) and *Doctor Kildare* (1961–66), also contained sub-plots concerning the doctor–nurse romantic encounter. In these highly popular shows, the doctor was the principal character and was frequently portrayed as a heroic figure, the competent and compassionate medic, and the playful but committed professional.[10] The television medical melodrama was an important vehicle for promoting a positive image of medicine and for advocating the benefits of medical technology; in order to achieve realism in the production of these programmes, the scriptwriters frequently engaged medical consultants.[11] However, through the lens the filmmaker could only ever produce a putative realism, a constructed version of reality. Later examples of the small screen medical melodrama continued the trend to achieve supposed realism, in such graphically 'real' US television dramas as *St Elsewhere* and *ER*, and their British equivalents *Casualty* and *Holby City*.[12] A characteristic and recurring trend of the genre has been the efforts to incorporate the latest advances in medical technology; in late twentieth-century versions of the genre, the 'medic' entreating all to 'clear!' before administering defibrillation in the ubiquitous 'code blue' scene typifies this trend.

It is in the putative realism of the medical melodrama that the image of the nurse is most widely represented. As the romantic interest and the subject of sub-plots in the early small screen medical melodrama, the nurse was portrayed as a subservient supporter of the medic in his work and, as Hallam writes:

> Nurses became background presences, translators of medical jargon for a surrogate audience of fictional patients who needed to be informed and educated about new developments in medical science.[13]

In early versions of the genre, the nurse is the physician's able and loyal ally, while later versions portray her as the quick-thinking and competent technician in an emergency. The gritty 'reality' of medical melodramas has also attempted to depict the juxtaposition of professional work and personal life; like the doctor, the nurse is frequently depicted as engaged in a struggle to cope with the demands of professional work, personal relationships, and family life. However, as Anne Marie Rafferty points out, in the genre, nurses are rarely given 'any good lines', unless they are breaking the mould of the (young white female) nurse.[14] Notable mould-breakers have included the sadistic Nurse Mildred Ratched in *One Flew Over the Cuckoo's Nest* (1975), the vixen Margaret 'Hot Lips' Houlihan in the subversive medical comedy drama *M*A*S*H** (1972–82) and the competent but fallible Charge Nurse Charlie in *Casualty*. The salacious nurses of *No Angels* (2004) returned to the clichéd stereotypes of nurses as sexual objects, but also conferred on them some of the attributes of the exuberant and playful doctor of earlier television melodramas.

Cinema and television thus offer a range of images of the nurse, variously portraying her as the romantic interest, the savvy technician, or the overworked multi-roled nurse, wife and mother. Nursing is variously depicted as a culturally esteemed and high status profession for respectable middle-class women or the loyal 'sister profession' of medicine.[15] On occasions, the nurse is the focus of sexual titillation and the sexual mascot of the doctor.[16]

The Irish and Women on Film

Any consideration of how the Irish nurse is depicted in film must take account of the wider trends in depictions of both the Irish and women in film. This is necessary since some depictions of the Irish nurse seem to represent these wider trends. Aside from the content of films made about the Irish and about women, the source of their production and genre conventions have constituted part of the context for the way that the Irish and women are depicted.

American and British films have dominated cinema in Ireland and, aside from some notable independent indigenous filmmaking, the most significant Irish film productions have been funded by international money. In the early non-indigenous films concerning Irish themes and produced by Hollywood, the Irish people were frequently portrayed as simple and idiosyncratic peasant folk; through the lens of the early filmmaker Sidney Olcott and directors like John Ford, Ireland was a romantic rural idyll, uncorrupted by foreign cultural influences.[17]

With the advent of more critical productions by independent filmmakers in the 1980s and 1990s, the less than idyllic aspects of Irish social life began to be represented in such films as *Our Boys* (1980), *Hush-A-Bye-Baby* (1989) and *I Went Down* (1997).[18] Critical counter-cinema and avant-garde productions led to re-evaluation and re-interpretation of Irish cultural identity and society, with productions on themes like the role of the family, urban poverty and crime, celibacy, sexuality and disability, and suicide.[19] From the (female) audience perspective, international cinema could provide Irish women with new and modern models of femininity, and permitted public expression of taboo subjects like sexuality and reproduction.[20] In Irish cinema, narratives concerning women have included *Anne Devlin* (1984) and *Agnes Browne* (1999), while the small number of films with a more feminist orientation includes *Hush-A-Bye-Baby* (1989), *Snakes and Ladders* (1996) and *Nora* (2000).[21]

Irish Nurses on Film

From the earlier definition of a 'nursing film', it is possible to find a large number of films, in all over 300, from both the United States and

Britain that contain images of the nurse. The United States has produced the greatest number of what are hospital-centred films, and their nurses appear in most of the main genres and sub-genres, even in horrors and musicals. In Britain, by far the most predominant genre is comedy, be it slapstick, bawdy or black; most of these productions appeared in the 1950s and 1960s.

A search of film archives from American, British and Irish studios yielded only a limited sample of what might be termed 'Irish nurse films' from the 1920s to the present day. Surprisingly, there are only three American 'Irish nurse films'. One is set in Boston and the other two are Westerns. There are three British and five Irish 'Irish nurse films', two of which only qualify as Irish films by virtue of Rockett's criteria of having an Irish director or being filmed in Ireland.

Kaitlin Costello Price is an ex-maternity nurse who gives evidence in a hospital cover-up of a medical malpractice case in *The Verdict* (1982), the courtroom drama set in Boston. The cavalry major and fort commander's wife, Abby MacAllshard, is seen doing some frontier nursing in John Ford's *She Wore A Yellow Ribbon* (1949); while Elizabeth Reilly is a full-time professional nurse ministering to a far flung local community in the frontier west in *The Revengers* (1971).

In a 1956 British nurses-in-training film, *The Feminine Touch*, student nurse Maureen O'Brien, newly arrived from Ireland, throws herself into her training in a large London hospital. Pauline Murray tries to bury herself in nursing so as not to become politically involved in a polarised British society after a successful Nazi invasion in 1940 in the documentary-style *It Happened Here* (1966); and Pauline Collins plays Joan Bethel, a nurse figure in the Calcutta slums in *City of Joy* (1992), cajoling Patrick Swayze, who plays a disillusioned doctor, into helping her work.

The first Irish film, or rather the first film with an Irish director, in Hollywood is reputed to be William Desmond Taylor's *Nurse Marjorie* (1920), a romance comedy using elements of the Florence Nightingale story; Nurse Marjorie is a rich aristocrat nursing against her parents, the Duke and Duchess of Donegal's wishes. In 1934, with its director, cast and setting all Irish, a truly Irish film, titled *Norah O'Neal*, was released. Often referred to as the 'first all Irish talkie', the film was another romance comedy with two nurses falling for the same doctor in a Dublin hospital. With an Irish setting at Crookhaven, *I Thank a Fool* (1962) featured Susan Hayward as Christine Allison, a Canadian doctor struck off for mercy killing but inveigled by the prosecuting attorney into acting as nurse companion to his Irish wife. Of more recent films there is the cameo role of Nurse Mary Carr in *My Left Foot* (1989). Although hardly on the screen in Jim Sheridan's biopic, Nurse Mary plays a pivotal part in introducing and linking the film's flashback scenes. *On the Edge* (2000) is a coming-of-age combined with a somewhat old-fashioned social commentary film about three suicidal teenagers in St Brendan's Grangegorman mental hospital. The film's portrayal of the male nurse is nominal. *Inside I am Dancing* (2004), which includes a portrayal of nurses at the Carrigmore Home for Disabled, appeared too late for inclusion in this chapter.

Factors Influencing Screen Portrayals

It is tempting to think that the screen portrayal represents the reality of nursing at the time the film was made; occasionally this may prove correct, but more often than not, the demands of the genre, studio and audience expectations, and stardom can prove otherwise. Film is a complex medium for historians, particularly as a single source is really a variety of sources that result from the collaborative nature of the industry. Sometimes, the initial script/screenplay is as important as the director's interpretation, or the influence of casting. Furthermore, the art director's sets might influence the audience as much as the actor's method and interpretation.

The Irish nurse films uncovered therefore need to be scrutinised in terms of genre conventions (i.e. iconography, theme, character, and narrative structure), ideology or historical setting, stardom, and source problems.[22]

Genre Conventions

To the audience, iconography is the easiest and the most obvious way of determining the genre they are watching. Iconography within genre is shorthand for recurring visual compositions like the saloon in the

Western, the tied down holster of the gunfighter, and so forth. Recurring visual compositions of nursing include hospital signposts, corridors, Nightingale wards, doctors and nurses' sitting-rooms, ward kitchens, operating theatres, uniforms and medical instruments. However, at the signs and meaning level, the camera often picks out religious imagery, such as the shadow of the cross cast by the ward window.

In our sample of Irish nurse films, just four are distinct hospital films, and in only two, *Nurse Marjorie* and *Norah O'Neal*, do we see Irish nurses working on the wards. Influenced by American films such as *Night Nurse* (1931) and *White Parade* (1934), *Norah O'Neal* depicts some of the first non-Hollywood civilian hospital scenes; by the 1930s, American cinema had discovered hospital nurses as opposed to First World War military nurses. As a predominantly courtroom drama, the film *The Verdict* contains only maternity ward scenes for background setting.

Uniforms and instruments are part of the visual compositions associated with the nurses in the two Western films in our sample. Elizabeth Reilly wears a uniform, has her own surgery and is familiar with medicines and instruments. While Abby MacAllshard wears cavalry trousers, she is seen assisting the doctor in an arrow wound operation, engaging in a little fevered-brow nursing and caring for a sick child. She is essentially a frontier officer's wife who, like her real-life counterparts, acquired some nursing skills as part of her social education back in the east.

Among the principal themes of the nursing film are self-sacrifice and dedication on the part of the nurse; in *The Revengers*, Nurse Reilly jettisons the chance of a relationship with her patient, the rancher, in order to permit him to grieve for his murdered family. An adjunct to these themes is a successful ending for the 'good nurse' and death or failure for the 'bad nurse'; witness the good nurse Norah O'Neal finally winning the love of the doctor by nursing him heroically through typhoid fever, whilst the manipulative bad nurse is rejected.

Narrative structure can affect a character's portrayal in films, including nursing films. Since former nurse Kaitlin Costello Price is the key surprise witness in a courtroom drama, it would not be possible to have flashback scenes to the ward, as this would weaken the denouement that revolved around report writing. All that was required of her was to stand up to the vigorous cross-examination of both prosecuting and defending lawyers and expose the cover up by the Catholic Church and the hospital authorities. *The Feminine Touch* (1956) owes much of its structure to the military platoon-in-training film, including mutiny against discipline, first death, court martial and so forth. Like the barrack room, the nurses' sitting-room needed not only a class mix but also a geographical one. Hence, it contains the rebellious, confident and talkative Irish nurse with her almost classless accent. She is the counterbalance to the star nurses, the middle-class idealist and the husband-seeking cynical nurse, the lesser jolly public school girl, and the working-class cockney.

Like *Girl Interrupted* (2000) or *I Never Promised You a Rose Garden* (1979), the narrative structure in *On the Edge* is the archetypal clash of the inmates against the psychiatrist until they (the inmates) leave hospital cured. Since one of the main protagonists in *On the Edge* is a doctor, it is usual that the nurse or nurses are marginalised – Nurse Ratched in *One Flew Over The Cuckoo's Nest* (1975) is an exception. So it is that the Irish male nurse hardly appears, and when he does, he is authoritarian, unsympathetic and menial. He is almost the muscle-bound custodian of the American film noirs of the 1940s.

In *My Left Foot*, using Nurse Mary as the chorus to the film by reading Christy Brown's autobiography is a clever filmic device. Nurse Mary is introduced at the start of the film and the film audience knows that she is Brown's future wife, thereby giving convenient closure when they go on their first date at the end of the film. The subsequent marriage affects her character portrayal; to appeal to Christy, she must be attractive, compassionate, thoughtful and quiet, but she must be strong-minded and firm enough to take on such a difficult person. She makes it clear that she is no mother substitute but an individual in her own right.

City of Joy is almost a Western with the town folk being persuaded by the protagonists to fight the Godfather and his gangsters for their livelihood, and Nurse Joan Bethel is a pragmatist who fights when her Irish blood is up!

It is in the character convention that representation and stereotyping are located. Here is found the entire spectrum of nurses from matron to nursing auxiliary, and the nurse's relationships with patients, doctors and administrators. Depending on their age, experience or rank, nurses are variously portrayed as naïve, vulnerable, clumsy, sexy, confident, authoritarian and embittered. The two early romantic comedies, *Nurse Marjorie* and *Norah O'Neal*, contain some of these elements, while *The Feminine Touch* explores the senior staff stereotype in a more sympathetic way.

With the exception of *Norah O'Neal*'s 'bad' nurse and perhaps the male nurse in *On the Edge*, all of the nurses in our sample are within the caring/compassionate stereotype; none of the films in our sample are horror or black comedy, which often deal in anti-myth. Apart from the hospital nurses, all of the nurses are aged over thirty and some are in their fifties. The Irish nurses are also the more mature version of the feisty colleen stereotype. Only Kaitlin Price – 'all red tresses and brogue' – and Maureen O'Brien are young nurses.[23] In *It Happened Here*, Pauline Murray might be older and more independent, but this merely heightens her political naïvety as she fails to realise that life will never again be normal in the dystopian society that exists following the Nazi invasion of Britain. In the new society, the fact that Pauline Murray is an Irish nurse is central to the film's theme. As a nurse she is indispensable to both sides, and in a commonsense way, she thinks that this fact will help her mentally to survive. However, all that it demonstrates is that, ironically, there are no neutrals, even those, like the 'Irish', who are technically neutral. Joan Bethell, a Mother Theresa-type in Calcutta, is middle-aged so that she can have the sort of missionary nun-drunken cynic conversations of films in the 1950s, but with no chance of being the love interest of the young doctor. She is Irish rather than East European, since Irishness and Catholicism are synonymous for cinema audiences, particularly Anglophone audiences, throughout the world.

Ideology or Historical Setting

Films are not made in a social or political vacuum and some contemporary trends may well influence production, but it must be remembered that this may not be the primary influence on the film's design, such is the conservatism of the film-making industry. The concerns about Ireland's rising teenage suicide rate might well have been the reason for the making of *On the Edge*, but, as already observed, the nurse portrayal owes more to American film noirs of the 1940s. *City of Joy* might have been inspired by the work of Mother Theresa, but the writers deliberately chose a lay nurse with religious and philanthropic impulses in order to underplay comparisons. Unlike the 1950s, the post-colonial 1990s was not the time for a film about a missionary nun–doctor relationship.

The Revengers is a typical 1970s revisionist Western, a genre that was influenced by Spaghetti Westerns of the 1960s and the Vietnam War. Cynical and bloody, these movies bred cynicism towards all institutions, especially political institutions, and heralded the anti-hero who, although outside the law, has justice on his side. Hence the protagonist in *The Revengers* is the bitter rancher. The women's liberation movement was well under way at the time of the film's release and with it came an interest in past witches, wise women and medicine women. This accounts for the independence of the nurse character Elizabeth Reilly who makes a professional living as a nurse, doctor and pharmacist, in the service of her small community. She is a strong character, both mentally and physically, and is portrayed literally digging her own smallholding. She is a true manifestation of the frontier spirit. Part of the revisionism of the 1970s was to use a fading female star who had previously played similar parts. Susan Hayward played the part of a nurse in *White Witch Doctor* (1953) and *I Thank a Fool* (1962). In *The Revengers* she becomes a middle-aged nurse in a cameo role playing a love diversion to a middle-aged William Holden. The use of an actress in her fifties might have been a studio reaction to the use of young actresses who played the part of saloon girls or school teachers – both western women stereotypes – or of nurses as doctors' handmaidens, amateurs all. It is possible to see Nurse Reilly as fitting the ideology of early 1970s filmmaking; she is a loner, an outsider isolated from the community by her sense of moral and professional self-sufficiency, and an anti-heroine.

It is probable that John Ford's love of the United States army was a result of his own Second World War service, and hence the post-war cavalry trilogy, of which *She Wore a Yellow Ribbon* (1949) was the middle film. However, Mildred Natwick's character Abby MacAllshard was not influenced by issues of the time. Rather, Nurse MacAllshard displayed her nursing skills in the comedic role of the slightly tipsy doctor's assistant, as befits a well-used John Ford character actress. After all, Natwick would play the widow Sarah Tillane in that apotheosis of Ford's American–Irish sentimentalism, *The Quiet Man*, some three years later.

Stardom

Casting and the star system can also influence character portrayal. Lindsay Crouse, who played Kaitlin Price, specialised in 'aloof no nonsense brainy types', while Mildred Natwick was one of John Ford's character comedy actors.[24] Mary Miles Minter in *Nurse Marjorie* projected innocence and naïvety, hence the comic possibilities of feigning ugliness and poverty to her socialist and semi-blind patient. In the 1940s and 1950s, female film stars were noted for playing victims, strong women or evil women; Susan Hayward for example frequently played strong female roles. Belinda Lee, the star of *The Feminine Touch* and a strong-woman actress, is the only student nurse to be shown doing nursing.

Source Problems

As a historical source, the feature film is a difficult source for the historian to analyse, and analysis requires the sort of rigorous scrutiny that the historian would bring to a written historical document. What appears on the screen is only one part of the source; the historian needs to consult as much extant written and oral material on each film before drawing any conclusions as to it relevance to its contemporary period. For example, *Norah O'Neal* was based on the novel *Night Nurse*, written by the surgeon James Johnston Abraham in 1908 while he was a student at Dr Steevens' Hospital in Dublin.[25] While the 1934 screenplay might show some updating, the prevailing attitudes contained in the novel and, consequentially, in the film were those of the period 1908. As a contemporary historical source for the 1930s, *Norah O'Neal* is therefore unreliable.

A director of the stature of John Ford can indirectly influence images, particularly in Westerns with his drunken doctor stereotypes and his stock Irish characters. However it is worth remembering that in studio history such Irish characters preceded Ford, appearing in Westerns as early as 1917.

In short, feature films can illustrate changes in occupational roles, but given the conservatism of the film business, they are just as likely to show continuities over time. While the image can change over time, it can also remain the same. Irish films are no exception, but given the very limited sample of Irish nurse films, it is difficult to draw definitive conclusions.

Why So Few Irish Nurses on Film?

Our sample of films contains most of the Irish-made feature films featuring an Irish nurse. It would appear that very few such films were ever made for or by the Irish. There is no one obvious explanation to account for such a paucity of films. The answer lies somewhere in the interplay between Irish culture and politics, international English-speaking audiences and their expectations, and distribution policies. There is, of course, a random factor in the nurse film trend, as it can often be a scriptwriter's whim whether or not a nurse appears in a certain genre. Unlike Ireland, films in England in the 1940s and 1950s were influenced by novel adaptation (often of the nursing autobiographical type), by the public debates on the introduction of the National Health Service, and by issues such as whether mothers should remain with their children in hospital. Irish audiences could view these 'medical' films made in England, especially the hugely popular *Doctor* and *Carry On* series. But since the Irish comprised only five per cent of the combined Irish–British box office audience, indigenous Irish nursing films could not be made for this audience alone. Apart from the comedies, medical films were usually not profitable material, even for the British box office.

One genre that produced a number of film nurses was the war film. In this genre, nurses are the love interest near the battlefield and are the symbols of what the boys are fighting for; they are their mothers, wives and sisters back home. This entire genre is excluded in Irish political history, at least until the late 1980s.[26] However, Ireland has its own entire sub-genre, the 'War of Independence' film. Yet even though

Irish nurses took part in the battles of the campaign for Irish independence, and women such as Constance Gore-Booth – who commanded infantry in 1916 – had nurse training, no nurse appears in these films, not even as a soldier's girlfriend.[27]

Another sub-genre that portrays nurses in feature films is that which deals with themes and plots concerned with infectious diseases. Apart from *Norah O'Neal*, Ireland has mostly produced documentary-dramas within this sub-genre.[28]

Following Irish independence, Éamon de Valera and many in the Fianna Fáil party believed that Ireland's image should be that of romantic pastoralism, an idyllic self-sufficient hardy agrarian culture for good Catholics. De Valera's favourite film was Flaherty's *Man of Aran* (1934) and he encouraged Irish filmmakers to emulate it.[29] Still there was not to be a film about the heroic district nurse ministering to the country folk in the west of Ireland. Nor was any attempt made to develop biopics of Ireland's most famous nurses, Catherine McCauley, Mary Aikenhead or Margaret Huxley. Perhaps Irish filmmakers believed that, with the exception of Ireland, there would be no audience for such films. Yet in 1947, French cinema had a huge international success with *Monsieur Vincent*, which, while not showing any nursing, does makes very clear what the Sisters of Charity stood for. Not even the much-vaunted Ardmore Studios encouraged indigenous films; the studio was merely a job-creation enterprise and a location facility for foreign film productions.[30]

It is not surprising therefore that there were so few indigenous Irish nurse films from 1922 to the present. But it is surprising there are so few Irish nurses in American and British films, since both countries, particularly Britain, employed large numbers of Irish nurses. There appears to be only two British films portraying an Irish nurse released in the heyday of nurse films: *The Feminine Touch* (1956) and *It Happened Here* (1966). This appears to be in direct contradiction to what was happening in reality. After a heavy recruitment drive to acquire Irish nurses in the 1950s, the 1971 census showed there were 31,000 Irish-born nurses in Britain, contributing to 12 per cent of the nursing force.[31] Although feature films in themselves are unreliable sources, there seems no adequate explanation for such an omission. Perhaps British audiences preferred the Irish to play comic patients, like in *Carry on Nurse* (1959) or the film *Life in Emergency Ward Ten* (1958), rather than be nurses whom they might have to rely on as hospital patients. From the late 1960s, the omission becomes easier to explain, as films emphasised ethnicity; Afro-Caribbean nurses almost became *de rigueur*. For example Nichol's *The National Health* (1973) or *Britannia Hospital* (1982) contained black nurses, while Puerto Ricans replaced the Irish nurses in the film version of Clarke's play *Whose Life is it Anyway?* (1981)

The Irish Nurse on Irish Television

While Irish audiences have consumed the medical melodrama of American and British television since the inception of Irish television in the early 1960s, no analogous Irish version of *ER* or *Holby City* has appeared on the small screen. Brenda Fricker's Irish nurse character in the BBC television soap opera *Casualty* is perhaps the best-known Irish nurse of the small screen in Britain and Ireland. Fricker plays the mature, steady, good and sensible Irish nurse, who is both firm and resolute in the face of adversity, and motherly to colleagues and patients in need of support. However, few other images of the Irish nurse are available in the medium of Irish television.

The most common contemporary portrayals of Irish nurses on television are found in archival footage used to complement the narrative in news items. The usual context for presenting these images is reportage concerning the Irish health services, the most common topics being related to health service problems, such as financial and staffing difficulties, medical malpractice, or an innovation in medical science. These images almost invariably depict nurses in (modern) tunic and trouser uniform, standing at the nurses' station and examining a document/chart, administering drugs from a drug trolley, or walking in a hospital corridor. Sometimes the nurse is seen doing a technical task, such as adjusting a drip rate or attending to an infant in an incubator. Rarely are nurses interviewed in this type of reportage.

During the first national strike by nurses and midwives in October 1997, images of Irish nurses were presented on each and every news bulletin for the period leading up to the strike and during the eight days of the strike. The two principal images of nurses were indoor footage of hospital nurses at work and outdoor footage of nurses on the picket line or attending public rallies. As a rule, these images made no distinction between nurses and midwives and no distinction between the various branches of nursing, such as psychiatric or public health nursing. Significantly, when the principal leaders of the nursing trade unions were interviewed, they were mostly men, and were usually filmed at the door of a building, either entering or leaving a meeting. In the reportage, the most enduring image of the nurse was that of the general hospital nurse. The implicit content of much of the reportage was that nursing was a highly technical activity associated with hospital medicine. The medical disciplines of accident and emergency, oncology and cardiology were frequently used to supplement reportage concerning the effects of the strike. As Jean Clarke and Catherine O'Neill observe in their analysis of newspaper reportage of the strike, 'the softer elements of caring were side-tracked, in an argument that seemed to focus on the "harder", so to speak "more scientific", elements of caring.'[32]

Aside from television news reportage, the three popular images of the Irish nurse on television are contained in the annual 'Lucozade Nurse of the Year' award (1974 and subsequent years), the documentary series *Nurses* (2001), and the images associated with the Irish Hospitals Sweepstake.

The 'Lucozade Nurse of the Year' award was launched in 1974 as a way of engendering greater interest in nursing as a career.[33] The award was conducted under the auspices of the Irish Nurses' Organisation (INO) and its sponsors were Independent Newspapers Limited and Beecham of Ireland Limited. The latter sponsor was a pharmaceutical company that had successfully marketed its product, Lucozade, as a health supplement. The candidates for the award were judged according to the criteria which the INO believed the 'ideal nurse' should possess, namely, 'nursing skills, compassion, personality, leadership, dedication, understanding and ambition in her career'.[34] The 'Lucozade Nurse of the Year' was a filler item on RTÉ's perennial *The Late Late Show*; the show's host, Gay Byrne, briefly introduced the finalists and announced the overall winner.[35]

The screening of the six-part documentary series *Nurses* (2001) aimed to portray the 'reality' of the working lives of Irish nurses.[36] Less in the tradition of cinema verité, the series derived its form and content from the popular British 'docusoap' format of such series as *Jimmy's* and *Airport*. In the six half-hour films, the lives of 'a diverse group of working nurses' at University College Hospital Galway and the experiences of some of their patients and families were depicted. With a nurse as the primary subject of narrative interest, each episode presented a series of scenes, involving a variety of nurse–patient encounters: Nurse Eóin treats a child with a head wound, Nurse Mary counsels a woman who is about to have chemotherapy, and Midwife Maureen examines a new-born infant. While some of the scenes are matter-of-fact, others are long and intimate. A quietly spoken male voice introduces each scene – 'student nurse Jeanie is about to start her first clinical placement ...' – and the voice-over and visual images are complemented by the voices of the nurses and midwives commenting and reflecting on aspects of their work. *Nurses* succeeded in portraying the many and diverse expressions of the role of nurses and midwives in a busy urban hospital. Its showing on national television in Ireland may have served to dismantle some stereotypes; nurses were not all females in white uniforms doing the doctor's bidding and they were not seen simply doing a range of medical/technical tasks, but were also seen assessing patients, planning and organising care, counselling and conducting research.

The Irish Hospitals Sweepstake was introduced under the Public Charitable Hospitals Act of 1931 to generate much-needed revenue for the Irish healthcare system.[37] The Irish nurse was closely associated with the various public representations of the 'Sweep', from the regular television advertising to the public sweepstake lottery draw. In addition, the actual lottery tickets incorporated an image of the head of a uniformed Irish nurse in its watermark. The nurses chosen to draw the winning tickets at the headquarters of the Irish Hospitals Sweepstake in Dublin were recruited from the voluntary hospitals and were carefully selected by their hospital matrons to partake in the drawing of tickets. Newsreel and later television images documented the sweepstake draw; the images featured a row of nurses selecting and holding aloft the winning tickets. As one nurse recalls: 'we wore the cleanest uniforms with the whitest gloves and we were coached in the technique of drawing the ticket.'[38] While the association of nurses with hospitals and with healthcare funding was rather obvious, the use of nurses in the public promotion of the Sweepstake lottery went far beyond this simple association. In her starched, whiter-than-white uniform, the Irish nurse could be trusted to objectively and honestly draw the winning ticket; she was a metaphor for purity and incorruptibility.[39]

Literal and Metaphorical Lens

Cinema and television became the principal media of popular culture in the twentieth century and these two visual representational forms provide a literal and a metaphorical lens on social, labour and women's history in which some notable trends emerge. There is evidence of a broad public consensus of the value of nursing to society, and there is evidence of a downward shift in the social status of nursing.[40] There is also evidence of shifting gender and race boundaries in popular portrayals of the nurse. The nurse has been predominantly a young white female, and while this white feminine ethos of occupational identity was one to which all nurses, including black and Asian nurses, were expected to conform, later medical melodramas and factual documentaries frequently included the non-white nurse and the male nurse in the narrative.[41] While international images of the nurse contain many common features, portrayals of the nurse can be culture-specific.[42] In cinema and television, portrayals of the Irish nurse reflect international nursing representations and stereotypes, but they also include representations that are uniquely Irish and/or are confirmatory of international stereotypes concerning Irishness.

In international film and television containing fictional portrayals of the nurse, there is evidence that nurses were represented according to extant historical visions of womanhood and the woman's role and status. For example, early medical melodramas portrayed nurses with reference to their relationships with doctors and these portrayals were inadvertent metaphors for the asymmetrical power relationship between men and women. Later examples of the genre self-consciously attempted to represent a more or less symmetrical configuration of power within the male-female relationship. Whether this succeeded in representing the 'reality' for nurses in their professional relationships is open to question. Efforts to represent the temporal transition towards gender equality may be simple window dressing or political correctness. The reality for nurses in this respect is much too complex to capture in any of the visual representational forms.

Conclusions

Images of the Irish nurse in film and television are related both to the social history of the era in which the particular image is constructed, and to the respective histories of the particular visual representational forms themselves. In film, factors such as genre conventions, studio and audience expectation, and the star system determine the sort of images that are available to the historian.

No popular visual medium is value-neutral and, like the language of everyday popular discourse, the process of visual representation is not a 'neutral information-carrying vehicle'.[43] Neither is it free from the constitutive capacity of other forms of human dialogue; the narrative that describes is also capable of creating.[44] Even in apparently innocent genres, such as television natural history, ideological self-interest is at work.[45] Thus, like the narrative of natural history, with its diet 'prepared according to recipes familiar to Western culture', the medical melodrama and the hospital documentary contain narratives that represent taken-for-granted gender categories.[46] These same categories are also constructed through the lens.

While books, newspapers and the Internet are important media for communicating factual information and popular culture, cinema and television remain the dominant popular mass media. These media are a powerful force in shaping people's attitudes and behaviour and they are the principal means through which the public develops its knowledge, beliefs and attitudes.[47] In the visual images that they employ to depict nurses and nursing, these media constitute an important part of the iconography of nursing. In this way, the nurse is represented in film within visual compositions that include Nightingale wards, doctors and nurses' sitting rooms, uniforms and medical instruments and, occasionally, alongside subtle religious imagery.

The consequences for nursing in the visual representations of nurses are not unproblematic. Crucially, in the popular visual media, audience positioning – the negotiated relationship between the viewer and the narrative – is as central as the representation itself.[48] The identity of the (film) audience is complex, contradictory and subject to a continuous process of negotiation.[49] Accordingly, the image of the nurse that the nurse receives gives rise to this negotiation of nursing identity, and the narrative that describes either the fiction or the putative reality of nursing may be figuring in creating nurses' professional identity.[50] In Julia Hallam's words, images of the nurse can be inseparable from the values that construct nursing and define its boundaries.[51]

CHAPTER 6

Irish Military Nursing in the Great War

Siobhan Horgan-Ryan

Records show that Irish-trained nurses enthusiastically volunteered for military nursing during the First World War, even after the 1916 Rebellion. Unfortunately, none of these nurses published memoirs, no doubt largely because of the tense political situation in Ireland at the end of the war, so we can only guess at the motivation which drove them to take up work which was physically and psychologically demanding and often dangerous. Many may have joined up in response to the fervent patriotism prevalent before the war, as well as the promise of a varied and exciting lifestyle. More pragmatic recruits may have been influenced by the relatively better employment conditions found in army nursing when compared with home civilian hospitals, especially with regard to salary and promotional prospects. Whatever their motivation, recent research shows that their participation in the war effort was far more widespread than has previously been recognised.[1]

Recruitment and Posting

A mix of official and unofficial organisations provided military nursing services during the Great War, but this chapter concentrates on the Queen Alexandra's Imperial Military Nursing Service (hereafter QAIMNS) and its reserve. The QAIMNS was set up in 1902 to replace the old Army Nursing Service and bring army nursing into line with the newly reformed civilian nursing profession.[2] The entry criteria were very strict and specified three years' medical and surgical training in a civilian hospital recognised by the advisory board, and also that 'as regards education, character and social status, she is a fit person to be admitted to the QAIMNS'.[3] One of the relatively few Irish nurses to join this service was Elizabeth Collins from Cork, who enlisted in the QAIMNS in 1912 and served in France during the war. Her brother was a major in the Royal Army Medical Corps and stationed at the Royal (Military) Infirmary Dublin at the date of her application, which may have had some bearing on her acceptance. In her application form, her father's occupation was given as 'gentleman', thereby satisfying the service's social requirement for entry. Elizabeth trained at the South Infirmary, Cork from 1907 to 1910 and afterwards worked as a ward sister in both medical and surgical wards.[4]

In 1908, the QAIMNS reserve was established and became very popular with Irish nurses. Requirements for candidates were similar to those for the regular service, but were less elitist and included at least three years' training in a recognised civilian hospital or poor law infirmary. If accepted, the initial enrolment was for three years, to be reviewed annually by the Army Nursing Board and renewable 'at their discretion'. Reservists had no military duties in peacetime and were merely required to report in writing annually to the matron-in-chief at the War Office, to remain in bona fide nursing duties and to notify the War Office immediately of any change of address. An annual retainer of £2 was paid to each reservist to remain on their books and to be available in the event of war, when she was liable to immediate call-up. This was a substantial sum of money, representing the difference in annual salary between a staff nurse and an assistant staff nurse in Irish voluntary hospitals, and may have been the inducement for some nurses to enlist.

Other nursing services included the Territorial Army Nursing Service, the British Red Cross Society and the French Flag Nursing Corps. The Territorial Army Nursing Service had been set up in 1907 to provide nurses for the newly formed Territorial Army, a part-time defence force established to free the army from home defence responsibilities in the event of war. Some Irish nurses later worked in this service, including three who died in service during the war, Eileen O'Gorman, Anne Cox and Hilda Garlick.[5] The British Red Cross Society supplied trained and untrained nurses for military hospitals to augment army nursing staff at hospitals in Britain, France, Belgium, Serbia, Russia, Romania, Italy, Salonika, Montenegro, Egypt and Malta.[6] The society also ran 'auxiliary' or 'ancilliary' hospitals throughout Ireland, including the

Dublin Castle Red Cross Hospital, which opened in February 1915.[7] The first matron of this hospital, Miss Annie Maria MacDonnell, had previously been matron at the Dublin House of Industry hospitals (Richmond, Whitworth and Hardwicke) for twenty-one years, during which time she had served in South Africa during the Boer War and had been awarded the Royal Red Cross Medal.[8] Other auxiliary hospitals were established for ordinary soldiers in Cork, Louth, Kildare, Kilkenny, Meath, Westmeath, and Wicklow; auxiliary hospitals for officers were established in Glengariff, County Cork and in Aut Even, Kilkenny.[9] Both categories were carefully segregated and even at the front there were special arrangements for the nursing of officers, either in special tents or in designated hospitals. An Irish unit of the French Flag Nursing Corps left Dublin for the front in early December 1914, made up of six nurses who, in addition to their nursing certificates, had recently attended first-aid classes run by the St John's Ambulance Association.[10]

During the war, the complement of the QAIMNS reserve rose from 800 in the summer of 1914, to 10,404 by the end of 1918, principally because recruitment was restricted to the reserve rather than to the QAIMNS regular service for the duration of hostilities.[11] Candidates were required to apply in writing and there is no evidence that any were personally interviewed. In spite of the potentially dangerous aspect of the work, the application form did not ask for the candidate's religion, but did request information on training and subsequent experience, including details of enteric fever nursing. Successful candidates were informed by letter and sent details about uniform and contract. Nurses had to arrange to have their uniforms made up by a special supplier in London, for which they received a refund of £8 on arrival at their first posting.[12]

Many Irish nurses applied to the QAIMNS reserve as soon as war was declared in August 1914, and there is some evidence that groups of friends applied together or one after another to the same unit. Six nurses from Dublin's Mater Misericordiae Hospital applied together to the reserve in August 1914, shortly after war was declared, but only four were accepted as there were insufficient vacancies at that time.[13] Thirteen nurses from the Royal City of Dublin Hospital, Baggot Street, joined the QAIMNS reserve between August and December 1914 and, by the end of the war, the Royal City of Dublin Hospital and the Meath

Hospital had each contributed twenty-six nurses in total to the service.[14] Successful applicants to the QAIMNS reserve had trained mainly in voluntary hospitals, including the Mater Misericordiae, the Royal City of Dublin, Dr Steevens' and the Adelaide hospitals in Dublin and the South Infirmary in Cork, but a small number had trained at workhouse infirmaries, including one at Waterford. They were the daughters of farmers, doctors, a jeweller, a stud farm manager, teachers, builders and shopkeepers, and they came from all over Ireland, including Dublin, Cork, Limerick, Kerry, Mayo and Waterford.[15] Many had recently finished their training but some were more experienced: Mary Chambers had worked in the private department of a voluntary hospital, while Nora Cremin had experience as a ward sister and home sister.[16] Some already had military experience, including Agnes Henderson, who had worked in the Tivoli Military Hospital, Cork, from November 1916 to July 1917 and had joined the QAIMNS reserve, serving firstly in a prisoner of war hospital in Surrey and later in Macedonia.[17]

In the rush to join up, many civilian nurses left hospital and district nursing posts, showing that there was no concept of essential employment in relation to civilian nursing work. Supervisory staff as well as ward staff volunteered for military nursing service. Volunteers included the matron of Cork Street Fever Hospital, Dublin, and the Irish superintendent of the Queen Victoria's Jubilee Institute for Nurses.[18] Sometimes this eagerness to serve led to nursing shortages at home at a time when hospital transport ships were bringing wounded soldiers from the western front to Irish hospitals for treatment.[19]

Service 'at Home' and in the Field

Irish nurses were sent to various military hospitals in England, including Devonport, Wiltshire, Staffordshire, Liverpool, Stoke-on-Trent, Nottingham, Winchester, York and Surrey.[20] In theory, nurses always served on what was termed 'home station', that is in a military hospital in the United Kingdom, before being transferred to foreign service. Eva Wolfe was posted to Devonport Military Hospital in the spring of 1915 and worked there for two and a half years before being sent to France, where she served in a casualty clearing station, as well as in various hospitals until she was demobilised in April 1919.[21] In practice, however, many nurses were posted immediately to France or another foreign station and some records indicate the nurse's start date as that of her arrival at the British Expeditionary Force Headquarters in Boulogne.[22] Nurses could request 'home' or 'active' service and some who were stationed abroad chose to return to the UK because of family illness.[23] There are some instances of friends being posted together for at least part of their service. Annie Grehan joined up in 1914 and served in Cork and southern England; her friend had the same postings until November 1916, when she was sent to Egypt.[24] Foreign service was usually in France, with the British Expeditionary Force, but Irish nurses also served in Macedonia, East Africa, Malta, Italy, Mesopotamia and Egypt.[25] Egypt was of immense strategic importance, because whoever controlled the Suez Canal, controlled access to the Persian Gulf and India. Military bases had been set up there to protect the canal, and the hospitals attached to them were used as base hospitals and supply centres for the Gallipoli, Salonika, Palestine and East Africa campaigns.[26]

Nurses worked in base hospitals, stationary hospitals, casualty clearing stations and in hospital trains. Base hospitals were large, with approximately 520 beds, well equipped, situated near a military base and roughly equivalent to a leading civilian general hospital. Stationary hospitals were smaller, of about 200 beds, and were situated on the lines of communication between the front and the military base. Their nearest equivalent in civilian life was the county infirmary. Casualty clearing stations notionally had approximately 200 beds but took in as many patients as necessary. They were highly mobile, sited close to the front and were often overwhelmed by the influx of wounded during a battle. They provided emergency treatment, passing the wounded on to stationary and base hospitals as quickly as possible.[27]

Base and stationary hospitals were sited in whatever buildings were available. Marquee tents, joined together by makeshift wooden walkways, were often used for the purpose. Number 14 Stationary Hospital was in a large hotel on the seafront near Boulogne. Number 13 Stationary Hospital was converted from sugar sheds at Boulogne's Gare Maritime, where 'the wounded were received by one door and were passed to the boats by the door opposite', and turnover was so fast that up to three groups filled the beds every twenty-four hours during a major battle.[28] Some stationary hospitals specialised in the treatment of certain conditions, such as fractures and fevers.[29] Irish nurses based in France worked in hospitals in Boulogne, le Havre, Abbeville, Camiers, Etretat, Etaples, Marseilles, as well as in the Rawal Pindi Hospital, Wimereux, which was under the control of Queen Alexandra's Imperial Nursing Service for India.[30]

At the outbreak of the war, the War Office had intended to staff casualty clearing stations with male orderlies, but within months had taken the more pragmatic view that service needs were more important than chivalry. The high casualty rate meant that the army needed to salvage as many of their wounded soldiers as possible so that they could be returned to the front, and skilled nursing was essential in the treatment and rehabilitation of the wounded. Gradually, a complement of seven nurses per casualty clearing station was established with a permanent reserve on standby for emergency relief. The onerous workload and the dangerous environment prompted the military nursing authorities to limit these postings to three (later increased to six) months at a time and, according to the British Expeditionary Force matron-in-chief, 'though there were many exceptions, particularly in the case of Sisters in Charge, this rule was kept throughout the war as strictly as possible'.[31] The Irish nurses staffed various casualty clearing stations including No. 44 with the army of the Rhine at Cologne in early 1919.[32]

From August 1914, specially adapted 'hospital trains' routinely received the wounded straight from the battlefield, where they might have lain for days before anyone could evacuate them. Luckier comrades had first received first-aid at a casualty clearing station or first aid post. These trains brought patients from the front to stationary or base hospitals for treatment or transfer home to the United Kingdom. On average, each train carried four to five hundred casualties, many of whom were critically ill. The general condition of the patients taken on board trains improved following the introduction of nurses to casualty clearing stations. On their arrival at the train, the nurses had to strip, wash, clothe and feed the injured men, as well as clean and dress their wounds.[33] The authorities used whatever rolling stock was available, including anything from cattle trucks to passenger coaches. Stretcher cases were placed on couchettes (sleeping platforms) to the front of the train and walking cases to the rear, in existing second and third-class seating. The sister-in-charge supervised the entire train, helping out where necessary and was also personally responsible for the officers' coach. Two other nurses looked after the men of 'other ranks', while the fourth cared for the 'sitting cases, i.e. those with relatively light wounds. The early trains had no communication between the coaches and it was often necessary for the nurses to jump between them to reach patients during the journey. This was against the orders of the train commanders, but necessary for the nursing care of the seriously wounded. Gradual improvements in the trains, which included the addition of communicating coaches and the replacement of couchettes by supported stretchers, reduced both the workload and the danger and enabled the nursing staff to be reduced to three per train.[34]

By 1917, arrangements were more streamlined. Patients were collected from casualty clearing stations located at railheads and loaded by orderlies onto the specially equipped trains for transfer to either a base hospital or to a hospital ship. The nurses were required to continue the treatment already begun at the casualty clearing station. They inspected the medical cards attached to the patients, gave food and any prescribed treatments and then handed out comforts such as sweets, cigarettes and books.[35] On arrival at the destination hospital or quayside, the wounded were unloaded, beds changed, wards scrubbed out and made ready for the next trip, and provisions were taken on board.[36]

The routine was similar for hospital ships, but there was the added responsibility of ensuring that all patients had their life belts to hand in case the ship struck a mine or was torpedoed. From the start of the conflict to early 1917, as many as 12,000 wounded were transported to Ireland on hospital ships and then sent to civil and military hospitals around the country. Many were suffering from the effects of weaponry never previously encountered, such as machine guns, flame-throwers and toxic gas. Many also had 'trench feet' from standing in waterlogged trenches for days at a time, 'trench fever' from infected body lice, and 'shell shock' caused by 'strain, exhaustion and horrifying and unnatural conditions and experiences'.[37]

Military hospital matrons sent periodic confidential reports on all their nurses to the matron-in-chief, either at the War Office or, if stationed in France, to the matron-in-chief of the British Expeditionary Force. Promotion was awarded on the recommendation of the hospital matron if a suitable vacancy was available.[38] Eva Wolfe was promoted twice, from a staff nurse to acting sister while stationed in England and, later, to full ward sister after working at a casualty clearing station in France.[39] If there was no vacancy available at the time of recommendation, a note was put into the nurse's service record, to the effect that she had been considered suitable for promotion.[40]

Conditions of Service

Compared to civilian nursing, army nursing was financially attractive and salaries were higher than those paid in the Irish voluntary hospitals for all grades. Salaries of matrons (superintendents) in Irish hospitals remained fairly constant at between £40 and £50 throughout the war, whereas equivalent army matrons saw their pay rise from a pre-war scale of £50 to £70 a year to £70 to £100. On average, a ward sister in the Irish voluntary hospitals was paid £35 per annum, while her army equivalent was paid £50 to £65. A qualified civilian staff nurse was paid £25 to £30 in comparison to an army staff nurse who got £40 to £45.[41] The army nursing salary scale was also clearly set down and the nurse knew exactly what she was due to receive, whereas salaries in civilian hospitals were more fluid, and any increases depended on the personal recommendation of the matron. Nurses stationed abroad also received a 'field allowance' of three shillings a day and 'colonial allowance' of one shilling a day on top of their board and lodgings.[42]

Nurses who remained in the QAIMNS reserve after their initial one-year contract were awarded salary increases of £20 a year thereafter.[43] On cessation of satisfactory army employment, reservists were entitled to a theoretical gratuity of £15 for matrons, £10 for sisters and £10.10s for staff nurses.[44] In fact, gratuities paid out at the end of the war were much higher than these figures. It appears that the military planners had not anticipated that the conflict would last as long as it did and had to increase the level of gratuities to match the long periods of service of many reserve nurses. Nurses who finished their service between August 1917 and June 1918 received a gratuity of between £15 and £80, not linked to rank. In this way, Sister Browning of QAIMNS reserve received £25, Territorial Army Nursing Service staff nurse D. Connor received £80 and Bridget Curtin, a staff nurse with QAIMNS reserve, was paid £50. This gratuity was paid in addition to other pay and pensions.[45] If the nurse died, her gratuity and any outstanding pay were paid to her next-of-kin.[46]

Annual leave entitlement was on a par with Irish civilian hospitals, theoretically six weeks for a hospital matron, five weeks for a ward sister and four weeks for a staff nurse, which compared favourably with the two weeks allotted to Red Cross nurses.[47] When the historical records are examined, however, an altogether different picture emerges. In practice, leave was not given as readily as the army regulations would suggest. Josephine Burke signed up in December 1914 and got one week off in February 1916 after fourteen months' continuous service, including four months in a casualty clearing station. She was later given a fortnight's leave in January 1917. Her friend, Ellen Byrne, also worked from December 1914 to February 1916, before getting a week's holidays and her next holidays were not until February 1918, when she had a fortnight of leave.[48] On the other hand, many nurses became ill at some stage and some were given special home leave afterwards to recuperate.[49]

Illness and Benefits

Most nurses seem to have had periods of sick leave, due mainly to infection. Conditions ranged from septic finger to influenza and meningitis. A septic finger necessitated one month off duty for a nurse in Salonika, as she would have been at risk of infecting her patients had she remained at work.[50] One nurse had three months off work for appendicitis and later contracted cerebral influenza caused by 'strain of nursing duties'. Another had five weeks' leave for quinsy.[51] Nurses working in Salonika in Macedonia were so badly affected by malaria, enteric fever and dysentery that a special one hundred-bedded hospital was set up for them and they were obliged to wear mosquito veils, mosquito gloves and puttees while working during the malaria period in the summer.[52] One Irish nurse who served in Salonika for ten months from May 1918 to March 1919 had almost two months' sick leave for dysentery, post dysentery debility and tonsillitis.[53]

Sick pay for army nurses was calculated at different rates, depending on whether or not the illness was related to service. When the nurse's illness was deemed to have been caused by military service, she was entitled to one year on full pay followed by six months on half pay. When not caused by service, she received full pay for six months, followed by half pay for six months if she had served for less than twenty years, or two-thirds pay for the same period if she had more than twenty years' service.[54] Notwithstanding this regulation, sick pay continued to be paid at the full rate for the duration of hostilities.[55]

Disability pensions for nurses 'who were disabled either by disease or accident wholly and directly due to service, or aggravated by service' were first introduced in 1916 and extended to include tuberculosis in 1917.[56] The pensions were variable and the amount paid appeared to reflect the length of service rather than the rank or grade of the pensioner. Pensions ranged from £100 to £300 per annum, representing the gross salary for periods of four months to three years.[57] Bridget Curtin was diagnosed with tuberculosis in July 1917 and died in January 1918. She was paid a disability pension at the rate of £100 per annum from July 1917 to March 1918, two months after her death. The balance was then paid to her father as next-of-kin. This disability pension was in addition to her 'end of service' gratuity of £50, paid to her in August 1917.[58] Eighteen serving Irish nurses died during the Great War. They had been stationed in Britain, France, Egypt, Malta, Salonika, Gaza (Palestine) and Bordighera (Italy). All died of disease, including meningitis, influenza, dysentery, malaria, and pneumonia.[59] This figure does not include those with chronic or terminal illnesses who resigned from the service and died before the end of the war.[60]

Nurses working near the front or on transport duty were vulnerable to injury by enemy fire. Nine nurses from Britain were killed on the western front, one by an artillery shell and the other eight by 'enemy aircraft bomb[s]'.[61] Mary Clarke from County Westmeath received facial wounds during an air raid on the 35th General Hospital in September 1917 and was sent home to Ireland to recuperate. She then volunteered to return to France, despite having been offered 'home service'.[62] Hospital ships were sometimes torpedoed by submarines or hit by mines in the English Channel and in the Mediterranean, resulting in the loss of thirty-six nurses. However, no Irish nurses were reported as killed in this way.

When a nurse or officer died, a 'Court of Adjustment' was convened for the purpose of sorting out their estate in accordance with the Regimental Debts Act, 1893. When there was a will, rather than handing over her total estate to an executor, the army authorities distributed the various bequests from the nurse's estate to her legatees.[63] When the nurse died intestate, her net estate was split equally between her surviving parents and siblings and distributed by the army authorities.[64]

Under the 1911 Insurance Act, employers were required to pay insurance contributions weekly in respect of all employees to a recognised insurance society. However, it is notable that the War Office did not pay any of the army nurses' contributions until 1920, but thereafter it paid the arrears owing for the full service time to whichever insurance society the nurse had been paying into when she joined up. Among the societies used by the Irish nurses were the Nurses' Insurance Society London, the Catholic Nurses' Insurance Association, 1 Mountjoy Street, Dublin, and the Nurses' Insurance Society of Ireland, 29 Gardiner Place, Dublin. Eva Wolfe's national insurance contributions were paid in arrears in August 1920 for the full period and amounted to £2.12 shillings and were paid to the Nurses' Insurance Society in London, presumably because she had been working there before the war.[65]

When a nurse fell ill with a longstanding illness, such as tuberculosis, her insurance situation was dealt with by the National Health Insurance Commission (Ireland), Pembroke House, Upper Mount Street, Dublin, which arranged for the claimant to be managed by a county insurance committee that had the power to arrange admission to a sanatorium in that county.[66] The Ministry of Pensions was responsible for disabled nurses and servicemen who had remained in the service and it established some long-term hospitals under the same rules and conditions as military hospitals.[67] Daisy Hayes applied for the QAIMNS reserve on completion of her training in early 1918 and was sent to military hospitals in Nottingham, Winchester and York. In April 1920, she signed on for another two years. She took a post in a hospital run by the Ministry of Pensions in 1922 and the end-of-service confidential report from her matron suggested that she was moving to more secure employment with better chances of promotion. It is noteworthy that her insurance payments were made in arrears in March 1922, which indicates that the army continued to postpone payment of employees' insurance contributions in peacetime, perhaps because the army provided hospital cover and sick pay when required.[68]

Discipline and Honours

Nurses on military duty were under the command of the local commanding officer who, when necessary, would institute disciplinary proceedings against a nurse and later report the matter to the matron-in-chief in London, who would then arrange for repatriation if required. Disciplinary action in one theatre of war did not necessarily have adverse effects on the nurse's future career in the army. One nurse was sent back from Malta after allegedly disobeying an order from the commanding officer to take charge of a hospital for sick nurses, but was later transferred to East Africa and continued to serve until autumn 1919.[69]

From February 1915 until the end of the war, nurses were mentioned in dispatches for reasons such as bravery under fire.[70] This distinction was then added to the nurse's service file. British honours awarded to nurses serving in the First World War were the Royal Red Cross, the Military Medal, the Albert Medal, the Medal of the Victorian Order, and the Order of the British Empire. The French and Belgian governments also awarded a number of honours.[71] Three nurses from the Royal City of Dublin Hospital, nurses Gordon, Johnston and Robinette, were awarded the Royal Red Cross for their war service.[72] Other Irish recipients included Elizabeth Collins, Mary Clarke (later wounded) and Mary Doherty. Elizabeth Collins had been one of the first nurses sent to France with the British Expeditionary Force in early August 1914 and she served there for over two years, during which time she worked in hospitals, casualty clearing stations, and ambulance trains. After the war, she continued to serve in the QAIMNS and was posted to Gibraltar, Egypt, Aden and India.[73] Mary Clarke trained in Liverpool, joined the reserve on 17 August 1914 and was posted immediately to France, where she worked in a base hospital and a casualty clearing station and was awarded the Royal Red Cross in July 1915.[74] Mary Doherty trained at Dr Steevens' Hospital and volunteered for army work at the beginning of the war. She was initially posted to a hospital in France, was mentioned in dispatches for her good work and devotion to duty and was awarded the Royal Red Cross. After her transfer to Salonika, she caught malaria, then dysentery, and died in September 1916, aged twenty-eight.[75]

Nurses serving in military hospitals in France and the United Kingdom were often kept on until the early 1920s, showing that there was still a continuing need for their services after the war officially ended.[76] The on-going treatment required by wounded soldiers as well as the 1918–19 influenza pandemic both contributed to this continuing need for nursing and medical services. On demobilisation, those who served with the QAIMNS reserve were offered a place on the permanent reserve provided that they continued in bona fide nursing practice in the United Kingdom. Those who later emigrated or who became unemployed had their names removed from the roll. Gertrude Twomey served in France from February 1915 until October 1917 when she was transferred to King George V Military Hospital, Dublin, where she served until demobilisation in April 1920. She was then maintained on the permanent reserve until emigrating to New York in June 1923.[77] Eileen Byrne worked for a private nursing agency in London after the war and was retained on the permanent reserve until 1938.[78]

Conclusions

During the Great War, army nursing was popular in Ireland and was viewed as an acceptable area of work for a trained nurse. The level of recruitment to military nursing service from a wide range of social and geographical backgrounds would seem to indicate an acceptance and indeed enthusiasm for the war within Irish society at the time of the outbreak of hostilities. Serving in a wide variety of services and in many theatres of war, Irish nurses contributed to the war in a way that was both significant and more widespread than has previously been recognised.

CHAPTER 7

'She must be content to be their servant as well as their teacher': The Early Years of District Nursing in Ireland[1]

Ann Wickham

In the early years of the nineteenth century in Ireland, the sick, whether rich or poor, were generally cared for in their own homes. The development of a system of trained certified lay district nurses of all denominations to serve the sick poor in their homes occurred towards the end of the nineteenth century, and only became possible due to the emergence of certified nurse training in hospitals and/or associated training institutions in Ireland and abroad. These institutions supplied the candidates for further training as district nurses. The system of district nursing remained a voluntary system, reliant upon local initiatives and fundraising. The financial and organisational characteristics of the various voluntary schemes, together with associated religious and class tensions, determined the extent to which the system could serve those most in need.

The Sick Poor and Medical Relief

Developments in nursing services for the poor in Ireland took place in a country divided by religious and political differences and characterised by extremes of rural and urban poverty. Although Roman Catholics made up the majority of the population, Protestants, of whatever persuasion, were the political rulers. Since the penal laws of the seventeenth and eighteenth centuries had restrained Catholics from gaining access to property and the professions, Protestants owned much of the wealth and property in Ireland.[2] While this situation had changed with the repeal of the penal laws and Catholics could, in theory, own property, the process of economic and social development was necessarily slow for Catholics. By the end of the nineteenth century, religious divisions had polarised around the issue of political union with Britain and all aspects of society in Ireland reflected deep religious differences.

The Great Famine of 1845–50 had greatly reduced the population of Ireland and the subsequent pattern of high emigration and low birth rate served to reduce the overall population further. At the same time, the population of the capital city Dublin continued to grow, fuelled by migration from rural areas.[3] While rural and urban areas suffered from extreme poverty, it was in Dublin, the largest British city after London, that the situation was particularly bad.[4] The conditions in Dublin slums, particularly in the tenements where whole families lived in one room with appalling sanitary conditions, were especially bad. Yet as Jacinta Prunty has shown, although there were numerous public and philanthropic organisations engaged in charitable activity in relation to the slums, effective action was long delayed.[5] As a result, Dublin went into the twentieth century with the fifth highest death rate of any city in the world.[6] Conditions for the rural poor were no better, only different. As James Tuke, a major philanthropist and ardent campaigner in relation to conditions of the poor, wrote of Donegal:

> thousands of people, not only the poorest, but even those in fairly good circumstances, are living in dark hovels filled with smoke, the one living room with its mud floor, occupied by large families … who squat at the one end around the peat fire, while the livestock … are herded together at the other.[7]

There was some medical relief available to the poor; in 1851, a system of 723 dispensary districts had been set up throughout Ireland to supply medical care, and each of the districts had a doctor. However, patients only had access to the service through a system of tickets and these could only be dispensed by a poor law guardian. Claims were made that these tickets were not necessarily used for the benefit of the poor but were instead handed, in certain instances, to voters who could well afford to pay medical fees.[8] In addition, the poor law guardians were often accused of sectarianism and of using appointments as a system of patronage.

As the cost of developments fell upon local rates, further initiatives were discouraged so when midwives were employed they were poorly paid and untrained. Treatment could often be cursory and was not supported by a nursing service.

Founded in the early part of the nineteenth century, two Catholic religious orders visited the poor, who were mostly Catholics, in their own homes.[9] The Sisters of Charity, founded in 1815 by Mary Aikenhead, a Catholic convert, included amongst their aims the visiting of the sick and the poor.[10] Later in 1831, Catherine McAuley founded the Sisters of Mercy. Initially hesitant about founding a religious order, she had hoped for a community of lay Catholic women to help the poor. In face of opposition to such a community, she established the Sisters of Mercy, another non-enclosed order. The Sisters of Mercy concentrated on the education and care of poor women and on visiting the sick poor and were active in providing sick nursing, particularly when epidemics of typhus and cholera swept Ireland.[11] Other philanthropic efforts were also directed at the sick poor, but often distinguished between those seen as 'deserving' and 'undeserving'.[12] When formally trained certificated nurses began to serve the poor, the first initiatives came from Protestant philanthropic efforts.[13]

St Patrick's Home

The use of trained lay nurses in tending to the poor came with the establishment in 1876 of St Patrick's Home, a Protestant institution for training district nurses. Stated to be non-sectarian in its operation and rooted in the Church of Ireland but with its nurses forbidden to evangelise, the home was established by Lady Plunket, wife of Archbishop Plunket and daughter of Sir Benjamin Guinness.[14] Lady Plunket had been instrumental in the charitable activities that became the Dublin Woman's Work Association. The association engaged a district nurse from London to provide a home nursing service. The Home for Nurses for the Sick Poor was set up as a branch of this organisation in 1876.[15] The home was established at 21 York Street with room for only three or four nurses and in 1881, it moved to 101 St Stephen's Green where seven nurses, including the lady superintendent, could be housed.[16] As well as employing nurses, the home began to train probationers for district nursing.

The home was a branch of the Woman's Work Association but over time it was felt that the non-sectarian nursing of the poor was hampered by this connection. It was decided that the home should be more independent and it ceased to be a branch of the association in 1887. However, in 1890 the home no longer operated independently when it became affiliated with the Queen Victoria's Jubilee Institute for Nurses (QVJIN).

Nurses taken on as QVJIN district nursing probationers had to be aged between twenty-five and thirty-five and already have at least two years of training from a recognised general hospital. They were paid a salary but were required to promise to serve the QVJIN for two years after their training was completed. Paying probationers not associated with the QVJIN were also taken on in the home.[17]

Queen Victoria's Jubilee Institute for Nurses in Ireland (QVJIN)

District nursing in Britain and the origin of the QVJIN structure are seen to have originated in William Rathbone's initiative in Liverpool in 1861.[18] In that year, Rathbone's wife died and he decided to retain the services of the nurse that he had engaged to care for her during her illness. Rathbone employed the nurse to attend the sick poor in Liverpool. Within a short period, this initiative had developed into a school of nursing from which both trained hospital and district nurses were emerging. Following this, a number of nursing associations developed in Britain with a mix of trained and untrained nurses supervised by 'ladies' (women of social standing in the community whose supervision was rooted in their social status rather than any formal nursing knowledge). In September 1889, the QVJIN was established by Royal Charter from monies collected for Queen Victoria's Jubilee celebrations of 1887 from the women's jubilee. The aim of the institute was to provide for the skilled nursing of the sick poor in their own homes. In February 1890, a central provisional council was set up and local committees were formed in Edinburgh and in Dublin. Existing nursing associations were invited to apply for affiliation to the new body.

Following much internal debate, the QVJIN sought to use only trained nurses in its district nursing services and also to employ as superintendents only those who were trained nurses. This represented a move away from the initial organisation of district nursing in England, which had focused on the role of 'ladies' as effective superintendents. This practice had reflected the belief that ladies' expertise in the home, and their moral behaviour, were sufficient and necessary in directing and improving the lot of the poor.[19] In terms of nursing, these attributes were now seen as insufficient. The transition to trained superintendents represented a move to a form of professional identity and responsibility. It was the start of a system of district nursing that was based on special professional training of nurses already certificated and managed by their professional peers.

However, the system itself remained a charitable service for the sick poor. As such, money was always a problem. Initially it was decided by the QVJIN council that the monies collected in each country should be used in that country.[20] Monies collected to mark Queen Victoria's Diamond Jubilee in 1897 provided further finance for the QVJIN. This system of reliance on local organisations to provide money for the employment of district nurses was to become a particular issue in Ireland.

From the start, it was envisaged that the QVJIN would include Ireland in its sphere of operations. In 1888, letters were exchanged between the provisional committee of the QVJIN and a Dublin committee on how the operation was to be set up in Ireland.[21] The governing body in London was prepared to devote one-third of its funds to Ireland; this was 'out of regard to the needs of Ireland, and is in excess of her proportion of the fund, whether calculated upon population or contributions from Ireland'. For Dublin, the conditions for affiliation were to be the same as those applying to London and Edinburgh. However, from the start religious issues that were to be a characteristic of developments in Ireland were brought up. At one point in the discussions, there was a suggestion from Dublin that Catholics should have a separate system of district nurses, but this was rejected by the QVJIN. Although first envisaged as a national scheme, it was eventually decided that the scheme should start with a centre only in Dublin because, even with the commitment of the central council to developments in Ireland, available funds were limited. The QVJIN was prepared to give £300 for Roman Catholic nurses, £200 for Protestant nurses, and £100 for lectures.[22]

There was further debate in Ireland as to how the system of nursing should be organised and who should be involved in its operation. The QVJIN initially relied upon existing nursing schemes joining the institute to get the whole scheme established in Britain as well as in Ireland. In Dublin, two pre-existing institutions put themselves forward in this regard. One was the Protestant institution, St Patrick's Home, the other was the City of Dublin Nursing Institution, which was devoted to the non-sectarian certified training of nurses, and the provision of trained nurses for hospitals and private nursing.[23] After considerable dispute over the allocation of areas of Dublin to receive nurses, the City of Dublin Nursing Institution withdrew from the embryonic scheme.

St Lawrence's Home

The establishment of the QVJIN in Ireland led to pressure for the setting up of a Catholic version of St Patrick's Home. There were already Catholic lay nurses in Ireland, some of whom had trained in Britain, but others who had trained through the non-sectarian schemes in the Dublin voluntary hospitals.[24] However, there had been no impetus to create a lay Catholic home visiting scheme, since the Catholic religious orders were meeting the needs of the sick poor. Yet Archbishop Walsh, the Roman Catholic Archbishop of Dublin, was sympathetic to the idea of lay district nursing. The archbishop's call for a separate Catholic superintendent was rejected by the QVJIN. However, the archbishop was adamant that Catholic nurses should live and train separately from Protestant nurses, even if working under superintendents who were Protestant.[25] Initiatives were always subject to the archbishop's approval, since he was most anxious that the home should not fail for 'want of public support', an important issue when private funds were needed to support such a home and when private funds had also to be found from within the Catholic community to employ the nurses, once trained. He didn't want a Catholic initiative to end in public failure.

In 1891, it was agreed that the City of Dublin Nursing Institution could undertake hospital training of Catholic nurses for hospital work but not their district training, and Archbishop Walsh gave his formal sanction for a Catholic home.[26] Initially located on Mary Street and later known as St Lawrence's, the home was to be ready by 1 June 1891. Miss St Clair, who trained at St Thomas' Hospital in London, was appointed as lady superintendent and Miss Noble as her assistant; both had trained as Queen's nurses.[27] By 1893, four nurses, including the lady superintendent were employed and the extent of their work can be seen from the fact that records for August, September and October of that year recorded 2,294 home visits.

Joint System under QVJIN Direction

From that time onwards, QVJIN nurses were drawn from St Patrick's and St Lawrence's homes. However, the resolution of the initial difficulties over districts, and the incorporation of the two homes into the QVJIN nursing system did not mean that problems for the QVJIN in Ireland were at an end; rather they were just beginning. Finance to employ district nurses, once trained, was always to be a major problem. In 1892, St Patrick's Home had five probationers, three of whom were Queen's probationers. At that time, there was a reported demand for district nurses, but many areas that needed them could not raise the finances to employ them. In addition, the QVJIN soon faced the difficulty as to which classes of women were to be recruited for training as district nurses. Although not the view of the council of the QVJIN (including Rathbone), the view of the committee of St Patrick's Home was that district nursing was an employment suitable for 'educated ladies'. Writing in February 1892, the honorary secretary of the home, Jane Thompson, noted that of the three Queen's probationers, two were thought by the committee not to be suitable by virtue of what seemed to be their lower social origins.[28] Thompson reported that the committee, '[do] not think it advisable to have Nurses of this class on the permanent staff of St Patrick's, [and] they wish for some guarantee that they will be provided for elsewhere when their training is complete'.[29] Miss Dunn, the superintendent of the QVJIN in Ireland, reported in a letter to Rathbone on 25 February 1892 that only pressure on the committee had led to them accepting as Queen's probationers 'candidates who appeared suitable for District work, without regard for their social position, thus anticipating your wishes on the subject'. She continued:

> I also agree with you in thinking that ladies, though perhaps actually not more expensive than Nurses of another class, would not always be content with the rough surroundings which I know they would meet with in many of the country branches. However, St Patrick's has consented to Nurses of both classes, but they are anxious to be assured that the Probationers will be passed on after their six months training is completed, as they wish their permanent staff, if possible, to consist entirely of ladies.[30]

For the next few years, the QVJIN was in dispute with St Patrick's Home about the refusal of some of those trained with QVJIN resources to move and work outside of Dublin. Rathbone wrote in 1894 that money for the home would only be given 'on the distinct condition that probationers thus trained shall be at the disposal of the Queens Institute for other parts of Ireland and that they distinctly understand and agree that they may have to go there'.[31] Correspondence on the matter continued between Rathbone and the home until Archbishop Plunket wrote claiming that there was a misunderstanding and that the dispatch of probationers would take place as the QVJIN wished in future.

St Lawrence's Home was not without its problems either. It seemed at first that many of Archbishop Walsh's fears concerning the viability of the home would be realised when there was concern as to whether the home would survive. By 1894, the QVJIN believed that St Lawrence's had not trained enough nurses when compared with the eighteen nurses that St Patrick's had trained. A Mr Teeling explained to the QVJIN council that this problem was related to the manner in which St Lawrence's had been set up.[32] He argued that when the home opened it had no support guaranteed except for £65 per annum. No committee had been set up until June 1892 and there were no district nursing posts available for nurses to go to. The Catholic community was required to use great exertions to get local committees formed. This lack of jobs for the nurses to go to because local associations had to raise the funds to pay for them was a grave problem for the home because it had already trained four nurses.[33] These nurses had to be kept and supported by the home for periods of between three and twelve months until places could be found for them.

Both training homes experienced problems in procuring places for their nurses. Miss Dunn, the QVJIN superintendent in Ireland, had foreseen this problem in 1892 when she wrote:

> The difficulty I now foresee, is the placing of these nurses in the future in suitable parts of Ireland. Though I have a list of twelve persons who have asked me for nurses, I fear very few of them will be able to guarantee the necessary funds, owing to the difficulty of getting all parties to work together, and the condition of actual poverty into which many of that class of persons (who will take most interest in such work) are thrown at present.[34]

Recruitment, Training and Placement

Despite the problems, the scheme continued and the respect in which the Queen's nurses came to be held is seen to lie in the fact that the two homes recruited only nurses who had already possessed a recognised certificate of training from a hospital. District nurse training in both of the Dublin homes was of six months' duration and the QVJIN gave an allowance of £35 to each home to cover the salary, board, lodging, laundry and authorised uniform of each probationer. Probationers were recruited following an interview and only after they signed a copy of the regulations, had their references checked and, where possible, had an additional interview with the Queen's Institute superintendent. Probationers were recruited for a one-month trial period. The homes could also train other nurses for district work, but the institute funded only the Queen's probationers and it was intended that these probationers would have their primary identification with the Queen's Institute and not with the home in which they trained.[35]

Most of the first district nurses appear to have been drawn from respectable backgrounds. Pauline Scanlan notes that these early recruits included the daughters of professional men, such as clergymen, army and navy officers, farmers or gentlemen farmers, businessmen and men of private means.[36] Recruits had received a private education, either abroad or at secondary schools in Ireland and amongst their number were a former teacher, a governess, and a student of the Academy of Music.[37] Margaret Preston has established that the largest number of early recruits were the daughters of farmers.[38] The central records of the Queen's Institute show that the first QVJIN nurses in Ireland ranged in age from twenty-two to sixty-two years and the average age at their time of registration as Queen's nurses, which occurred after they had completed both their initial training and their training as district nurses, was thirty-one.

In view of the different circumstances between the Protestant and Catholic training homes that existed when the QVJIN was established in Ireland, and in view of the problems with financing nurses in districts, it is not surprising that in the first decade of the scheme almost twice as many Protestants as Catholics were trained.[39] However, this situation changed after the turn of the twentieth century, the balance began to shift and more Catholics than Protestants became district nurses in the period from 1900 to 1909.[40] By the end of the first two decades of operation, almost equal numbers from the two religious groups had been trained.

Although it is not possible to be definitive as to the nationality of the district nurses, it is possible that the place of initial nurse training is indicative of their place of origin. In the first decade of its operation, one hundred and four women became Queen's nurses, or 'Jubilee' district nurses, in Ireland.[41] Almost half (forty-nine) had received their initial nurse training in Ireland, fifty-three trained in Britain and two had arrived from the United States.[42] There were differences between the two religious groupings; although the number of Catholics was smaller in the first decade, they were much more likely to have received their initial nurse training within Ireland. Almost two-thirds (twenty-four) of the Catholic nurses trained in Ireland and a little over one-third (twenty-five) of the Protestant nurses had their first training in Ireland. In the following decade the picture remained similar with over two-thirds of Catholic nurses having trained in Ireland compared with one-third of Protestant nurses.[43]

The advent of the QVJIN in Ireland was fortunate in that it coincided with the introduction of lay nurse training by the major Catholic nursing orders, the Sisters of Mercy and the Sisters of Charity. The

Sisters of Mercy began training nurses at the Mater Misericordiae Hospital and at the Charitable Infirmary in 1891, and the Sisters of Charity introduced nurse training at St Vincent's Hospital in 1892. These developments broadened the opportunities open to Catholic women who were previously required to seek 'non-sectarian' training offered by the other voluntary hospitals in Dublin, such as the City of Dublin Hospital or Dr Steevens' Hospital. The impact of the training offered to lay women by the Catholic religious is evident in the fact that half of the Catholic Queen's nurses in the first decade had received their initial training with them.

In the first ten years of its operation, the QVJIN nursing scheme was provided in many parts of Ireland but did not become fully established as a national scheme. For example, by 1897 there were twenty nurses in the Dublin area, but only forty in the country as a whole, and these were mainly clustered in the north and the east.[44] Not surprisingly, it was common practice for nurses of a similar denomination to be sent to areas with specific denominational majorities, which meant that those going to the north and to Dublin were mainly Protestant, while those sent to other areas were Catholic.[45]

A large number of counties in the west of Ireland and in the midlands did not benefit from the Jubilee scheme. Nurses, such as those preferred by St Patrick's Home, showed themselves less than willing to serve outside Dublin, and although it was acknowledged that a demand existed, the main barrier to their employment was financial. Local nursing associations were required to support their employment by paying their wages and expenses. Outside of Dublin, those who could best afford to support district nurses lived in areas in the eastern part of Ireland and in Ulster. However, there were large areas of the west of Ireland, which were the poorest and the least populated and, therefore, could not provide enough local inhabitants of sufficiently good means to support a district nurse. The QVJIN in Ireland was aware of this situation and, although one nurse was sent to Achill Island, the institute could not effectively address the situation, given its own limited resources.

Other Voluntary District Nursing Schemes

The lack of finance for poorer areas led to three initiatives to help provide some nursing assistance for the western areas. These were the West of Ireland Association in Manchester, the *Irish Homestead* nurses, and the Lady Dudley Nursing Scheme. During a period of distress in the west of Ireland in 1897–98, a group in Manchester was established to raise money to help alleviate the problems. A large and influential committee of thirty-four ladies was set up with Lady Leigh as its president and led by Miss Southern (later to become Mrs J. Brown). Two members of the ladies committee, Mrs Hyland and Mrs Handel Booth, were sent over to Ireland on an inspection visit. They reported:

> ... we can declare that in our experience as members of English Poor Law Boards, we never saw such evidence of want as came under our observation on this visit.[46]

The ladies came to the conclusion that the inhabitants could not deal with the problems by themselves and that help had to come from outside:

> if a number of district nurses were permanently provided, who would give instruction and assistance, much benefit would result. Owing to the want of sufficient and proper food and a general ignorance of sanitation, illness is very prevalent, especially typhus, black measles, and phthisis. In many cases doctors have to come as far as thirty miles to visit their patients. It is obvious that poor people living in remote districts cannot pay for the services of medical men, therefore when sickness overtakes them they simply lie down and die.[47]

This belief in the apathetic nature of the peasantry was a not uncommon view amongst contemporary commentators, who tended to ignore the social and economic structures that constrained the people.[48] Also ignored was the extent to which the poor might have resorted to other forms of healing, such as herbal or folk cures.[49]

The response to the report of the ladies committee was immediate and the association decided to appoint two nurses, one to Oughterard, County Galway and one to Burriscarra, County Mayo. The nurses would be Queen's nurses and would receive the support of the West of Ireland Association, working under the supervision of the QVJIN. The association established local secretaries who were expected to offer sympathy and help to the nurses, but were not expected to control their work. Mrs Jackson was appointed supervisor in County Galway, while Miss FitzGerald Kenny was appointed to County Mayo.

The district nurses were immediately effective with, for example, a Nurse Bird undertaking 1,500 visits in her first year. However, despite the efforts of the West of Ireland Association, finance for the nurses remained a problem; the cost of the two nurses was approximately £221 per annum or £120 each after furnishings and supplies were deducted.[50] The QVJIN initially contributed £20 per annum towards the cost of each nurse.[51] In 1901, the association requested the QVJIN to continue this grant, as the association's funds were very low.[52]

In the March 1901 issue of *The Irish Homestead* (the official publication of the Irish Agricultural Organisation Society),[53] Miss FitzGerald Kenny wrote a letter in response to earlier correspondence that had called for nurses for the poor in Ireland.[54] In the letter, Miss FitzGerald Kenny reflected on the impact of a West of Ireland Association nurse from St Lawrence's Home, stating that over a thousand visits had been undertaken by the nurse in just ten months. She suggested that, as the finance for nursing associations was not available in such districts and since the Poor Law boards were not taking initiatives, supporters of *The Irish Homestead* should act to raise the funds to secure such nurses. An editorial in *The Irish Homestead* agreed with the proposal and called for subscriptions to establish, through the QVJIN, a nurse for a single poor district, with more nurses to follow once the first was well established.[55] The scheme would cost about £100 per annum to set up and to maintain a nurse in such an area, including her salary, living, supplies and associated costs.

The finance came in slowly throughout 1901, and it was not until the December issue that *The Irish Homestead* was able to announce that definite arrangements were now in progress and that the first meeting of the new committee to run the scheme had been held on 13 December.[56] The committee resolved to select Kilcommin-Erris as the first district to which an *Irish Homestead* nurse should be sent; a Nurse O'Shea was appointed to the post. The nurse would receive the support of a local secretary, the Reverend Mr J. J. Hegarty, and she would also receive the assistance of the central committee, a medical sub-committee and a clothes guild.[57] Since there was no certainty as to what extent donations received in 1901 would be repeated in subsequent years and since there was also a wish to supply additional nurses if possible, a call for subscriptions to the scheme continued to be published in each issue of *The Irish Homestead.*

Like the West of Ireland Association, another voluntary district nursing scheme, the Lady Dudley Nursing Scheme, was concerned with the western counties of Ireland, but the nurses provided by this latter scheme were placed all along the entire western seaboard from Donegal in the north to Kerry in the south. The scheme was set up in April 1903 on foot of an appeal from Lady Dudley, the wife of the lord lieutenant of Ireland, when she wrote a public letter to the Irish newspapers in order to raise money. Lady Dudley was a Quaker by birth and, like many others of superior social standing in Ireland, was active in many philanthropic activities. At the time of her appeal, there were only four certificated district nurses in the west of Ireland, the two supported by the West of Ireland Association, one supported by *The Irish Homestead*, and the nurse on Achill Island supported by the QVJIN. In her letter, Lady Dudley outlined the continued inability of many areas of greatest need to support a nurse:

> ... it is just in those places where the need for nurses is greatest, on account of the extreme poverty of the people, that it is impossible to obtain the necessary funds locally. In many of the very poor districts there are no resident gentry and no well-to-do inhabitants of the middle classes, and because of their poverty the people themselves are not able to make any contribution.

The QVJIN had agreed to provide £180 per annum towards a separate fund for nurses for such districts and Lady Dudley appealed to the public for funds to provide nurses who would each cost approximately £100 per annum. Sufficient funds were forthcoming to send twelve nurses over the first four years, a number that was to expand over the following decade.

The Role and Status of District Nurses

In their day-to-day practice, nurses of the QVJIN were seen to have two roles, those of servant and teacher. A district nurse was not only expected to carry out direct nursing care but she was also required to undertake activities that in more prosperous homes would have been the responsibility of the servants. Although their role incorporated an element of 'service', the district nurses' supervisors regarded them as the 'teachers' of the poor. The nurses were to do in practice what it was hoped the women that they attended would subsequently do in order to improve the standards of their homes and the lives of their families. This dual role was expressed in the QVJIN pamphlet:

> … the Nurse washes and arranges the patient, makes the bed, applies the dressing required, dusts the room, ventilates it and washes all utensils, dirty glasses, etc., and, when necessary, disinfects utensils and drains, sweeps up the fireplace, fetches fresh water and fills the kettle. So far as is practicable, the Nurse does all of this, while she also seeks to inculcate lessons of self help amongst those whom she visits, persuading the mother, wife, daughter, or neighbor of her patient to see that order and cleanliness are possible in all circumstances, and themselves to put and keep things right in the sick person's room. Besides nursing the patient, she shows them in their own homes how they can help in this nursing – how they can be clean and orderly – how they can call in official sanitary help to make their one poor room more healthy – how they can improvise appliances – how their home need not be broken up. She can, in short, 'teach without seeming to teach.'[58]

This view was reiterated in the documentation on the Lady Dudley scheme, but in this case there was also an emphasis on 'civilising' as well as educating:

> The extension of a system of trained nurses is regarded as of inestimable value in more than one respect. First as a mitigation of the sufferings of these poor people in times of sickness, in child-birth, and during epidemics caused by neglect, through ignorance of the simplest precautions. Second, as a civilizing and educating influence, which shall do something towards raising the standard of living in these districts.[59]

The appeals for further funds to continue both the work of the QVJIN and that of the other organisations associated with district nursing stressed the importance of the work that district nurses were doing. The large number of visits and the long hours of work recorded by the district nurses attest to the fact that they were busy in their work. Their nursing treatments were welcomed by the poor that they visited and much of their work involved teaching the poor about hygiene and sanitation. Descriptions of district nurses' work in urban areas reiterate the extent to which nursing care involved washing and cleaning patients and their homes.[60] In remote rural areas, this was also the case. Miss Kenny, familiar with the work of the nurses funded by the West of Ireland Association, wrote:

> A nurse ... is a refining and education influence. She comes as an apostle of cleanliness. She sees her patient's house is swept and cleaned and that drinking vessels, etc., in use for a patient are not used by the healthy members of the family, and so saves them from contracting the illness ... fresh air and daylight let in ... a proper system of ventilation introduced.[61]

However, the extent to which this 'teaching' was accepted and acted upon by the poor is less certain. Although the nurses themselves, in their reports, reflected on some teaching successes and the adoption of new levels of cleanliness and hygiene, the poor, whether rural or urban, remained poor. All of the elements with which women had to struggle in their impoverished homes, including the lack of sanitation and water, remained, despite the nurses' visits. In these circumstances, the message regarding cleanliness and health that the nurses brought would only bring for many poorer women the 'pressure to increase their obligations and workload'.[62] Therefore, the role of the district nurse as teacher was less likely to be successful until the wider structural elements that created the poverty and poor sanitation were acted upon, and the women were better placed to act upon the ideas put before them.

There is little doubt that district nursing was a calling only for women with particular characteristics. In urban areas, commentators stressed the extra 'vocational' nature of district nursing when compared with nursing in general. There was a belief that district nurses had to be better equipped with nursing skills than hospital nurses, since they were fulfilling the dual role of servant and teacher, and their wide range of duties and responsibilities placed more demands on them than on their hospital nurse counterparts.

The regard in which the district nurse was held could vary. Where local associations had to raise the money to fund a district nurse, social status could be an important element in the way in which she was regarded. Annie Smithson, a writer and former district nurse, remarked in one of the few-recorded instances of the experiences of a Queen's nurse, that the president of her nursing association in County Down treated her (Smithson) as 'some kind of upper servant whom she was engaging'.[63] However, unlike in England, where some of the district nursing associations remained under the direct superintendence of 'ladies', those who were presidents of nursing associations in Ireland were not persons with responsibility for the district nurses.[64] The QVJIN had insisted from the start that certificated QVJIN nurses should undertake all superintendence. The superintendent and deputy superintendent for the QVJIN in Dublin were also responsible for nurses throughout the country and there was a system of regular inspection visits to QVJIN nurses. Thus, while those who raised money for the establishment of district nurses might not always regard them as social equals, within each QVJIN district, the nurses worked within an organisation run by their peers. In this connection, their training and their value was recognised and was not subject to social vagaries. If district nurses were looked down upon in some more affluent areas, in the remote areas of the west of Ireland which lacked nursing associations and had few resident middle- or upper-class inhabitants, the nurses were more likely to enjoy high social standing in the community.

The Work of District Nurses

Whilst battling against urban poverty and the additional health hazards created by slum conditions, district nurses working in Dublin had the comfort of St Patrick's and St Lawrence's homes, to which they could return. Those nurses working outside Dublin had to be rather more independent in spirit and action, especially those who went to the poorest districts of the west. While some kind of community and social life might be available to district nurses in the eastern and northern areas of Ireland, this was not available to their counterparts in the west, where community and creature comforts were lacking. Nurses tended to live by themselves, often in homes that were inadequate. Travelling to visit patients frequently involved additional hardships, as one nurse recorded in her report:

> A child with double pneumonia, to which I was called on Christmas day. She lived three miles out with no road going to within a half mile of the house. To get there, one had to walk through a swamp part of the way, and then climb up the mountainside to this house, which was most difficult in this wet and stormy weather.[65]

Nor did they always receive a welcome; their presence was a challenge to those women in the community who, without certificated training, had traditionally provided assistance, particularly in childbirth:

> The night was so dark and raining sleet and snow ... still I persisted in going. I'm sure it took me a full 2 hours to walk. When I got to the house there was great indignation on the part of the old handy woman, who informed me the patient never had a nurse or a doctor for six in the family.[66]

Once at her patient's home, the nurse could encounter extremes of poverty:

> Pneumonic fever: boy, 9 yrs, very ill and filthy dirty. Only one apartment in the house and no window. Two adults, five children, as well as a cow, calf, two dogs, two pigs and the fowl all sleep in the house.[67]

While district nurses were expected to work in cooperation with the local doctor, in isolated areas they were required to act on their own initiative. This was particularly so with the numerous maternity cases, where nurses frequently acted by themselves, each having received midwifery training in the course of their training as district nurses.

The role as teacher of the poor was also an important part of the activities of the district nurse. One nurse recorded:

> I found the patient, a woman aged about 35 in bed in a very small room which besides lacking ventilation, was in a very dirty condition. After attending to the patient I cleaned the room and succeeded in opening the window, which she informed me had never been opened before. I spoke to

her on the subject of fresh air and explained its beneficial effects. I was greatly pleased to find that every time I visited the window was open and the room very clean and tidy.[68]

Another district nurse recorded the success of her efforts in instructing mothers in her care:

Whooping cough is very prevalent amongst the children of my district. Have been called out frequently to cases where they only want just advice, some which were very glad of, as they kept their children stuffed up indoors near the fire wrapped in blankets. This I persuaded the mothers to give up and follow my instructions, which they are doing and their ideas are very much altered.[69]

The records of another nurse encapsulate the hardship that the district nurse could endure:

A maternity case to which I was called at 9 p.m. The woman lived four miles out. She had been my patient on two former occasions and it was gratifying to see how nicely she had prepared this time. She always has the most difficult labours. At 3 a.m. I sent her husband for the doctor, he came at once and a son was safely born at 7.30 a.m. Both mother and child are now getting on nicely. The day of her confinement was very wet and stormy and after the men had taken the doctor home in the boat they lost their courage and would not put out again to take me home even though it only meant coming along the coast. I was disappointed as I was very tired after having been up all night, and on duty twenty hours but there was nothing for it except to walk the five miles across the cliffs in the pouring rain and wind … This has been a very heavy month. The midwifery calls came one after the other. I was on duty without sleep or returning home for nearly 52 hours, all the Christmas in fact. The condition of the roads made it much more hard, as in some places the snow was four feet deep which made it impossible to take a car or ride a bicycle, and you had to struggle as best you could.[70]

What attracted women to such work? While hospital and district nurses served the poor of Ireland, the district nurse had a degree of freedom and responsibility in her work that was not available to the hospital nurse. In the period in question, hospital nurses worked long hours with little leisure time, they were subject to the supervision of the lady superintendent and were also under the close scrutiny of the medical staff; in the hospitals, strict rules and regulations governed their days and their actions, including their work and leisure.[71] In contrast, district nurses were independent and self-reliant, they knew their own worth each day that they worked. Whilst highly visible in the community and, in theory, subject as nurses to the directions of any local members of the medical profession, district nurses could still choose their own ways and control their own work. Working in an organisation run by their peers, the early district nurses of the QVJIN in Ireland were subject to professional inspection and direction only by their peers.

District nursing was a hard life but was an attractive proposition for nurses who sought some independence in their working lives.

CHAPTER 8

'Heading into the Wind': The Work of District Nurse Mary Quain[1]

Therese Connell Meehan

As the new light dawned on the Galway village of An Cheathrú Rua on the first day of October 1937, Nurse Mary Quain prepared with pleased anticipation to commence her new position as the district's third Dudley nurse. She was beginning to get the feel of her new home, a furnished, two-bedroom stone house with a coal range, paraffin oil lamps and nurse's surgery in the front hall. She had in a good supply of provisions and her cart of turf had been stacked close by. Several new navy cotton uniforms and warm coats hung in the wardrobe, her black leather nursing and midwifery bags had been carefully checked and her sturdy new bicycle stood ready near the door.

Aged twenty-six, she was relatively young and inexperienced for a Dudley nurse. She had known little about nursing and nothing about midwifery when she started her nursing training in 1932. Her view having completing her training in 1935 was that she loved nursing but not the strictures placed on nurses' practice in hospitals. In 1936 she undertook her midwifery training at the Rotunda Hospital in Dublin and while there heard about Jubilee nursing. Mary really liked the idea of nursing people in their homes and for the first half of 1937 did her Jubilee nurse training at St Lawrence's Home. Upon completion, she decided to work wherever she was needed and was assigned to the Lady Dudley Scheme.

Jubilee and Dudley Nursing

Jubilee nursing was established in Ireland in 1889 to provide home nursing for the sick poor.[2] It was named in honour of the financial support it received from Queen Victoria on the occasion of her silver jubilee. The service operated initially from St Patrick's Home at 101 St Stephen's Green, Dublin, where the nurses became known as 'the nurses out of the Green'. A few years later, St Lawrence's Home at 39 Parnell Square was added. The homes served as Jubilee nursing administrative centres, practice bases, training schools, and nurses' residences.

For a city or country district to have Jubilee nurses, local financial support was required. However, people in poor country areas with non-resident landowners could not raise financial support and were left without a home nursing service. In 1903 this deficiency was recognised by Lady Rachel Dudley, wife of the lord lieutenant. In response, she founded Lady Dudley's Nursing Scheme for the Establishment of District Nurses in the Poorest Parts of Ireland. The scheme employed Jubilee nurses who became known as Dudley nurses. This desperately needed service spread rapidly and by 1910 supported nineteen nurses in districts along the western seaboard from Donegal to West Cork and at the peak of its work in the 1940s it employed around fifty nurses.[3]

Jubilee and Dudley nurses were required to have completed registered general nurse training, midwifery training, the six-month Jubilee nurse training course, and be unmarried and of excellent character. Dudley nurses provided home nursing and midwifery over large districts. Their work was hard and demanding but their role in improving people's health was significant.[4] This is reflected in a tribute paid to them by a former chief secretary of Ireland, Augustine Birrell, when in 1937 he recalled, somewhat romantically:

> [a district in Connaught] supplied with a pious and sensible priest, a devoted and skilled 'Dudley' nurse, and a sober dispensary doctor attained as nearly to Paradise as is possible for any place on earth to get.[5]

An Cheathrú Rua, West Galway

In 1937, An Cheathrú Rua was a lively coastal village and district of some ten square miles with a population of about 4,000. The population was Irish-speaking but also spoke some English. Families lived on small stony holdings, making their living from farming and fishing. Those who lived closer to the village could earn additional income keeping summer visitors to the Irish college. Some, whose income was inadequate for basic daily needs, received state assistance. Houses were of stone and thatched, usually with three or four rooms with small windows, and held great warmth from well-stoked turf fires. Clothes were mainly woollen and homemade. Water was drawn and carried from wells, cooking done over open fires, and lighting provided by candles or paraffin oil lamps. The principal means of transportation was a donkey-drawn cart, but there was a frequent bus service between villages and to Galway town, twenty-five miles away. A telephone was available at the post office or garda station.

Families were usually large and extended families lived in one house. Family animals were likely to include hens, a dog, a donkey, one or two cows and perhaps a horse. People were generally relatively healthy and accustomed to hard physical work. Meals consisted of homemade bread, porridge, milk, tea, eggs, fish, a little meat, various types of sea plants and vegetables. However, malnourishment was not uncommon. Healthcare needs related mainly to childbirth, infectious diseases and injuries. There were approximately eighty births each year. Illnesses associated with aches and febrile symptoms, usually referred to as 'the flu', included relapsing fever and mild and chronic forms of typhus. Although pneumonia was not common, when it occurred it was serious because there were no antibiotics. Tuberculosis was common but less so than in other parts of the country. Outbreaks of measles, chicken pox and mumps took their course, but diphtheria and whooping cough were in decline due to new vaccination schemes. As in all poor communities of the time, lice were an inevitable fact of life, and scabies and impetigo were difficult for children to avoid. Injuries included burns, cuts and broken bones. Chronic conditions included arthritic pains and leg ulcers. Nonetheless, families had great initiative in coping with life's vicissitudes. They looked out for one another and there was always acceptance and support for any person in need.

Collaborations

Mary Quain kept her nursing and midwifery textbooks and Jubilee training notebook close to hand. However, except for tuberculosis, she was not particularly concerned with the exact nature of an illness and generally left medical diagnoses to the dispensary doctor. But she was acutely concerned with individuals' and families' responses to pregnancy, childbirth and illness. She carefully observed physical details and signs and symptoms of illness and emotional details of family and group interactions. Equally important was prevention of infection to every extent possible. In addition, respect for and sensitivity to the needs and feelings of each individual person as well as those of families was central to her work. Imagination and practicality had to be balanced to accommodate a variety of home circumstances, so that the very best possible nursing and midwifery care was always provided. Families naturally participated in their own care and no opportunity was lost for health teaching. A deep appreciation of the spiritual dimension of life underlay Mary's dedication to and love for her work.

Mary worked closely with the dispensary doctor who was based in Béal an Daingin and who covered four Dudley nursing districts. She had great respect for Dr Bourke and Dr O'Malley, who later succeeded him, because she observed them to be very skilled and conscientious in their work. While she paid particular attention to following their instructions, she also had a relatively autonomous relationship with them. Usually, families called Mary first for a woman starting labour or for an illness or injury, and she determined if and when to call the doctor. She would send someone for him if the need was urgent, or talk to him by phone from the post office or cycle to his house in Béal an Daingin if the need was less urgent.

Nurse and doctor would sometimes meet on the roads while doing their rounds and always stopped to talk over their patients, particularly any problems or puzzling situations. Some problems could be resolved by talking them through, and for some, each might ask the other to make a visit to the patient and do a separate assessment before talking again. While the doctor gave some instructions for treating patients, he left the treatment of many problems to Mary's discretion. She valued greatly the doctors' trust in her professional work and judgement, particularly because it gave a boost to her somewhat shaky professional self-confidence.

This collaboration also involved a third member, the parish priest, and was probably a good example of Birrell's idea of 'paradise' in the west of Ireland. Father McHugh had great concern for the physical and emotional health of the people as well as their spiritual health. Eight years earlier, and through considerable effort, he had been instrumental in securing a separate Dudley nurse for the An Cheathrú Rua district. Any time Mary saw him on her rounds they stopped for a chat about how his parishioners were doing, and he would make suggestions about who needed a visit from the nurse. While Mary had immense respect for him, she also used her own judgement regarding his suggestions. One bleak, stormy winter afternoon she encountered him on her way to a new mother she had delivered that morning. He insisted that there was no need for her to make another visit that day with the weather being so rough, and escorted her back to her house. She waited a half-hour after he had gone and went out on her way again; she wanted to see the mother feed the baby before nightfall. Although exacting in manner, Father McHugh was not without a sense of humour. When Mary once told him during a very busy period that she had not attended Sunday mass for three weeks, he replied with a twinkle in his voice that she must have been out too late dancing.

Methods of Organising Work

On a normal day, Mary arose at 6.30 a.m., attended Mass at 7.30 a.m., ate a substantial breakfast at 8.00 a.m., opened her surgery between 9.00 and 10.00 a.m. and then went on home visits. She planned each day by prioritising her most important visits and fitting less important visits around them. Among her most important visits were a woman starting labour or a person seriously ill or with a new illness. Next in importance were checks on ill patients and new mothers and babies, dressings and injections. Fitted around this work were longer-term mother and baby visits, school visits, child welfare scheme visits, and informal assessments and health teaching over cups of tea.

Three additional factors determined how she organised her work. These were: the need to try to visit non-infectious patients before infectious patients; where in the district the patients lived; and the weather. Some days she could cycle up to thirty miles. Some visits required leaving her bicycle and walking across a stony bog, and a boat was needed to reach a patient on an island. While the weather could be bright and gentle, it could also be grey and stormy. The wind had always to be reckoned with; it could be hard and constant, or it could be biting, gusting and whirling with lashing rain. Heading into the wind on her bicycle was an experience that was to remain with Mary for the rest of her life. Invariably, it seemed, she would find herself riding into a headwind on her way to visit a patient and on her return find that the wind had changed and she would be heading back into it again.

Most days, in fact, were not normal. Circumstances were constantly changing. She was the only nurse and midwife available and could be called upon at any time, day or night. If she was not at home, her neighbours knew the direction she had taken. During a busy period she might have to work almost continuously for two or three days, catching a little sleep here and there. She had to get the most important work done as carefully and safely as possible and she had to be practical.

Midwifery

No sooner had Mary begun to organise her very first day's work when a young man came to tell her his wife was starting labour. Off she went with her midwifery bag. In its outside pocket were a thermometer, and soap and a towel so that she could wash her hands before opening the bag. Inside were sterile swabs, pads, squares of cotton material, scissors and forceps, bottles of sterile saline and methylated spirits, handmade sterile cord ties, and a clean handkerchief to place over the mother's abdomen if she wanted to put her ear down to listen to the baby's heartbeat. She always wore a watch with a second hand and carried a good supply of newspapers for placing on the mother's bed to save the sheet and on the floor to receive soiled items. She was known for being 'good to the grannies' because she would ensure they had the least possible extra washing after a delivery.

When she arrived to a mother, she conducted an assessment to determine whether a normal delivery could be expected and how far labour had progressed. If the baby was not lying normally and could not be manoeuvred or there were any other untoward signs she would immediately send for the doctor. Although pregnant women were expected to see the dispensary doctor at least twice during their pregnancy, not all would do so. Mary did as much antenatal checking and teaching as she could fit in around her other work. Occasionally the doctor delivered a baby with Mary's assistance or a mother was sent to the hospital in Galway, but most labours were normal and she assisted with them by herself. An enema was given, water was boiled and all was made clean and ready. The bag was not opened and its contents laid out until delivery was near. She would discuss the process of labour with the mother and then they let nature take its course. If it was not a first labour and was in its early stages, she might leave for short periods to make other visits nearby.

Upon delivery, the usual baby checks were made. Clamping, tying and cutting the cord were quickly accomplished and baby given to the mother to hold. A baby slow to breathe would likely have a dab of poitín applied to its lips, which would have it 'roaring in no time'. The placenta was delivered and examined. Episiotomies were not done and occasionally a perineal tear would occur, which would be sutured by the doctor. The mother was helped to put the baby to her breast. Instructions were given as needed but usually the grannies knew well how to care for mother and baby. When she was as sure as possible that all was progressing normally, she departed with an arrangement to return to check mother and baby later the same day or the next day.

New mother and baby visits were made daily for ten days, each visit taking about one hour. Usually, Mary would bathe the baby each day and examine it carefully. These visits tended to be family affairs with everyone, especially the children, inspecting the new arrival. She observed particularly how the children reacted to the baby. They were great little chatterers and much was asked and learned about babies and boys and girls, and ideas voiced about how the baby would fit into the family and what each child could do to help look after it. She discussed with the mother the baby's care, breastfeeding, and how she should care for herself, emphasising the importance of a good diet of milk, eggs, fish and vegetables. Typically, women breastfed a baby for at least a year and sometimes for up to four years.

Mary recalled very few midwifery emergencies and no babies being stillborn or dying shortly after birth. Once, when she was waiting with a woman in labour, she had a 'strong feeling' to check on another woman about a mile away whom she knew had been delivered by a nurse from another district some hours before. At times when several women were in labour at the same time nurses from other districts would try to help one another. Mary found the woman haemorrhaging severely without anyone in the house realising what was happening. She sent urgently for the doctor and priest, massaged the fundus and got the woman into a head-down position. The woman survived and Mary got back to the first woman in time for her delivery.

Deliveries by handywomen had been illegal for several years, but in parts of the west of Ireland some women who 'had the gift' still helped in an emergency. Once when Mary had three women in labour at the same time and only one other nurse to assist her, she assented to a handy woman attending the third delivery. The handy woman was extremely worried afterwards that word would get out, but Mary assured her and took measures to make sure that it would not. A nurse-midwife had to be practical and do the best she could in all circumstances.

Nursing

Nursing took place in Mary's surgery, on home visits and in relation to various health schemes. Everyone who was able came to her surgery for check-ups, dressing changes, attention to injuries, injections or advice. Her surgery was furnished with a table, two chairs and a cupboard containing an array of lotions, dressings, bandages, bowls, instruments, syringes and needles, and the ever-useful sheets of newspaper. It also contained a stand for a bowl and jug of water, soap and towel, and a bucket for soiled items.

Mary's nursing bag contained the essentials for her visits. It had an outside pocket for soap, a towel and thermometers. Inside were bandages of varying sizes, clean and sterile squares of cotton sheeting, and tins of sterile cotton pads, dressings and swabs. She prepared sterile cotton items herself by baking them in a cotton-lined tin in a moderate oven for one hour. Her bag also contained sterile scissors, forceps, a probe, syringes and needles, bowls, medications, bottles of Dettol, methylated spirits, sterile saline and water; it carried lotions including iodine, mercurochrome and gentian violet, and ointments including Vaseline, sulphur ointment, and Queen's Ointment. Queen's Ointment was a special Jubilee nursing ointment made from lard, Vaseline, zinc oxide, carbolic acid and creosote.

People were resourceful and usually coped themselves with minor injuries, short-lived aches and pains and heavy colds. Mary was called for anything more serious. When making a visit the first thing she would do was wash her hands, and people knew to have water ready for her. For a person with a fever, she listened carefully to the history of the illness, recorded temperature, pulse and respirations and observed and assessed carefully factors such as type of breathing, skin condition, sweating, type and frequency of urine and bowel movements, pain, vomiting, ability to move and the state of consciousness. Based on this assessment, she would judge how seriously ill the person was and whether the doctor should be called; Mary remarked: 'you got to know ... to recognise serious symptoms very quickly.'

If the person were seriously ill or 'heading towards it', the doctor and priest would be sent for immediately. Everything possible would be done in the meantime, including trying to administer fluids and giving a sponge bath to bring down the temperature. The doctor would decide about additional treatment and whether to try to get the person to the hospital in Galway. Any person seriously ill was automatically anointed by the priest; anointing was associated more with healing than with dying because people had great faith in its curative effects. Mary firmly believed there was a cure in anointing and was often amazed at how it would help a person to recover from a serious illness.

If the person was not seriously ill, she had the family 'pour in the fluids', encouraged nourishing food, gave simple verbal instructions about additional care and visited again later the same day or the next day. While patients generally had to 'ride an illness out', careful nursing was key to facilitating this process. The patient was warmly covered and the room kept warm with a good turf fire. An antiflogistine poultice might be applied for chest congestion. Poitín was used medicinally, but she left the family themselves to administer it because they knew best how to use it. A punch was made from the poitín by adding hot water and sugar. Although it was illegal and Father McHugh was trying to eradicate it, Mary thought it very beneficial in many cases, especially for fevers, and she fully supported its judicious use.

Everything possible was done to prevent the spread of infection. Drinking water was boiled, and Mary strongly encouraged the use of Jeyes Fluid to clean everything in the house. However, people did not always have the price of it, especially during the war. In addition, overcrowded conditions often made it difficult for an infected person to have a separate room or even a separate bed.

Wounds, burns and ulcers were usually cleansed with sterile saline and, if appropriate, iodine, mercurochrome or gentian violet was applied. People took comfort in the colours of these lotions, which they believed promoted healing. If hot compresses were indicated, a bread poultice would be made by wrapping a good slice of bread in a square of sterile cotton and soaking it with hot, boiled water. Mary often used Queen's Ointment around a wound or to rub on aches and pains; she considered it to be great for almost everything. Poitín was also put to use as a lotion and it gave great relief from muscle and joint pains.

Health teaching and emotional advice were constant themes in Mary's work. She was an enthusiastic proponent of a healthy diet, encouraging families to eat their own eggs, milk and butter, rather than selling them for the money to purchase processed shop food. She emphasised the benefit of home-baked bread compared to shop bread, and the importance of eating every possible type of vegetable. She explained in simple terms how to minimise infection and cross-infection. She was attuned to the nuances of emotional difficulties and thought it important to know when to say yes to a cup of tea:

> You could go through an awful lot of work with a cup of tea under certain circumstances ... sometimes it gave people the opportunity to screw themselves up to unburden themselves ... you could give very valuable help to a family under those circumstances.

Mary made child welfare scheme visits to all children up to five years of age and kept a record card for each child, about four hundred at any one time. During her time in An Cheathrú Rua, the school health scheme was introduced and she organised it with the help of the priest. There were three schools with about one hundred and forty children each and one smaller one with about fifty children. She tried to visit one school a week, usually on a Friday afternoon to minimise disruption, and on each visit inspected one class. She observed for general cleanliness, malnourishment, problems with vision, hearing or teeth, and infections such as lice, scabies or impetigo; teachers would alert Mary to any child who they were concerned about. She examined all children for all problems so that attention would not be drawn to any particular child. When a class was coming up for First Holy Communion or Confirmation, she took a large bottle of paraffin oil and pieces of cotton wool and treated every child for lice, whether or not they had lice, so that every child was treated equally. The children usually enjoyed the distraction of a visit by the nurse. One day, a little girl stopped her on the road and enjoined her to visit her class the following afternoon at 2 p.m. When Mary suspiciously inquired what class she would be having at that time, the child's innocent reply was 'sums, Nurse'.

Mary's role as both nurse and midwife brought her close to the heart of her families. She was often a confidant and was very careful never to break a confidence. She was thoughtful, respectful and ever-watchful in ways that gave her great insight into her patients, and she looked for the individual human person in each patient. At the same time, she was careful not to become personally involved with her families. She tried to treat everyone equally and to be impartial and judicious in her care. This was not always an easy role to maintain. For example, it was not unusual when she was biking purposefully on her rounds to be greeted with waves from houses she passed and the call 'Are you coming in to see your baby, Nurse?' She would stop for a few minutes. As much as she loved her families, she remarked: 'it could be an awful nuisance, you know.'

Documentation and Accountability

Record-keeping took up a considerable amount of Mary's time. She kept a general register with patients' names and medical histories and diagnoses. This was carefully guarded, confidential information available only to some county medical personnel. She also kept a daily visits book, in which she described her nursing and midwifery care, referring only to 'a family' or 'a case'. This provided an account of how she spent her time and it documented her actions so that if anything untoward occurred she would be able to describe the situation in detail and verify her actions. Reports were sent to the county medical authorities and a monthly report was sent to the Lady Dudley Scheme central office in Dublin, where it was shared with the Jubilee Nursing central administration. The reports included details of the numbers of new visits and types of care given, deliveries, postnatal visits, mother-child visits up to one year and those from one to five years, children referred from the school health scheme, and descriptions of any notable events.

Mary also kept a payment book and prepared a monthly financial report. The Lady Dudley Scheme provided a free nursing service but people knew that donations to the scheme were appreciated if they could afford them. Many people liked to pay even a small amount for the delivery of a baby, for example a half-crown or five shillings. During one of her first deliveries, the mother who was very poor and had a very large family handed Mary a half-crown the moment the baby's head was delivered. Somewhat startled, Mary explained that the service was free and, as she continued the delivery, protested strongly at taking the money, but the mother insisted. Gradually Mary realised how important it was to the mother that she could pay her way and accepted the donation graciously. Later, as always, she provided a receipt stamped with the Lady Dudley Scheme stamp, which the mother accepted with great satisfaction. Subsequently, Mary made sure that the family received an additional supply of children's clothes, which were available for 'needy cases' from the Lady Dudley Scheme Clothing Guild.

Both the Jubilee nursing organisation and the Lady Dudley Scheme sent inspectors to the districts about every six months. Mr Pym, the treasurer of the Lady Dudley Scheme, was an engaging and welcome visitor. He examined her financial records and was concerned primarily with how well the scheme was supporting her. Miss Bourke, from the Jubilee nursing organisation, was a native of Galway, an experienced Jubilee nurse and a fluent Irish speaker. She made an overnight stay, examined the daily visits record and accompanied Mary to her surgery and on home visits to assess the amount and quality of her nursing knowledge and work. Mary was sometimes cautioned for falling behind with her record-keeping, but generally passed muster and even won some accolades for her work.

Social Life and Health of the District Nurse-Midwife

Mary had great enthusiasm for her work. She was always 'on duty' and took relatively little time for socialising; in Mary's words, 'the work was there to be done and there was no one but yourself to do it'. Dr Bourke once observed that An Cheathrú Rua was the 'busiest little corner' of all his Dudley districts and Miss Bourke noted that for a time An Cheathrú Rua was the heaviest midwifery district in the county. Mary did not have a maid, as did the two previous nurses, and aside from sending out most of her laundry, she looked after herself. She was a physically strong and resourceful woman, but at times became exhausted from her work. Sometimes she worked almost continuously for days at a time with breaks only for a few hours of sleep. Winters were especially hard. She had five heavy coats, but it was not always easy to keep at least one of them dry. Sometimes she had to don a saturated coat and cycle for miles in cold, wet weather to attend a woman in labour. She would pray urgently to Our Lady to protect her and hope that there would be a good fire at her destination. In early 1939, Mary bought a car, thinking that this would help lighten her work. She found instead that her work increased and that she had to do a lot more walking. When the war started and petrol was rationed, she sold the car and returned to her bicycle.

During her early months in the district, she felt lonely at times and somewhat isolated, partly due to not having much spoken Irish. Although she tried to improve her Irish, she was never very fluent. However, over time she came to know everyone in the district and made several special friends including a neighbour, an artist, the doctor's wife, and a former Dudley nurse who had married a schoolteacher. Always an avid reader, she usually read two newspapers a day and enjoyed reading novels. She also enjoyed listening to the radio. Friends and family members visited during the summer and once a year she took a short holiday. However, toward the end of 1943, there was concern about the toll her work was taking on her health and, following discussions with Miss Bourke, she decided to transfer to a less busy district.

Heading into the Wind: Lessons for Contemporary Practice

This biographical history is based on interviews with an eighty-seven year old nurse who was remembering events which occurred sixty years previously. However, it is consistent with her earlier general description of Jubilee nursing.[6] It is also subject to the rendition of the author. Nonetheless, within these possible limitations, the biography offers contemporary nurses and midwives in Ireland some opportunity to know themselves in relation to an important part of their history. As Mary Grossman (1994) has observed:

> Discovering how others must have thought about the trials and tribulations of life tells us something of our potential as a discipline and of our individual possibilities as emissaries of that discipline.[7]

There is marked similarity between how Mary thought about her practice, and the ideas which should guide contemporary practice, but are not always adhered to. Mary had great respect for the 'medical model' but she did not use it as a basis for her practice. She observed, assessed, diagnosed and treated human responses to actual and potential health problems. Her emphasis was on fostering health in every possible way and on health teaching. She was attuned to the influence that emotions could have on health and the importance of knowing when to take time to listen and offer counsel. She developed good insight into intrapersonal and family dynamics and considered this essential to effective practice. In contemporary education, much emphasis is placed on concepts such as professional autonomy, collaborative practice, documentation and health promotion, almost as though they are new ideas. But this portrait of a Jubilee-Dudley nurse-midwife illustrates how these concepts were in daily action many years ago.

The practice of the Jubilee-Dudley nurse-midwife anticipated that of the contemporary public health nurse. However, while Mary's practice was broad-reaching and more or less autonomous, contemporary public health nurses have been divested of any meaningful role as midwives and are restrained in their ability to be self-directed by medico-social vested interest groups. The role of the community midwife is only just returning after a long and unjustified absence. Mary's relationship with her families also identifies her as a prototype of the family nurse practitioner, one of the most effective nursing speciality roles in the US. In light of Mary's work, it is interesting to observe that in the US it is possible to earn a dual master's degree as a family nurse practitioner and midwife. Mary's role could also be viewed as a prototype for another nursing role popular in the US and Australia, that of the parish nurse. While An Cheathrú Rua was not technically a parish, practically speaking it was. Mary worked within a parish structure and it was the parish priest who originally secured a Dudley nurse position for his parishioners.

Obviously, Mary engaged in what is often referred to as 'real nursing', but she also had great enthusiasm for intellectual endeavours. She loved ideas, was always thinking and did not in the least consider this inimical to her practice. Her natural enthusiasm for thinking coupled with her skill in observation and her quietly questioning attitude engendered in her a propensity for independent thought and judgement, what is currently referred to as 'critical thinking'. While these characteristics did not endear her to the matron or nurse teachers in her hospital nursing school, they made her a skilled and innovative professional nurse and midwife. Today, some nurses and midwives still appear to think that excellence in practice and intellectual enthusiasm are mutually exclusive endeavours, but Mary would have disagreed vigorously.

Grossman's reference to the trials and tribulations of life brings to mind the ubiquitous presence of excessive stress in the lives of nurses and midwives. Mary experienced a fair amount of work-related stress; some stress resulted from her very heavy workload, but another and more subtle source of stress was her inveterate lack of self-confidence. Despite her intelligence, skill and ingenuity, a feeling of being not quite acceptable or good enough was often lurking beneath the surface. Such experiences may resonate with some nurses and midwives today. They may experience stressors as a weight of circumstances opposing them, which they must nonetheless bear up against to continue their work.

The motif of heading into the wind can symbolise this experience. Literally and figuratively, Mary spent much of her professional life heading into the wind, but she was not one to let a strong head wind divert her from her purposes. She thought carefully about the sources of her stress and recognised why she lacked confidence in her own ability. She did everything possible to change the sources of her stress and what she could not change she put philosophically aside. She believed in her work and had great faith that the Star of the Sea would guide and protect her. This approach gave her an inner sense of calm and resilience, which together with her quiet determination and perseverance, fuelled her ability to head into any wind and persist, no matter how hard it blew.

Postscript

Mary Quain subsequently worked in other Dudley Scheme districts. Following further education, she became the superintendent (principal tutor) at St Patrick's Home. She went on to become the last Dublin-based general superintendent of Jubilee nursing in Ireland, before it was merged with the public health nursing system. Until she passed on, in November 1999, she continued to take a keen interest in nursing and midwifery ideas and practice.

CHAPTER 9

Scene and Obscene: Childbirth in Ireland, 1650–1750

Declan Devane and Jo Murphy-Lawless

The history of childbirth is a complex one. In this chapter, having set out some of the themes attached to this history, we will principally explore the changing attitudes and language of James Wolveridge, who wrote in the seventeenth century, and Fielding Ould, who wrote in the eighteenth century, in the hope that readers might be encouraged to read some of these texts themselves. Their texts on childbirth and the practice of midwifery were both written in Ireland with an Irish focus. Although they are separated by seventy years and have differences in emphasis, they represent a trend towards a more scientific approach to birth that would be disadvantageous to midwives and would have mixed consequences for women. In many ways, the practice of midwifery is only recently beginning to free itself from the constraints of medical science that began to emerge in the period in which the key texts were written.

Childbirth 1650–1750

The period of the seventeenth and eighteenth centuries was a time of transition for childbirth throughout Europe. Although the vast majority of women in early modern society, which was predominantly agrarian, would continue to give birth at home with the local midwife in attendance, two new types of professional men with an interest in childbirth were making their appearance. Firstly, there were the scientists who were part of the seventeenth-century revolution enquiring into the origins of life, including Francis Bacon, Robert Boyle, William

Harvey, Regnier de Graaf and Anton von Leeuwenhoek. Following on from René Descartes, these men were establishing methodical, experimental forms of enquiry as the basis of knowledge that would eventually displace the last vestiges of the old scholasticism of the late Middle Ages entirely. The views of these scientists on sexuality and reproduction were to have an enormous impact on the perceptions of and attitudes toward women as mothers and women as midwives. Secondly, a new kind of trained medical man emerged. This was the barber surgeon who had learned his medical skills not in the universities, but in the many European wars on land and at sea and to whom the midwife turned when she required emergency assistance with a labour where the woman's life was at risk. Although midwives were forbidden to use instruments, barber surgeons were permitted to perform so-called 'destructive operations', using crotchets, fillets, hooks, scissors and, later, forceps, to release a trapped or obstructed foetus from the woman's body in order to save her life.

By the sixteenth century, midwifery had recovered from the terrible ravages of the witch hunts of the previous century, which had, in part, been constructed and ignited by James Sprenger and Heinrich Kraemer's infamous *Malleus Maleficarum.*[1] In many parts of urban, continental Europe, midwifery had become highly organised with corps of trained midwives practising in Holland, Germany and France. However, the vast majority of midwives came from the untrained village tradition, in which a woman of good character and kindness dealt with a task that still attracted considerable stigma. For example, assisting at childbirth was considered filthy work.[2]

This perceived need for a woman of good character to carry out filthy work betrayed the continuing influence of a Christian sense of sin connected with sex, pregnancy and birth. In the wake of the witch trials, there was still a concomitant and strongly expressed need on the part of men to control the activities of midwives involved so directly and intimately with birth. Therefore, it fell to the Church to take up the issue of untrained midwives and, after the Council of Trent in the 1540s, midwives were issued with a licence by Church authorities, detailing their duties. This licensing of the midwife was tied to the absolute necessity of baptising a baby if the baby were dying and if no priest were available.[3] A flavour of this can be gleaned from the case of a licence issued to a midwife in 1740 in Kilkenny, Ireland, by the bishop of Ossory. The licence was issued to a Widow Elliot to enable her to practise as a midwife, but only after she had sworn not to 'use any sorcery, divanation, magick, incantations, witchcraft or any superstitious, hellish or horrid methods' to help the women under her care, and undertake that, should 'any distemper grow dangerous … [she would] send for a clergyman, the physitian of the soul'.[4]

The Church's insistence on baptism is thought to have had a major influence on the teaching of barber-surgeons in France and it advanced French obstetric thinking dramatically by the seventeenth century. The need to get a baby baptised, even though it was dying or dead, led to many more instrumental deliveries, and this aided the observation and understanding of the birth process, which was viewed at that time as a rational and predictable mechanical process. In addition, the practice of dissection was established in France earlier than in the British Isles, and was to become central to building clearer understandings of birth.[5] These circumstances led to many more practitioners publishing texts in France in the seventeenth century.

Wolveridge: Texts and Contexts

Little is known of James Wolveridge's life except that he was born in England, practised as a physician in Cork, Ireland, and graduated from TCD in 1664. Wolveridge published one of the earliest texts on midwifery in English and its rarity in this respect is chiefly why he is remembered today.[6] In 1932, Professor Elis Essen-Möller of Lund in Sweden[7] described his acquisition of the second-known copy of the text on midwifery by Wolveridge, titled *Speculum Matricis Hybernicum; Or, the Irish Midwives Handmaid* (1671).[8] Möller's edition is currently held at the University of Lund and the only other known original copy of the text is held at the Bodleian library at the University of Oxford.[9]

Wolveridge's book added to a handful of seventeenth-century texts in English with a focus on childbirth. Preceding Wolveridge's text by over a century was *The Byrth of Mankynd* (1540), an English translation of Eucharius Roeslin's *Der Swangern Frawen und Hebammen Rosegarten*

(1513).[10] Other texts published in the seventeenth century included the English translations of Jacques Guillemeau's 1609 text *De l'Heureux Accouchement des Femmes* (1612) and Harvey's *Exercitationes de Generatione Animalium* (1651),[11] *The Compleat Midwife's Practice* (1656),[12] and Nicholas Culpeper's *A Directory for Midwives* (1656).[13] Percival Willughby, a contemporary and friend of William Harvey, wrote his *Observations in Midwifery, as also the Country Midwife's Opusculum or Vade Mecum* in the 1660s,[14] while a translation from Latin to English of Jacob Rüff's text, *The Expert Midwife*, was published in 1637.[15] These texts can be said to represent two ends of the spectrum in a trend towards a scientific approach to childbirth. This spectrum ranged from a highly scientific approach, based on empirical observation, to an approach based on conjecture and restating and/or interpretation of the ideas of other writers.

During the seventeenth century, concepts were slowly assuming the recognisably scientific view of birth that has dominated our perceptions in modernity. However, this scientific view also contained the basis for an ideology about women that would contribute to the creation of deeply unequal relationships between male-dominated medicine and women as midwives and as mothers.

Roeslin's text *The Byrth of Mankynd* was at the more speculative end of this spectrum. The text was the rewritten Latin *De Partu Hominis* that largely comprised corrupted fragments from Galen and Hippocrates, with details of ancient Greek and Roman practices on birth. The misjudged accounts of the physiology of birth contained in Roeslin's text reflected the status of medical doctors in this period who lacked direct empirical knowledge and who practised at arm's length from their 'patients'. As Edward Shorter has noted, academic medicine was just coming out of a thousand-year twilight in its thinking on birth.[16]

In addition to its re-circulation of outdated ideas, Roeslin's text is notable for two other reasons. Firstly, its translation into the vernacular languages of first German and then English evoked widespread dismay. Churchmen objected to formal knowledge of a woman's body being made available in any language but Latin, the teaching of which was inaccessible outside the Church and the universities where gentlemen physicians learned medicine. Part of the churchmen's objection was related to the strongly misogynistic discourse referred to above, which held that women's bodies were a source of threat, sin and pollution, and the masses, therefore, needed to be regulated in their acquisition of physiological knowledge about women.[17] Secondly, and for somewhat different reasons related to professional boundaries, 'gentlemen' physicians dismissed midwifery as contemptible and beneath their notice. So Roeslin's text is also noteworthy for the inclusion of the following ditty, which reveals the impoverished and degraded status attributed to midwives by academic medical opinion of the day:

> I'm talking about the midwives all
> Whose heads are empty as a hall,
> And through their dreadful negligence
> Cause babies' deaths devoid of sense
> So thus we see far and about
> Official murder, there's no doubt.[18]

This entrenched opposition to midwifery dated from late medieval times and from the era uncomfortably close to the witch burnings instigated by the Church.

In contrast to Roeslin's work, which looked back in time for its legitimacy and authority, the importance of William Harvey's text was that it contained an accurate description in English of women's reproductive organs derived from his own dissections. Such knowledge would eventually help to set aside some of the morass of myths about childbirth. Perhaps of more immediate importance to midwifery was the translation into English of the work of Louise Bourgeois. *The Compleat Midwife's Practice* made available to an English readership Bourgeois' extensive empirical experience. Bourgeois worked first as a pupil of her husband, a barber surgeon who had studied under Ambroise Paré and, subsequently, she became head midwife at the Hôtel-Dieu in Paris in the early seventeenth century, where she was responsible for the training and supervision of the hospital's midwives. She had a long-term influence on childbirth management and, as a result, the renown of the Hôtel-Dieu reached well beyond France. The works of Roeslin and Bourgeois contributed to the beginning of a protracted discourse in English on the proper conduct of the labour process that still constitutes an unresolved and often bitter debate amongst childbirth professionals.

In the spectrum of writings on childbirth in the seventeenth century, Wolveridge's text is closer to the work of Roeslin and conveys an absence of awareness of the changing debates in relation to childbirth, although it does convey an awareness of the growing client base for medical men. Wolveridge's text provides insights into the social relations between midwives and medical men in the period. The text was published in two editions; the first one, printed in 1670, was titled the *Speculum Matricis Or the Expert Midwives' Handmaid*, and the second, to which we refer, was titled *Speculum Matricis Hybernicum; Or, the Irish Midwives Handmaid* and was printed in 1671. Although he trained and practised in Ireland and despite the title's 'home-spun dress', Wolveridge avers that his book is aimed, predominantly, at an English readership:

> It hath an English dress under an Irish mantle; it being never intended for the Irish (though I heartily wish it may be serviceable to them also, if occasion be,) whose fruitfulness is such, that there is scarce one barren among them; and whose hardiness, and facility in bringing forth, is generally such, as neither requires the nice Attendance of diligent, vigilant Nurse-keepers, or the Art of expert Anatomists, or the unwearied pains and skill of dexterous Midwives; being, more like the Hebrew women, than the native Egyptians; delivered before the Midwives can come to them.[19]

He bases his opinion of the reproductive competence of Irish women on a story that was said to come originally from Sir George Carew, president of Munster and one of the architects of Hugh O'Neill's defeat at the Battle of Kinsale in 1601. Wolveridge acquired the story from William Harvey, to whom it had originally been recounted.[20] The story is about an Irish woman who, on accompanying her soldier husband to camp, goes into labour as the army is delayed from crossing a flooded river:

> [The woman] … withdrawing herself to the next thicket of shrubs (without the help of any Midwife …) there, all alone, brings forth Twins … both which she brought down to the River presently, and there washed both herself, and them; which done, she wraps them up (not swaddled at all) in a coarse Irish mantle, and carries them at her back, marching with the Army

> the same day barefoot and barelegg'd (as she was) twelve miles, and that without the least prejudice to her health, or to the lives of her children.[21]

Like all colonisers, the Tudor English, as they set about the re-conquest of Ireland, invented myths about the people they conquered; in the sixteenth century, the native Irish were consistently described as 'wild' and 'savage'.[22] These descriptions generally brought with them an implication that women of other ethnic groups and even lower-class women of their own ethnic group were far more powerful sexually and reproductively than women of the middle- and upper-classes. While it may be true that lower-class Irish women of that period frequently gave birth on their own and returned to their duties and work as soon as possible after birth, it was not their 'wildness' but absolute necessity that made this possible. Nevertheless, the pain and danger thought to afflict women in birth was consistently seen as reserved for upper-class women, while 'hardy Scots, wild Irish, working countrywomen, whores and doxies [trollops]' all had nearly painless labours.[23]

In directing his book to the 'grave and serious matrons' of England, Wolveridge was merely repeating a common perception of the day, that women of the upper-classes were more delicate and needed greater tending. Of course, upper-class women were also a well-paying clientele, so it was worthwhile underlining the specific need for 'skilled Anatomists'. Even Louise Bourgeois noted class differences, arguing that after birth upper-class women or women of 'quality' must not be treated like country women. While upper-class women had 'delicate' stomachs, women of the lower-classes were used to eating heartily to enable them to work hard and needed to be restored quickly from the rigours of birth to do that work.[24]

Wolveridge's *Speculum Matricis* relies on the same range of debased Greek and Roman fragments that mark Roeslin's text; the Irish medical historian T. P. Kirkpatrick characterised the *Speculum Matricis* as mainly plagiarised.[25] In his text, Wolveridge uses a fictional dialogue – a common device in writing from that period – between a midwife (Eutrapalia) and a doctor (Philadelphus), and its purpose is to describe the attributes of a 'good midwife' and the practice of midwifery.

We should not assume that the practices denoted in the *Speculum*

Matricis reflect to any significant degree the practice of midwifery in Ireland during the latter part of the seventeenth century. However, what is notable is that Wolveridge portrays midwives in a broadly positive light as competent practitioners. He also appears to have been keen to gain a reputation as a doctor to whom rich English clients might turn if they encountered difficulties in childbirth which midwives could not or were ill equipped to deal with. Despite the fact that Wolveridge had the perceptiveness to seek, fictionally at least, the advice of a midwife on the role and practices of midwifery, throughout the many dialogues between Eutrapalia and Philadelphus, the midwife is subservient to the doctor. The structure and content of the dialogue poignantly illustrates the power relationships between the female midwives and male doctors at that time. For example, accepting the doctor's invitation to enter into conversation with him, Eutrapalia states:

> I should be willing (if your Worship, and other Learned Physicians think me fit) to be serviceable to my generation [midwives], and to take upon me that employment [midwifery].[26]

It was not only midwives who were subservient, so too were childbearing women. In discussing the 'Rules for Child-bearing Women', Eutrapalia asks of Philadelphus:

> I beseech you, Doctor, lay me down some Rule to be observed by Child-bearing women.[27]

In discussing techniques for assisting at births with complications, the midwife is consistently, albeit courteously, interrogated by the doctor. It is much later in the dialogue that the doctor attempts to redress the burden of his many questions to the midwife. As he does so, he indicates that he will use his professional status to help legitimate her status as a good midwife:

> I have hitherto troubled you with many Questions, that I might not only be sure of your abilities but also give testimony of your sufficiency, if need require.[28]

The power imbalance here is hardly surprising, being strongly rooted in perceived differences of physiological and mental capacities. For example, many early modern writers attribute excessive sexual passions to women, not because of their 'temperament', which was thought to be colder than that of men and thus less inclined to passion, but because women were 'the weaker vessels'[29] and men were 'commonly endued with greater presence of Mind'.[30] Helkiah Crooke's anatomical text of 1615 describes women as:

> ... more wanton and petulant then Males, wee thinke hapneth because of the impotencie of their minds; for the imaginations of lustfull women are like the imaginations of bruite beastes which have no repugnancie or contradiction of reason to restraine them.[31]

Women were consistently seen to be laden with emotion and excess sensibility. This perceived problem profoundly affected the practice and thinking of medicine in the eighteenth century.

Ould and Other Eighteenth-century Doctors on Childbirth and Midwifery

Fielding Ould was born in Galway. Having qualified as a doctor from Trinity College Dublin, Ould went to Paris where he trained at the Hôtel-Dieu for perhaps a three-month period. This was the fashionable option in the mid-eighteenth century. The Royal Charter, which incorporated the Rotunda Hospital, drew attention to the need to provide training for doctors in Ireland in order to stem this outward migration, and to ensure that potential doctors might not be lost to other countries.[32] Ould did return from France and became the second master of the Rotunda Hospital from 1759 to 1766. He was eventually knighted and otherwise pursued a lucrative private practice among the wealthy in Dublin, including apparently attending the Countess of Mornington when she gave birth to the Duke of Wellington.

A More Scientific Method

Ould was only thirty-two when he wrote his *Treatise of Midwifery*. As with most of the writing from this period, the text was, in part, an effort to establish his name professionally. The treatise owed much to his observations in Paris, where he benefited from the wide exposure to clinical material through births and dissection:

> I cannot help declaring the Necessity of being indebted to France for the true Knowledge of practical Midwifry; for the Opportunities which are there to be met with, are no where else to be found, without which, it is hardly possible to be an Adept, namely those of ocular Demonstration of women being delivered both in natural and preternatural Labours where as well the external Parts of the Patient, as every action of the Operator, are the whole time in view.[33]

The commercial state, with the French state as the model *par excellance*, welcomed and supported the contribution of hospitals to the growing demographic and disease surveillance systems of monitoring population and health data that were deemed necessary to exert direction and control over the population. Medicine also derived a second crucial benefit from the poor who entered the hospitals for care, as they became part of the clinical material on which medical knowledge was to advance.

The 'gaze' of the eighteenth-century clinician that dissolved the opacity of the body[34] came to rest soonest on the pregnant and labouring female body, resulting in a dramatic escalation of knowledge on childbirth.[35] Thus, moving through the eighteenth century, the previous trickle of books on midwifery and midwifery practice had become a deluge.

By the time that Ould was writing in the fourth decade of the eighteenth century, obstetric medical knowledge had begun to assume contours more familiar to us now. For example, Ould, and later William Smellie, the London midwife, in his *A Treatise on the Theory and Practice of Midwifery*,[36] considerably advanced our understanding of the mechanism of normal and difficult labours.[37] Ould is possibly best remembered for his description of the mechanism of labour:

> First, it is evident that the Head, from the Os Frontis to the Occipitis, is of an oblong Figure, being very flat on each Side: Secondly, that the Body, taking in the shoulders, makes still a more oblong Figure, crossing that of the Head; … the Head coming into the World, is a Kind of Elipsis in a vertical Position; and the Shoulders of the same Form in an Horizontal position: Thirdly, that the Pelvis is of an Eliptical Form, from one to the other Hip [and] … the oblong Figure of the Head must cross that of the Pelvis … so as to admit of its [the fetal head] Exit, it must of Necessity … acquire another Form for the Admission of the Shoulders; … it is evident

> that when the Child is turned, so as to have the Chin on one Shoulder, all the above Objections are removed; for the Head and Shoulders are on a parallel Line, in respect of their Shape, and at the same Time, both answer the Form of the Passage from the Pelvis.[38]

This level of objective analysis was inseparable from the philosophy of the Enlightenment. By the eighteenth century, Europe had eagerly claimed the scientific Enlightenment, which held that human life at the social and individual levels could be understood in the same way the natural world could be analysed. In other words, human life could be measured and core truths established. These truths, once understood, could be used to help shape human life. This reliance on the scientific method is reflected in Ould's treatise where, admonishing those that seek to perfect the art of midwifery, he quips that:

> For many of their (other writers on midwifery) Schemes are like those of some Navigators and Geographers, who never made use of a Compass, but in their Closet.[39]

Ould's writings of course had 'Truth and Demonstration on their Side, being confirmed by Practice'.[40]

However, the complexities of the Enlightenment philosophy ensured that 'Truth and Demonstration' did not necessarily promise greater equality for women or more rational considerations of their positions in society. In fact, Enlightenment ideologies decreed a set of social relations that privileged the male over the female. For example, the nervous system of the body was feminised, with strong linkages between women, nerves and passions that required containing and direction, as contrasted with the masculinising of the body's musculature.[41] These complex associations attributed to men the capacity for rational thought, while women by comparison, whether as midwives or women giving birth, were viewed as physically weaker, emotionally wayward, if not insatiable, and superstitious. This was a secular scientific dress for an ideology not dissimilar to that of the late Middle Ages. As for the disavowal of women's rational capacities and intelligence, this was a strand of inegalitarian thinking that stretched as far back as Aristotle. Not only did this perspective go unchallenged, but new experiments, measuring brains and comparing musculo-skeletal features, were devised to 'prove' that women had less mental capacity than men.[42]

Characteristics of a Midwife

These ideas had a decisive impact on how doctors, accoucheurs (or male midwives), depending on how they styled themselves, wrote about their immediate professional rivals, the midwives. Ould characterised midwives in a negative light, as being rescued from their ignorance, finally, by the new male scientific empiricism:

> … as medicinal Knowledge increased, it became very apparent, that there was more Learning and Dexterity required, in the prosecution of this Art [of Midwifery], than could be expected from ignorant Women, who generally had the meanest Education; And then it was, that Men, who were well acquainted with Operations in general, applied themselves to the Improvement of this Art.[43]

The contrast with Wolveridge is striking. Seventy years earlier, even if midwives were subordinate to doctors, Wolveridge painted a more sympathetic portrait:

> The best Midwife is she that is ingenuous, that knoweth letters, and having a good memory, is studious, neat and cleanly over the whole body, healthful, strong, and laborious, and well instructed in women's conditions, not soon angry, not turbulent … hasty, unsober, unchaste; but pleasant, quite, prudent; not covetous.[44]

While many early modern writers expended considerable effort in describing the characteristics required in what was perceived to be a 'good' midwife, few extended this requirement to the descriptions of surgeons and physicians. Of notable exception is Daventer's *The Art of Midwifery Improv'd*, wherein he exalts the characteristics of *all* who might attend a woman in labour. Women in labour should, he states, be treated 'gently and modestly as [they] ought to be'.[45] Male surgeons and physicians were rebuked, particularly if they handled the woman cruelly or roughly. For him, it was essential that a surgeon 'behave himself … in words and actions', and his intolerance for ineptness is palpable:

> How could he otherwise but afflict the Woman in Labour, as well as the Standers by, when they saw a Man in Liquor, almost void of the use of his senses, both void of Pity and Compassion, furnished with a Knife, a Hook, and Iron Forceps, and other Instruments horrible to fight, to come to the Assistance of one in Agony, who commonly begins … to hurt the Mother, then kill the living Infant, then with a great deal of Pain to draw it out in Pieces, and at last to think no Reward satisfactory for such an extraordinary piece of work. I could wish such Surgeons would change their Office with a Slaughterer of Oxen and Sheep.[46]

Writing ten years after Ould, Smellie was somewhat more optimistic and balanced in his depiction of the relationship between a male midwife and a female midwife. Smellie's thinking was based not on mutual respect however but on what he perceived as the need to make allowances for the inherent weaknesses and ineptitude of female midwives:

> A midwife … ought to avoid all reflections upon men-practitioners; and when she finds herself at a loss, candidly have recourse to their assistance … this confidence ought to be encouraged by the man, who, when called, instead of openly condemning her method of practice (even though it be erroneous), ought to make allowance for the weakness of the sex, and rectify what is amiss, without exposing her mistakes.[47]

Failure by the male midwives to 'cajole' the female midwives thus would be disadvantageous for both:

> These gentle methods will prevent that mutual calumny and abuse which too often prevail among the male and female practitioners, and redound to the advantage of both.[48]

Ould clearly had little time for traditional midwives. Referring to a woman with a difficult delivery in which he assisted, his antipathy is evident when he states that all the adverse outcomes associated with the woman's labour were as a result of 'the Ignorance of the Midwife' who had, he claims, lacerated the 'orifice of the womb'. In the management of labour with twins, he charged, midwives would leave up to a week between delivery of the first and second twin and frequently two or three days. This miserable situation arose, according to Ould, from her 'Ignorance'. Another example of the incompetence of some 'female' midwives is given in Ould's discussion of a retained placenta, 'left behind by some Malpractice of the Female Midwife'.

Evidently, the relationship between the male and female midwives was often disharmonious. Although this trend was mainly seen in the writings of the male midwives, a handful of female midwives also wrote about what was a fierce rivalry and sense of competition. A famous example from the mid-eighteenth century was Elizabeth Nihell, who was married to a surgeon-apothecary; a midwife herself, she had studied in Paris at the Hôtel Dieu and returned to London to practise. She argued that women, and not men, should practise midwifery. Not only did Nihell deride the involvement of male midwives in childbearing, but she was also not averse to defamatorily naming those for whom she had little respect. William Smellie was frequently the subject of her rebuke:

> If on the contrary, and what the most frequently happens, you fall into the hands of one of the common men-midwives, either of that multitude of disciples of Dr Smellie, trained up at the feet of his artificial doll, or in short of those self-constituted men-midwives made out of broken barbers, tailors, or even pork-butchers (I know myself one of this last trade, who, after passing half his life in stuffing sausages, is turned an intrepid physician and man-midwife) must not, I say, practitioners of this stamp be admirably fitted, as well for the manual operation, as for the prescriptions? … I should be almost as much afraid of the prescriptions of these mock-doctors as of their operation. I should have more confidence in the advice of a discreet matron, or of a skilful midwife …[49]

Perspectives on Birth: Wolveridge and Ould

Wolveridge's seventeenth-century view of childbirth is generally more optimistic and physiologically focused than that of Ould. In the management of labour, Wolveridge's discussion is principally devoted to the management of difficult labour with referral to male physicians and surgeons where 'Chirurgical Instruments, or other Physical means must be used'.

In eighteenth-century Ould's treatise, there is, however, a shift in the view of natural childbirth, which by now has become wrought with the potential of complications and thus he advances that the 'assistance of a Surgeon particularly instructed in the Art of Deliveries, is generally necessary in the most natural Labours'.[50] Such assistance would not only benefit the mother by reducing the pain of her labour, but would also prevent normal labours from becoming abnormal, the cause of the latter being the incompetence of female midwives:

> … by their [Surgeon] preventing Labours originally natural, from becoming the contrary, which is too often the Case under the Misconduct of Female Midwives, of which we have frequent Opportunities of being convinced.[51]

Wolveridge's traditional view, that women were best suited 'to help women in their [natural] deliveries',[52] was to become completely displaced by the male midwife or accoucheur. For example, writing in 1724, John Maubray insists that men were of better assistance by far to the labouring woman than female midwives:

> And indeed MEN … being better versed in Anatomy, better acquainted with Physical Helps, and commonly endued with greater Presence of Mind, have been always found readier or discreeter, to devise something more new, and to give quicker Relief in Cases of difficult or preternatural BIRTHS, than common MIDWIVES generally understand.[53]

These male medical practitioners tended to have a greater degree of anatomical knowledge because they were able to engage in dissection, which formed the larger part of their training. The 'training' itself in this period rarely extended beyond two or three months and therefore, unsurprisingly, Smellie claimed to have trained hundreds of male midwives in his teaching rooms. Midwifery, as a subdiscipline within medical training (rather than as we know midwifery today), was only slowly offered in university or through professional medical training courses in the eighteenth century. Yet, as seen in their writings on midwifery, male medical practitioners of midwifery regarded anatomical knowledge as the foundation on which midwifery should be built.[54] Indeed, it might be argued that their access to anatomy classes and practical dissections was critical to their professional success because women were excluded from such teaching in Ireland and Britain and from the universities as well.

Such qualifications and knowledge built this new professional power of obstetrics and, allied with the Enlightenment philosophy about the starkly different mental capacities of men and women, allowed these nouveau obstetricians to claim superior ability to female midwives in all areas of childbirth, including normal childbirth. As a result of these developments, midwives were to become the butt of some male writers' satire. No distinction was made between trained, urban, midwives in the continental European pattern and untrained midwives.

Intervention in Labour

Contrary to the writings of many feminists in the 1960s and 1970s, the polarised view that all early modern male accoucheurs were far more inclined toward intervention in labour than their traditional female counterparts does not present the full picture.[55] According to Edward Shorter, well-trained urban midwives were less likely to intervene than male midwives and were, on balance, the safest practitioners for a woman, whereas untrained rural midwives were as likely to use interventionist practices as many of the male midwives were.[56] Shorter's thesis is borne out by the scrupulous historical and folkloric research of Jacques Gélis, who concludes that untrained midwives feared long labours and this led to their interventions.[57] Ould criticised the interventionist practices of traditional midwives:

> For want of this Knowledge [of interutero foetal position], many Labours prove dangerous and tedious, that might have been very successful, had they been committed to Nature.[58]

Nevertheless, despite his assertion that he brings 'Nature for my Advocate', Ould conflictingly and frequently illustrates that he is not adverse to significant intervention in labour.[59] For example, he advocated that, on spontaneous rupture of the membranes, the hand should be introduced into the vagina and do all that is possible to facilitate the passing of the cervix over the presenting foetal head.[60] To facilitate delivery of the foetal head, Ould promoted the introduction of the thumb into the rectum to retract the coccyx. Where a mother is unable to push to effect delivery of the placenta, she should be 'compelled to it, by putting a Finger into her Throat', which no doubt would cause an increase in intrathoracic pressure as a result of her unnecessary vomiting and thus facilitate delivery of the placenta in 'about Five Minutes'.[61]

Episiotomy

Routine episiotomy has been a passionately contested intervention in contemporary childbirth management. Although it is not precisely known when this practice of incising the perineum during childbirth first began,[62] the operation and the indication for episiotomy[63] was first described by Ould in his *Treatise on Midwifery*:

> It sometimes happens … the Labour will become dangerous, by the Orifice of the Womb contracting about the Child's Neck; wherefore it must be dilated if possible by the Fingers, and forced over the Child's Head; if this cannot be accomplished, there must be an Incision made towards the Anus with a Pair of crooked Probe-sizars; introducing one Blade between the Head and Vagina, as far as shall be thought necessary for the present Purpose, and the Business is done at one Pinch, by which the whole Body will easily come forth.[64]

Despite Ould's description, the use of episiotomy remained relatively infrequent until the mid-twentieth century.[65] Prompted by the recommendations of prominent obstetricians, episiotomies became re-popularised and were to become routine practice in Europe by the 1930s.[66]

In Ould's text, social class continued to be used as a way to measure how 'natural' births could be. While he acknowledged that it was commonplace for women to deliver without any assistance other than nature, this predominantly happened to those of a lower social ranking. Here Ould assimilated the ongoing discourse about the greater physical capacity of lower-class women to give birth, in this instance women who were rendered socially unacceptable because they were prostitutes or because they had given birth outside marriage:

> This [delivery without assistance other than nature] happens chiefly to those who have Bastards, Women at Sea, and in Camps.[67]

Birthing Position

Another widely debated issue in contemporary practice has been the value of the upright position or vertical axis in giving birth. The encouragement of the use of upright positions features in Wolveridge's writing:

> Women are variously delivered, some, on their bed, that is to say, o'rethwatt the hardest bed, with their faces upward, with their feet closed, doubled, and covered. But if she not so tired out that of necessity she must be delivered on the bed, remove her to the [birthing] stool.[68]

The use of the birthing stool in Ireland in the late 1600s appears, by Wolveridge's account, to have been widespread where 'all Midwives (nay few) have them, or use them'.[69] The upright position advocated by Wolveridge had, by the 1740s, been replaced with the recommendation that women be preferably delivered in a lateral position in the bed, which Ould asserts, is 'the Posture for natural Deliveries'. Ould justified his assertion about the value of a horizontal, lateral position on grounds that it preserved the mother from attendees' 'remarks and whispers' and optimised pelvic diameters. This is a good example of the ideology of male medical practitioners overcoming accurate observations of anatomy. Somewhat contradicting himself, Ould recommends the retention of an upright, kneeling position for abnormal presentations. Gélis laments the fact that, by 1914, very few women in European countries were able to make a choice about birth position, so extensive was the medicalisation of birth.

This medical preference of the birth position continued to be reflected into the mid-twentieth century. In a 1952 textbook from the Rotunda Hospital, Dublin, which was aimed at student midwives, illustrations depict the birthing woman lying on her left side and the text advises that women be kept in bed during the second stage of labour. The adoption of an upright position for childbirth was seen as crude and primeval. As late as 1981, referring to positions for delivery, the ninth edition of *Myles Textbook for Midwives* confidently asserts:

> Where doctors and trained midwives are in attendance and when analgesics and anaesthetics are administered the dorsal or left lateral position is employed but a squatting attitude is the one adopted by primitive tribes.[70]

We have referred above to the tendency of those who are successful colonisers to dismiss the ways of life and approaches of those whom they colonise as wild and savage. The use of the word 'primitive' in the Myles text illustrates how mainstream obstetric practice successfully colonised women and midwives so that its way of thinking predominated and any alternative was rejected as uncivilised.

Conclusions

JoAnne Brown writes how professional language succeeds in convincing a wider society of its authority and correctness by a skilful combination of 'ideology, legitimation and persuasion'.[71] Brown also argues that emerging professions have to try and sway potential clientele about the value of their work.[72] We can see these strategies in the texts on midwifery and birth that mark the beginnings of the profession of obstetrics. Some writers we have examined use language that is more benevolent and kind. A writer like Ould tends to use more forceful language about female midwives, almost as if such linguistic practices are required in order for him to assert his authority. Ould does the same with many of the interventions in the birth process that he describes, such as that with vaginal examination where he speaks of having 'to *thrust* the Edge of the Orifice up'[73] or his delivery techniques in a normal birth where the doctor must 'losing no Time … *pull* the child forward'.[74] These descriptions also lend an edge of drama and haste, as if the process of childbirth is not a reliable one, but requires active and immediate intervention. So wealthy women are thus convinced of this logic and turn to the accoucheur in his private practice, while many poor women choose to go to the new lying-in hospitals where they gladly accept the charity of shelter and care, while becoming the basis for extending medical dominance.

Overall, whether kindly or more forcibly expressed – and the history of obstetrics contains many examples of both – the objective of this professionalising project is the same.[75] The objective is for male midwives to secure their presence as the most legitimate professionals in the field of birth, at the expense of the older practitioners, namely the female midwives. As we have indicated above, the new professionals were aided greatly in being able to use an ideology about women that emphasised the destabilising impact of female emotions. Even Wolveridge declared that there were risks to birth extending from 'the woman, as when she is too angry, too fearful, or too modest, or if she be in age above 40 … or when she be so thick and fat, that the passages be narrow'.[76]

At first sight, this caution appears good common sense. The issue, however, is how women's emotional lability was increasingly used to justify the control rather than the support of women during childbirth. This should come as no surprise, since the control of women in childbirth was aligned with the larger project of state control of the people. In this connection, Ludmilla Jordanova points out that there were deeply powerful interests in overseeing reproduction in the eighteenth century and the flood of treatise from pregnancy to childrearing indicated the profound concern of those who saw themselves as protecting the interests of the state.[77] Ordering reproduction, a term that began to enter the language in the late eighteenth century, also meant ordering social relations to impact on the political order.[78] This is illustrated in Ould's work, where he implies that medicine is a God-given tool that enables its practitioners to correct flaws in the natural order of things, to make a more perfect world:

> … as an Instance of his great Benevolence to Man kind, he (God) has supplied us with artificial Means, whereby we may remove Grievances to which it (nature) is obnoxious; and none more extraordinary than those, by which Nature is assisted in those Operations which are to be the Subject of the following Discourse (childbirth).[79]

As male midwifery gathered greater professional power to itself, midwifery, as an independent practice undertaken by female midwives, sank into ignominy in Ireland and Britain. As Brown states, 'language is not merely another kind of activity, but is the repository of history'.[80] The early treatise on birth helps us to trace the elements in this history that set the scene for unchallenged professional hegemony until the late twentieth century when midwifery began to redefine professional boundaries and reclaim its mission to care for women in childbirth with new terms of reference.

CHAPTER 10

Regulating Midwives: The Role of the Royal College of Physicians of Ireland

Anne McMahon

There is evidence that both Church and municipal authorities have attempted to regulate midwives in the pre-modern (1400–1800) period. By the latter half of the nineteenth century, state regulation of midwives was a political issue in Britain and in other European countries. The Royal College of Physicians of Ireland (RCPI) was among those active in agitating for midwifery legislation in Britain and for its subsequent extension to Ireland.

The Royal College of Physicians of Ireland (RCPI)

The Fraternity of Physicians was established in 1654 and was granted a Royal Charter by King Charles II in 1667. This gave the fraternity control, nominally at least, of the practice of 'physic' in Dublin and within a seven-mile radius of the city. At the request of the college, a new charter granting wider powers was given by King William and Queen Mary in 1692 and this charter still governs the college.[1] The charter gave the college the authority to license the practice of medicine in Ireland and it entrusted it with the supervision of apothecaries, surgeons and midwives.

Training and certification of female midwives was available from the Rotunda Lying-in Hospital, the Coombe Lying-in Hospital, Sir Patrick Dun's Maternity Hospital, and the Royal College of Physicians of Ireland.[2] This training was of three to six months' duration and women, usually older, married, and frequently with children themselves, were trained as midwives. With their training, they could work independently or as nurse tenders or monthly nurses, attending women in childbirth in their own homes, usually under the supervision of a doctor.[3] However no system of formal statutory regulation of midwives existed and the majority of women who practised as midwives in their communities were without any formal training. In the absence of evidence specifically related to the Irish context regarding their training and practice, it is presumed that these were married women with their own children who gained their experience by attending women in childbirth, and were recognised in their communities as having some skill in this area. The title 'midwife' was used to refer to female practitioners, but frequently it has been used interchangeably with the title 'nurse' or 'midwifery-nurse', even before it became common for midwives to have previously qualified in nursing. Prior to regulation, this interchangeable use of terms led to a degree of confusion with regard to the precise parameters of the role.[4]

The minute books of the Parliamentary Committe of the RCPI in the RCPI archives provide evidence of the college's interest in the matter of the training and regulation of midwives. The committee comprised a small group of senior members of the college who met regularly to discuss the implications for the RCPI and for medical practice of any pertinent legislation coming forward for debate in parliament. Arising out of its deliberations, this committee made recommendations that were raised at the business meetings of the RCPI.

The Select Committee, 1893

By 1890, and with the introduction of the second midwives bill to the House of Commons, the RCPI became actively involved in the debate on midwifery regulation and the evidence indicates that the issue of midwifery registration was a prominent matter on the college's agenda for debate. The parliamentary committee met on 22 December 1890 and invited Dr Lombe Atthill, former master of the Rotunda Hospital, fellow of the RCPI, and a member of the General Medical Council to attend.[5] The meeting was held in response to the resolution adopted by the RCPI at its business meeting of 17 December 1890, which instructed that the parliamentary committee be directed 'to take all necessary steps to carry out the view of the college regarding the Midwives Registration Bill'.[6] A statement and petition were approved and Attorney General D. H. Madden, MP, was requested to present the latter to the House of Commons on the re-assembly of parliament in January 1891. This statement and petition expressed the view of the president and fellows of the Royal College that:

> registration of midwives as proposed in the said Bill will not tend in any marked degree to render more efficient the women practising as midwives unless steps be first taken to improve their education.[7]

They recommended that the whole subject of the education and registration of midwives be referred to a select committee of the House of Commons. On 11 February 1891, the parliamentary committee was informed that a deputation was to meet with the lord president of the privy council on 13 February, with regard to the matter of the Midwives Registration Bill.[8] This meeting was regarded as significant and the RCPI wished to be represented. The attorney general was telephoned and confirmed the meeting and, at short notice, the president of the RCPI and Dr Atthill prepared to travel to London in order to represent the RCPI on the deputation.[9] However, the attorney general telegraphed in reply that he would act for the RCPI and save the members from travelling.[10]

The midwives bill of 1890 failed to get the support of parliament and, after its failure and that of a subsequent midwives bill of 1891, a reformulation of the medical position on midwives and their sphere of competence occurred.[11] It was broadly accepted that some form of registration was inevitable.[12] Dr Atthill represented the RCPI to the select committee, which met in 1892. His objection to midwifery regulation was primarily to registration in the absence of an appropriate system of education; midwifery instruction for the London Obstetrical Society's diploma was of just three month's duration. An additional concern was the possibility of registration for those midwives currently untrained but having empirical experience as midwives, i.e. those in bona fide practice; this concern was an ongoing bone of contention. Dr Atthill expressed his point of view on the matter:

> It is absolutely essential not to put a certain number of women who are now in practice and who are wholly illiterate, and many of them of very doubtful character, on the register, thereby giving them the proposed privileges of very considerable value.[13]

The main thrust of his argument was the concern that in the eyes of the public registration would confer a certain status on midwives:

> I think it is a pity to put the midwives on a par, in any way, with medical men. Let them practice as much as you like, but I think you ought to make a difference between a fully qualified practitioner, whether male or female, and one who is only qualified in one department, and therefore if there is to be a register, which is to be the same in the eyes of the public as the regular medical register, the public would not be able to make a distinction between them.[14]

The select committee of the House of Commons reported in 1893 and it recommended the registration of midwives. The General Medical Council was invited to frame rules for admission to the register, both through practice and through examination. The privy council would then confirm such rules. The select committee took into account the apprehension expressed by some members of the medical profession, 'lest their interests might be injuriously affected by an improvement in the status of midwives'.[15] However, the select committee expressed the view that, although the fears of some medical representatives were considered, nevertheless the overwhelming evidence pointed to the necessity for registration, which could be of benefit to the medical profession. In this regard, the select committee was of the opinion that:

> medical men will not only be relieved of much irksome and ill-paid work, but that improved knowledge on the part of midwives will induce them to avail themselves more frequently, and at an earlier stage than at present, of skilled medical assistance in time of emergency and danger.[16]

The select committee had accepted the principle of midwife registration, the attainment of which was now just a matter of time. The broad parameters of possible registration legislation were laid out, which would include mechanisms for control of midwives by the medical profession, a system of training and examination which would be under medical control, and a sphere of practice limited to normal labour. Midwives thus registered were seen as having a role to play in providing services for the poor, who could not afford the fees of a medical man, and would thus not constitute any competition for patronage of women who could afford to pay fees for attendance in childbirth. One of the nagging fears of the medical profession, and articulated by Dr Atthill, was that the registration of midwives would effectively constitute another order of medical practitioners. This was once again the position articulated by the RCPI in 1900, when the issue of registration of nurses began to feature on the political horizon. Following its deliberations, the parliamentary committee of the college resolved that:

> [it] cannot recommend the College to support the movement for the State Registration of trained nurses, which would not be for the public interest while it would tend to create a new order of practitioner.[17]

Further, in response to the concerns expressed regarding the possible privileges conferred by registration, it would eventually be agreed that midwives would enter their names on a roll, not a register, which would not mislead the public into thinking that they provided a service equivalent to that provided by the registered medical practitioner.

Following the involvement of the RCPI in the issue of midwifery registration in the early 1890s, the minute books make no further reference to the matter until it is again raised in 1898. This is not to suggest that the members of the RCPI were not involved in or concerned with the issue. It is likely that the RCPI's position was represented through members' activities on, for example, the General Medical Council and through other avenues; most medical representative bodies were deeply engaged with the issue of registration.

Changing Views

At the meeting of the parliamentary committee in April 1898, the proposer and seconder being Dr W. J. Smyly, from the Rotunda Hospital and Dr Andrew Horne, joint master of the National Lying-in Hospital, respectively, recommended that the RCPI 'oppose any Bill for registration of women as midwives or midwifery nurses being carried into law, the provisions of which would extend to Ireland'.[18] The argument advanced by the RCPI and articulated by Dr Atthill during his evidence to the select committee in 1892 was that the situation in Ireland with regard to maternity services for the poor was adequate. He claimed that the Rotunda Hospital and the Coombe Lying-in Hospital trained more midwives than were required and that a midwife was attached to virtually every dispensary district.[19] These midwives were paid a small salary from the rates, administered by the relevant Poor Law Union, and they supplemented this small salary with an income from private practice. The dispensary system provided a minimal level of medical care for the poor.[20]

However, the RCPI could revise its opposition to midwifery regulation very rapidly, depending on whether or not its interests were represented. It approved of the position of the Midwives' Bill committee of the General Medical Council regarding midwifery registration, which had been represented to the lord president of the privy council. This legislation would restrict the midwife to attendance on natural labour and would require the midwife to send for medical aid in difficult cases, thus making explicit her inferior status. The RCPI also approved the proposal of banning the unqualified woman from the opportunity of enrolling under a bona fide clause of experience and practice.

The General Medical Council had also managed to have a clause regarding good character reinserted in the proposed bill, this clause having been previously opposed and dropped in 1890. All of the above legislative proposals met with the assent of the RCPI. At its meeting of 11 May 1898, the parliamentary committee expressed the opinion that legislation on the lines indicated should be extended to Ireland.[21] However, by May of the following year, the RCPI once more revised its position. It seemed that in the matter of the recognition of the licence awarded by the RCPI, the Rotunda and the Coombe Lying-in hospitals would not be recognised under the proposed legislation, thereby reflecting adversely upon the prestige of those institutions.[22] Thus, at the meeting of the parliamentary committee on 1 May 1899, it was recommended that the RCPI adhere to the resolution of 1 April 1898, which supported the General Medical Council's suggestions. The college would support the legislation containing the clauses relating to Ireland, but with the following resolution:

> that the Bill will have the effect of disqualifying from practice in England and Wales (after … two years from the commencement of the Act) women holding the certificate of midwife and nursetender of this College as also those of the Rotunda and Coombe Lying-In hospitals. The Committee recommends that the College oppose any Bill containing such an unjust provision.[23]

The RCPI lobbied vigorously through the members of the Irish Parliamentary Party at Westminster, through prominent members of the Midwives' Bill committee, and it communicated directly with the clerk of the privy council in making its views known. Support was sought through these bodies for an amendment which would recognise the awards of the Irish licensing institutions as equivalent to any examination which would be held under the auspices of the proposed Central Midwives' Board (CMB), and which would enable holders of those same certificates to be enrolled, both retrospectively and in the future.[24] The argument was that a large number of women came from England to Ireland in order to undertake training as midwives in the Irish institutions.[25]

In the event, the 1900 bill was talked out and a further bill was introduced in 1902 and, once again the RCPI supported the extension of the bill to Ireland, if certain conditions were fulfilled. However, they objected to the title 'midwife' being adopted, preferring the title 'midwifery nurse'.[26] The thrust of the legislation was to place the regulation of midwives very firmly under medical control, and it may be that the use of the latter title more clearly represented the reality of what the RCPI had envisaged, i.e. a practitioner who would have a very clearly demarcated function, under medical supervision. In the resolutions adopted at that time, the reference is to 'midwifery nurses', as distinct from midwives.[27] According to Robert Dingwall *et al.*, with increasing medical involvement in childbirth, a demand was generated for a reliable person to relieve the doctor of the labour-intensive task of monitoring the labouring woman's condition, and sitting with her in an inactive way until she was ready to deliver.[28] It is likely that this type of practitioner equated with the preferences of the RCPI. The RCPI remained concerned regarding the recognition of the certificates of the

Irish awarding bodies and it was determined to ensure that the awards of the Dublin midwifery training institutions, along with the certificates awarded by the National Lying-in Hospital and Sir Patrick Dun's Maternity Hospital, should also be recognised. Their interest was in ensuring that candidates for enrolment on the English roll, in possession of Irish certificates, should be in a position to so do without further examination.[29]

The 1902 bill reached the report stage in the House of Commons in early June. T. P. O'Connor, MP for the Scotland division of Liverpool, who had led the opposition to other bills, in conjunction with other Irish MPs, also led opposition to this bill. There were a total of sixty-five amendments on the order paper and only three hours at the disposal of the promoters, so it seemed that, like the previous bills, this bill would also fail.[30] In the event, a compromise was reached on one of the main amendments and Mr O'Connor withdrew his opposition to the bill and the other amendments, principally in the name of his Irish supporters.[31] In the Midwives Act 1902, the certificates awarded by the Irish training institutions were recognised for enrolment, without the necessity for further examination. This principle, established through the activities of the RCPI, assumed substantial importance for Irish midwives when registration legislation was extended to Ireland.[32]

The Role of the RCPI in Midwifery Regulation, 1902–18

No further minutes relating to the registration of midwives were entered into the minutes book of the RCPI until 1906. However, it is unlikely that the RCPI lost interest in the matter and it is probable that the effectiveness of the English legislation was observed with interest, both through professional contacts and through the medical press. For example, from the inception of the Central Midwives' Board (United Kingdom), *The Lancet* regularly published news relating to that body's activities, including reports of the penal cases committee.

In October 1906, the RCPI was approached by letter by T. J. Stafford, Medical Commissioner of the Local Government Board (LGB).[33] According to Ruth Barrington, the Local Government Board was at the 'apex of the poor law, dispensary and public health structures' and, since 1898, the LGB had been placed at the head of the new system of local government, which gave it an interest in all activities carried out by what were then the newly formed county councils and county borough councils.[34] The LGB was to take a direct and ongoing interest in the regulation and supervision of midwives. Dr Stafford proposed that 'possibly a short act making it illegal for unqualified persons to practice for hire as midwives in Ireland would be sufficient for the requirements of this country, and would be desirable'.[35]

He sought the RCPI's views on the likelihood of such a measure finding general favour in Ireland. Such support could not be assumed. The Irish Medical Association, representing mainly general practitioners, the group most likely to be threatened from any improvement in the status of midwives, had written to the RCPI in 1900, seeking the RCPI's support for the Irish Medical Organisation's opposition to the midwives bill, then under debate in parliament. The support of the RCPI was not forthcoming at that time.[36] However, the RCPI did reply favourably to Stafford's letter, expressing its support in principle for the extension of the Midwives Act 1902 to Ireland, and once again emphasising the importance of the principal of reciprocity for the licensees of the English and Irish Midwives' boards.[37]

By December of 1906, a special business meeting of the RCPI was considering a letter from Dr Stafford, requesting the RCPI to draft a midwives bill for Ireland.[38] At that meeting, the matter was referred to the parliamentary committee and doctors Horne, Tweedy and Jellett, senior obstetricians associated with the National Lying-in Hospital and the Rotunda Hospital, were asked to draft a bill and to report back to the committee.[39] A draft bill was presented to the RCPI at a monthly business meeting early in January 1907 and was accepted subject to a minor alteration.[40] In early February, the RCPI instructed the parliamentary committee to forward the draft bill to Dr Stafford of the LGB.[41] Dr Stafford met with the parliamentary committee, and some amendments were made to the draft bill on Dr Stafford's suggestion, including a clause relating to good character. The amended bill was once again returned to the RCPI for consideration and approval.[42]

However, there was no further movement on the bill until 1910. In April of that year, Viscount Wolverhampton, lord president of the privy council, had introduced a midwives bill to the House of Lords, its purpose being to amend the Midwives Act 1902.[43] A departmental committee had reviewed the workings of the 1902 act and significant amendments were required. Among the required amendments were the reconstitution of the Central Midwives' Board, additional provision to deal with the enrolment and suspension of midwives and the notification of their practice, and the further regulation of the power of the local supervising authorities. Another amendment was the need to provide for the payment of the fees of medical practitioners called in to assist in cases of difficulty.[44] Alice Gregory, a prominent member of the Midwives' Institute and active in the campaign for midwifery registration, had noted that the 1902 act had made it compulsory for midwives to call in a doctor when difficulties arose. However, no provision had been made in the legislation for the payment of his fees, which many poor women could not afford, and frequently midwives ended up paying the fee out of their own pockets or risked being reported to the CMB penal committee for not observing the rules.[45] The medical press held the provision of payment for medical men as being the most important element of the proposed amendments to the Midwives Act, and framed the response of the medical man to the summons for medical aid from a midwife as an altruistic act. The medical press also made it clear what it perceived the midwife's role to be, that of 'the care of mothers of the poorer classes in the cases of normal childbirth'.[46]

It may be the case that this heightened debate in Britain once again encouraged the interests of Irish medical men to press for a midwives act for Ireland. The parliamentary committee recommended that the RCPI take steps to press for an extension of suitable legislation to Ireland and suggested that a conference of the interested Irish medical bodies be held to press for a suitable act.[47] This conference was held under the auspices of the RCPI at the Royal College of Surgeons in Ireland on 3 June 1910. Representatives of the Dublin maternity hospitals, the RCPI, the Irish Medical Association, the Royal Academy of Medicine, the registrar-general, the LGB, and the universities attended. A decision was made at the conference to demand that the provisions of the Midwives Act be extended to Ireland and a committee was formed to communicate this demand to the chief secretary for Ireland.[48] According to *The Lancet*, the decision of the conference represented the expression of Irish professional opinion and could not be ignored.[49]

In the meantime, the governors of the Rotunda Lying-in Hospital had also lobbied Irish members of the House of Lords, requesting action on the matter.[50] During question time in the House of Commons on 14 July 1910, Viscount Castlereagh asked the chief secretary for Ireland, Mr Birrell, MP, if the government proposed to introduce a measure dealing with midwives in Ireland similar to that introduced in England. In response, the chief secretary made it clear that this was not one of the government's priorities and that there was no immediate intention to introduce such legislation. The reason given was that the same urgency for such a measure did not exist in Ireland as in England, due to the power of the boards of guardians of the Poor Law Unions in employing midwives.[51] A letter was sent by Dr Andrew Horne, president of the RCPI, to the chief secretary on 22 July, appraising him of the Dublin conference and informing him that a resolution for the absolute necessity for a midwives act for Ireland had been passed at the conference. The letter also noted Mr Birrell's reply to Lord Castlereagh in the House of Commons, which, he stated, differed markedly from professional medical opinion.[52] Mr Birrell replied promptly, noting the concerns of the college and the resolution passed at the conference. However, he stated that his reply in the house only referred to the possibility of legislation being introduced in the current session, as this was not planned.[53] The government appeared to be stalling on the matter. Nothing further was accomplished at that time.

Towards Registration Legislation

In 1915, the Midwives Act 1902 was extended to Scotland and, in 1916, the parliamentary committee of the RCPI once again took up the agitation for the extension of the act to Ireland, urging the government of the 'pressing necessity' existing for the passing of a bill for Ireland. The committee declared:

> such a bill is needed to protect lying-in women, to control infant mortality and to enable Irish trained midwives to take their proper place in the ranks of the registered midwives of the U.K.[54]

By July 1916, the RCPI had received a letter of support from the Irish Medical Association, containing a resolution passed at the association's AGM and requesting the RCPI to nominate a member to act on a committee to draft a midwives bill for Ireland. Sir Andrew Horne, master of the National Lying-in Hospital was appointed to represent the RCPI.[55] Letters were also received from the Irish Matrons' Association and from the Irish Nurses' Association, expressing the urgent necessity for such legislation and expressing pleasure that the RCPI had had such legislation under discussion.[56] It is worth remembering that in April 1916, a military uprising against British rule in Ireland had occurred. Much of the country was in ferment, with the tide of public opinion going against the Westminster government, following the executions of several leaders of the uprising. The profile of women was also at its highest point at the time, since many women had played an active role in the campaign for suffrage, in the labour movement, in the pacifist movement, and in the republican movement.[57]

Pressure from various interests forced the government to act and a 'Bill to Consider the Better Training of Midwives in Ireland and to Regulate their Practice' was introduced into the House of Commons in November 1917. At a parliamentary committee meeting on 23 November 1917, the bill was considered and a special subcommittee of obstetricians was convened to consider the bill and suggest amendments.[58] The subcommittee recommended to the parliamentary committee that representatives of the Royal College of Surgeons in Ireland, the Irish Nurses' Association, the Irish Matrons' Association, the National Union of Women Workers, and the Civic Union should be asked to meet with the committee. The various representatives should meet to discuss suggested amendments, and 'to try to obtain as large a co-operation as possible in any representation which the college should see fit to make to Parliament'.[59] The proposed meeting was held on 4 December 1917. While there is no record of the discussion, the amended bill, as presented to the meeting, met with the 'unanimous approval of those present'. In presenting the bill to the RCPI for adoption, the parliamentary committee stated that it was desirous that it should become law, as there was an urgent necessity for such a measure for the protection of the mothers and children of the country and for the welfare and education of the midwives.[60]

The amendments suggested by the subcommittee and accepted by the college are noteworthy in that they reveal the position of the subcommittee regarding midwife representation on the proposed Central Midwives Board for Ireland (CMBI), which they (the subcommittee) considered to be insufficient. They recommended that the number of midwife representatives be increased to three. In order to do this without increasing the size of the board, it was recommended that the number of medical practitioners be reduced to four.[61] This was an advance on the constitution of the CMBI as evident in the draft bill which provided for a Central Midwives Board, whose membership included just a single midwifery representative. Four members would be LGB appointees, eight would be registered medical practitioners, four would be representatives of the universities, and there would be one representative of the RCPI, one representative of the Royal College of Surgeons in Ireland and two further representatives, one each to be appointed by the Irish Committee of the British Medical Association, and the Council of the Irish Medical Association. The sole certified midwife representative provided for in the draft Bill would be appointed by the lord president of the council, 'when, in his opinion, midwives so qualified are available in numbers sufficient to warrant the appointment'.[62]

Therefore, the amendment suggested by the subcommittee was an improvement on the draft, but yet it was not as radical as it might appear on first reading. The number of medical practitioners to be elected by the medical profession was indeed four. The LGB was to nominate three persons, one of whom should be a registered medical practitioner, and the other two appointed after consultation with the county councils and county borough councils. In the event, one of the latter two appointees was also a medical practitioner. The LGB also appointed four women, referred to in the act as 'midwives' representatives'. Three of these were to be appointed following consultation with recognised nursing associations in Ireland. Three of the appointees were matrons of maternity hospitals and one was the superintendent for Ireland of the Queen Victoria's Jubilee Institute for Nurses.[63]

The trajectory for development for midwifery as an occupation was set at this point. The medical representation on the CMBI was substantial, representing a total of six out of a board of eleven members. It may further be argued that the interests of the nursing associations would also be closely aligned with the medical interests, with the path of development for midwifery in the future being closely identified with nursing. This is indeed the route that was subsequently taken by midwifery.

The issue of reciprocity of certification was of ongoing concern for the RCPI, since the prestige of the training institutions, such as the Dublin maternity hospitals, was at stake and the members of the parliamentary committee of the RCSI were leading obstetricians in these same institutions.[64] However, the issue of reciprocity was an important one which was factored into the legislation, and assumed ongoing importance throughout the life of the CMBI.[65] It assumed special importance in 1950, when the title of 'midiwfe' was once again under threat, and the functions of the CMBI were being amalgamated with the General Nursing Council for Ireland under a new generic nursing board (An Bórd Altranais).

The amendments proposed by the subcommittee were carried, and the Midwives Bill quickly passed through parliament, with some trade-offs being negotiated. At the monthly business meeting of 1 February 1918, the registrar informed the RCPI that the bill had successfully passed through all stages and was awaiting the royal assent.[66] At a meeting of the Irish Midwives Act committee at the Royal College of Surgeons on 14 May 1918, four medical men were put forward for election as representatives for the CMBI. Among those elected were Sir Andrew Horne, Master of the National Lying-in Hospital and Sir W. J. Smyly of the Rotunda Hospital, both fellows of the RCPI and active in securing midwifery registration legislation for Ireland.[67] Of the medical representation on the CMBI, of whom there were a total of six, five had associations with the RCPI.[68] The Midwives (Ireland) Act was placed on the statute books on its passing on 6 February 1918, and the statutory regulation of midwives was a reality. The Central Midwives Board for Ireland was established to oversee the implementation of the legislation, and to control and regulate midwifery practice, until its incorporation with the General Nursing Council into An Bord Altranais (The Nursing Board) in 1950.

CHAPTER 11

Being a Psychiatric Nurse in Ireland in the 1950s

Ann Sheridan

For Ireland, achieving political independence from the United Kingdom in 1922 resulted in more than political and economic separation. The desire of the newly established Irish Free State government to further Ireland as a separate nation that was 'Gaelic and Catholic' frequently resulted in its rejection of initiatives from outside the new country. The nature and pace of change within psychiatry in Ireland was affected by this, as well as being influenced by the Catholic hierarchy and its antipathy to socialism, behaviourism, psychoanalysis and dynamic psychologies in general.[1] Ireland's position as a devoutly Catholic country and the dominance of the Church in State matters, and in particular those relating to education and healthcare, mitigated against the introduction of a range of therapies in Ireland that were becoming accepted practice elsewhere.

Coupled with the desire to establish an independent Irish nation, the early years of Irish government were associated with improving the general living standards of the population. Major projects, including the extension of electricity and water supplies to rural communities, were undertaken as a matter of priority. The most significant changes in the health system in Ireland focused on public health issues, including preventative services, maternity and child health schemes, and schemes to deal with tuberculosis and infectious diseases. While these years saw no fundamental change in the system of care of the mentally ill, the nomenclature associated with insanity and the insane did begin to change; gradually 'asylums' became 'hospitals', 'insanity' was renamed 'mental illness' and 'lunatics' were now called 'patients'.[2]

It was not until 1945 that a Mental Treatment Act was passed in Ireland. This act, which repealed all previous legislation other than that related to the care of criminal lunatics and wards of court, firmly established the jurisdiction of the medical profession as the sole legitimising force in determining the existence of mental illness and the detention of patients in mental hospitals, a situation which had been the case in England since the 1930s. Similarly, with regard to nursing, the legislative arrangements established in 1919 while Ireland was still under British rule, continued to operate to regulate education, training and the registration of nurses in the new independent state until 1950.[3] Only in that year was a new Nurses Act introduced. This act dissolved the existing regulatory bodies, including the General Nursing Council of Ireland and the Central Midwives' Board, replacing them with a single regulatory body, An Bord Altranais (the Nursing Board), established in June of 1951.[4]

During this period when psychiatric services were themselves not afforded high priority, in terms of attention or development in the emergent state, the work of Irish psychiatric nurses likewise went, for the main part, undocumented and unpublished.

International Developments in Mental Healthcare

In the post-Second World War period in Europe, there were significant challenges in the treatment of persons with mental illness; there were alarming rates of overcrowding within psychiatric hospitals, shortages of staff, particularly psychiatric nurses and a serious lack of financial resources. Together, these issues converged within the international context to provide the momentum for a fundamental review of the existing systems of psychiatric care.[5] During the 1940s and 1950s, the care of the mentally ill and the existing systems of care provision began to attract more attention. However, in spite of the emergence of new treatment approaches during the war years, the existing care and treatment of the vast majority of the mentally ill remained mainly institution-based. More and more hospitals were being identified as inappropriate and indeed dysfunctional places of care and were associated with harsh régimes, resulting in a range of damaging effects collectively termed 'institutionalisation'.[6]

The recognition of the importance of the care environment as a key factor in achieving a positive outcome in the treatment of mental illness was, however, not a new concept. The 'moral' management of patients, promoted by William Tuke at York and Phillipe Pinel in Paris in the eighteenth century, had recognised the value of providing an environment in which patients benefited from being exposed to friendly association, discussion of their difficulties and productive and purposeful activity.[7] The re-emergence of interest in this concept of the care environment began during the early years of the twentieth century. However, the writings of Maxwell Jones,[8] Russell Barton, and Erving Goffman[9] in the 1950s and early 1960s are identified as significant in focusing the attention of policy-makers and professionals on the negative effects of institutional care, while promoting a recognition of the care environment as a potential therapeutic entity. Inherent in the concept of therapeutic community was the requirement for its occupants, both patients and staff, to behave in prescribed and organised ways, based on the dual concepts of permissiveness and democratisation. This process of liberalising the care environment coupled with the focus on providing interventions aimed at developing the patient's personality, became a primary focus for debate surrounding developments in psychiatry and the role of the psychiatric nurse during the 1950s.

Re-directing Psychiatric Nursing

In 1956, through an expert committee on psychiatric nursing, the World Health Organisation (WHO) addressed specifically the issue of psychiatric nursing and provided a seminal international report on the matter.[10] The report of the expert committee was to prove instrumental in directing changes in psychiatric nursing globally over the coming two decades and an explicit intention of the report was the desire to drive change away from the predominant custodial-based approach in psychiatric nursing towards an approach that was therapeutic and interpersonally based. While recognising the limitations in terms of national, local, social, cultural and economic determinants, and the impact of these on the eventual role of the psychiatric nurse, the expert committee warned that failure to move in the direction being proposed would almost certainly result in the custodial role of psychiatric nurses being reinforced. It also warned of the possible emergence of other groups of workers who would assume the more therapeutic functions of the nursing role, leaving psychiatric nurses to care for the chronically ill and the elderly.

In delimiting the future role of the psychiatric nurse, the expert committee drew heavily on the dual theoretical concepts of interpersonal relations and therapeutic community, and this is evidenced in the elements of the nurse's role outlined in the WHO report. This role was envisioned as being an integral part of the therapeutic programme of the hospital, concerned with the promotion of individualised care and developing competence in the use of group therapy skills. The report of the WHO expert committee identified the nursing structures required to achieve these desired changes. Likewise, the educational preparation and training of nurses at different levels within these structures was identified. Other issues addressed, albeit briefly, by the WHO report included the need for personal, professional and practice development in psychiatric nursing, coupled with the development of specialist nurses, who were recommended as a means of achieving changes within the profession. The need for interaction and liaison between psychiatric nurses and other nurses in both primary and secondary care settings was highlighted, and particular examples of how these relationships might be beneficial to patients were presented.

While the structure of psychiatric services and the role and function of psychiatric nurses were beginning to be examined in other countries, as yet in Ireland no systematic study of either the psychiatric services or the role of the psychiatric nurse had been undertaken. While the recommendations of various international reports regarding psychiatric practice were enlightening, the existing structures and functioning of the Irish psychiatric services and their relative isolation from international practices made the adoption of such recommendations problematic.

In Ireland, it was not until 1961 that the first comprehensive report since the founding of the Irish state dealing specifically with the needs of the mentally ill was commissioned: The Commission of Inquiry on Mental Illness, established by the minister for health in 1961, produced its final report in 1966.[11] This report provided an overview of the state of psychiatric services in Ireland during the 1960s and it clearly indicated a legacy of inertia, which had prevailed since the turn of the twentieth century. When the commission produced its report in 1966, Ireland had the highest rate of bed provision in the world for the mentally ill, at 7.3 per 1,000 of population, and it was estimated that approximately 18,000 beds were provided in district mental hospitals, excluding private institutions, which provided approximately another 1,000. The majority of these institutions had been built in the previous century. It was also acknowledged that these facilities were more often than not 'barrack-like structures characterised by large wards, gloomy corridors and stone stairways ... [and that] too many had inadequate facilities and services, and lacked the purposeful activity and therapeutic atmosphere considered necessary in a modern mental hospital'. It is evident from these descriptions that in the majority of cases, very little had changed in either the physical make-up or the therapeutic milieu of the mental hospitals of Ireland from those prevailing in Irish asylums at the beginning of the twentieth century.

Being a Psychiatric Nurse in Ireland in the 1950s

Relatively little is known about the work of psychiatric nurses practising in Irish mental hospitals during the period of the 1950s and accounts which do exist tend to be presented as part of the wider history of psychiatry, narratives of particular asylums, or within social policy research concerned with service provision to the mentally ill in Ireland. While these accounts provide useful insights into aspects of asylum life and of prevailing social conditions and attitudes, they do not specifically focus on the work of psychiatric nurses *per se*, or on the nature of care provided by them. The history of psychiatry is also generally one that presents the views of those individuals who are recognised as important or great, and this often fails to address the accounts of the 'ordinary' participants in that history. I have undertaken a study which has attempted to address this imbalance in historiography and to bring to light new evidence about psychiatric nursing in Ireland from the perspective of psychiatric nurses.[12] Combining an examination of the records made by nurses in the period with oral testimonies provided by retired psychiatric nurses who had worked during the period, the study provided accounts of 'ordinary nurses' concerning their role. The study attempted to interpret the changes that have occurred in this role since the 1950s, probing relationships between these role changes and the wider social, political and economic context of Irish mental health policy. Presented as themes concerning the role of the psychiatric nurse and the context of professional practice, the following accounts are part of the findings of this research.

Segregation

A key theme to emerge from the historical study was that of 'segregation'. Segregation occurred at both macro and micro levels. The nature of segregation at a macro level was based primarily on the diagnosis of mental illness and the consequent removal of the patient from the wider population. Thus for the individual, the diagnosis of mental illness operated as a segregating force, separating them from family, community and wider society. This macro-level segregation was the initial and most significant process in that it brought with it a number of consequences related to the removal of the person from society. Once the person was segregated within the mental hospital, he/she became a 'patient' who was subject to institutional or micro-level segregation.

From the nurses' descriptions of the organisation of the hospital, the theme of segregation is strongly evident. The hospital consisted of 'two sides', the male side and the female side, with a head male nurse and a matron independently operating each respective side. Apart from sexual segregation, patient segregation occurred at a number of other levels. Patients were segregated within the hospital based on their length of stay, their type of psychiatric illness or related condition, their ability to work, their treatment regimen and the nature of the care that they required.

Both student nurses and registered (qualified) nurses tended to spend extended periods of time in a small number of areas within the hospital, frequently returning to the same ward. This fact, when coupled with patient segregation, had implications for the work of nurses, in that their role, as well as being segregated on the basis of sex, was also highly segmented. This segmentation was based on the specific activities engaged in within a restricted range of practice sites. Furthermore, it was possible for nurses to progress through their training and beyond without having gained experience in the full range of activities undertaken within the psychiatric hospital and, as a consequence, their practice skills were limited.

Institutional Agents

A primary feature of the role of Irish psychiatric nurses during the decades of the 1950s and 1960s was, what I have termed, 'institutional agent'.[13] As an agent of the institution, the nurse ensured that patients adhered to the prevailing system of rules and regulations. In particular, these rules dictated that patients be occupied, and this was to be achieved principally through utilising patients as the primary workforce of the institution to ensure its efficient running. Through this process of acting as an agent of the institution, primarily through supervising and reporting on the patient workforce, nurses perforce were also directly engaged in these activities with patients.

The compliance or non-compliance with the rules of the institution was evident in the form of attaching labels to individual patients. Patients were considered as compliant if they were productive members of the institutional community through engagement in 'work', and this level of compliance was viewed as an important indicator of adherence to the rules. Patients who complied were labelled as 'helpful', 'good' and 'well behaved', while those who did not engage in productive work were viewed as 'lazy', 'un-cooperative', 'resistive' and 'troublesome'. The role of the nurse as the agent of the institution appears to have focused on achieving this compliance by ensuring that patients were engaged in work activities and by supervising that work. There was also a sense of patients being viewed by nurses as a homogenous group or 'collective', with all requiring the same approach; patients were viewed as either 'good' or 'bad', 'worker' or 'non-worker', 'compliant' or 'non-compliant', with the demands of maintaining the institution dominating over the individual needs of patients.

This position of the nurse as institutional agent serves to illustrate the existing system of hierarchical relations within the institution and the position of both the patient and the nurse within that system. This hierarchy appears to have been largely dominated by a three-tier system, with the rule makers at the top, rule enforcers in the middle and rule adherents at the bottom. The role of the nurse as institutional agent is further emphasised through the activities of observing and reporting patient activity and behaviour. The frequency with which nurses recorded entries related to patients' behaviour and their activity related to level of compliance with the rules emphasised the high degree of importance with which this was viewed by the rule enforcers. The accounts of the daily work of nurses and patients show that it consisted of engagement in domestic type activities, which included both indoor and outdoor activities; females (nurses and patients) engaged in the indoor activities and males (nurses and patients) in the outdoor activities. Indoor activities included cleaning, cooking, attending to fires, laundry and sewing, while outdoor activities included farm work, grounds maintenance, tailoring, and shoemaking.

Student nurses were often given particular jobs to undertake and be responsible for, while registered nurses were responsible for supervising students and making sure that these jobs had been undertaken correctly and completely. Moreover, different jobs were associated with particular wards or units. In certain wards, the student nurse was responsible for collecting milk from the kitchen, slicing bread and removing the bones from meat prior to patients receiving it. In one area, the lighting of gas lamps in the ward and adjacent corridors was the responsibility of the student nurse. The student was given a lantern and taper and had to light and quench the gas lamps on a daily basis. Nurses were assigned to the laundry or kitchens and worked there under the direction of a ward sister or senior nurse alongside groups of patients. Attending in the dining-hall appears to have been an activity engaged in by all nurses. Assisted by patients, nurses were responsible for cooking, preparing and serving meals, and washing up afterwards. Patients were counted on leaving the ward, on entry to and exit from the dining-room and again on returning to the ward. Registered nurses observed patients closely, monitoring what they ate, ensuring that they did not choke, remove cutlery from the dining-room, or fraternise with patients of the opposite sex.

Doctor's Assistant

A significant aspect of the work of psychiatric nurses was associated with acting as an assistant to or supporting the work of the doctor. From the notes made by nurses, it was evident that the model or approach to care and treatment adopted by the medical staff in the institution influenced to a great extent what nurses recorded. The primary focus on physical aspects of care was evident in the nurses' notes and the majority of entries made by them concerned this aspect of care. Likewise, the focus on physical interventions tended to dominate accounts of treatments prescribed and received by patients.

In these physical treatments, the role of the psychiatric nurse was that of assistant and the work usually involved sterilising equipment such as needles, setting up trays or preparing the area where treatment was to be administered. Nurses also assisted with treatments such as insulin therapy, electro convulsive therapy, malaria therapy, and deep narcosis therapy. These treatments were generally provided in wards or units specially designated for the care of patients undergoing them. The registered nurses who worked in these units were usually trained in general nursing (i.e. registered general nurses), as it was considered that nurses so trained had a better understanding of and greater competence in physical treatments.

Psychiatric patients who were physically ill were also treated within the psychiatric hospital and nurses assisted with a wide variety of treatments in the infirmary ward, including some minor surgery. The type of physical illnesses encountered in the infirmary ward included cardiac conditions, pulmonary tuberculosis, fractures, typhoid, skin conditions that were frequently the result of newly-admitted patients having flea and/or body lice infestations, and 'general paralysis of the insane', the end stage of syphilitic infection. Again, the infirmary ward was generally staffed by registered general nurses and was organised and run along the lines of a general hospital.

Physcial Care

The provision of physical care to patients was a role and responsibility designated to all nurses. For the most part, this physical care was described as 'basic care'. Basic care appears to have consisted of a range of activities in which nurses either assisted patients with activities or undertook them completely for those patients who were unable to do so for themselves. Included in descriptions of basic care were activities such as attending to patient hygiene, which included a range of discreet activities. While in training, students nurses were taught to be observant when bathing patients and to note and report any skin abrasions, bruising or rashes. Likewise, attending to the care of patients' hair was seen as especially important and particular attention was paid to identifying if patients had head lice or nits; cutting patients' finger and toe nails and inspecting the condition of their mouth were also included in the instruction given to students. Other basic care activities included feeding patients and supervising their food and fluid intake. Patients who were fed were either unable to feed themselves due to physical or mental infirmity or were considered unsafe to do so on the grounds that they might self-harm using cutlery.

The entries made in nurses' records relating to patients' mental state tended to be less descriptive and consisted mainly of one-word statements. These statements were almost always written from the perspective of the nurse and there was no evidence of any attempt to present the patient's perspective. A range of terms was used to describe patients' mental state, including 'sad', 'cheerful', 'elated', 'depressed' 'very deluded' or 'anxious'. From the entries, it was clear that the notes made by nurses about the patient's mental condition were based on a limited range of terms and were consistent with those used by medical staff.

Social and Leisure Activities

In addition to work-related activities, nurses were charged with the responsibility of engaging patients in various leisure and social activities. At ward/unit level, these activities included knitting – men's socks were knitted by female patients – sewing, various board games, such as draughts, card playing and reading. Other leisure activities included taking patients to the 'airing courts' (separate for male and female patients), walking in the hospital grounds, participating in hospital sporting events and accompanying patients to hospital dances and performances such as plays and concerts. These social events were as important for the nursing staff as they were for patients in that they provided one of the few legitimate opportunities for male and female nursing staff, as well as male and female patients to meet.

Nurses also had a role in accompanying patients to religious services. Two separate places of worship existed within the hospital, one Roman Catholic and the other Protestant, and each week a number of nurses were assigned to accompany patients to their respective religious services. In the case of male nurses, part of their role was to assist the priest or minister with church services as an altar server. The same nurses tended to be selected for these duties on a regular basis and, according to some nurses, it appeared that this type of duty was considered a 'perk'.

Ward Administration and Supervising Students

The role and responsibilities of the registered psychiatric nurse also involved aspects of ward administration. While primarily the responsibility of the ward sister or charge nurse, certain aspects of this role were delegated to registered nurses. For registered nurses, ward administration included assisting the ward sister or charge nurse with tasks such as stocktaking of ward equipment, ward clothing, furniture, bedding, crockery and cutlery. Stocktaking of such items was generally undertaken on a monthly basis and those requiring replacement had to be returned to the stores before a replacement was provided. In addition, registered nurses were involved in ordering weekly ward supplies of items such as cleaning fluids, disinfectants and special food provisions, as well as supplies of items such as dressings and medications from the hospital pharmacy.

Other ward administrative duties of the registered nurse included counting items of bedding and clothing prior to dispatch to and on return from the laundry, maintaining records such as temperature charts and bowel books, and reporting any incidents, such as falls or altercations between patients. Registered nurses reported to the ward sister or charge nurse any information relating to patients' dietary intake, their behaviour and their participation in work activities. Registered nurses were also responsible for ensuring that student nurses learned the job and did the work that was required of them. The supervision of student nurses work was based on assisting them to quickly learn the routines of the specific ward, in order to enable its smooth and efficient running.

Conclusions

When taken together, the findings from the nurses' notes and the interviews with retired nurses provided a description of the origins of the contemporary role of the Irish psychiatric nurse. The origins of the role were firmly based in the institution of the large mental hospital and its function emerged from a predominantly custodial and disease-orientated approach to the treatment and care of the mentally ill. The role of the psychiatric nurse was multi-faceted and involved a range of activities relating to the maintenance of the environment in which care was provided and the provision of physical care. A further dimension of the role was concerned with a range of other activities not directly related to patient care but supportive of it, such as ordering ward supplies and teaching student nurses. Certain activities were often directly associated with the particular ward or unit in which the nurse was working. Likewise, within each ward area there appears to have been a hierarchical division of work, in that different grades of nurses were responsible for particular tasks or duties. The sexual division of patients and nurses also contributed to a sexual division of labour consistent with that of the wider society.

The medical model was the predominant model of care operating within the mental treatment setting, and the impact of this model was evident in the ways in which psychiatric nurses in Ireland perceived and constructed their clinical role. While international literature on psychiatric nursing demonstrates that alternatives to institutional care were being developed in Europe and the United States during the 1960s and 1970s, which facilitated the implementation of other models and approaches to care in addition to the medical model, the psychiatric institution continued to be the predominant means of care provision for the mentally ill in Ireland as late as the 1980s. This effectively inhibited similar developments in Irish mental healthcare.

Little attention has been paid to the segregated and segmented nature of psychiatric nurses' work and how these aspects of care impacted on both role and practice development within psychiatric nursing. While David Towell has identified that the label 'psychiatric nurse' encompassed a cluster of different roles that were determined by the nature of the practice setting in which nursing took place, findings from the present study indicate even greater role segmentation in Ireland.[14] The role clustering suggested by Towell presumes that, regardless of where nurses worked, there was an underlying or grounding set of core principles and competencies, which were identifiable as psychiatric nursing skills. While Irish psychiatric nurses might well have possessed some of these skills, the absence of an identifiable or clearly articulated set of principles or core competencies in which psychiatric nursing practice was grounded suggests that rather than psychiatric nursing comprising a cluster of different roles, the nursing role was strongly segmented according to the nature of the tasks to be undertaken.

Thus the predominant activities of psychiatric nurses during the period under review were those associated with a static and deterministic context, and there is little evidence of the need for nurses to have an identifiable body of knowledge to undertake these activities. Even for those medical support activities, which were of a limited nature and undertaken according to medical direction, the need for professional knowledge was commensurately limited. This concurs with previous narrative accounts by Thomas Murphy *et al*[15] and Hanora Henry,[16] which indicate that the type of knowledge valued by the institutions was knowledge related to social and functional activities, such as cooking, sewing, farming, carpentry, music and sporting activities. Nurses were often employed based on the possession of such knowledge and skills, giving further testament to the perceived need to maintain the institution rather than engage in distinctly therapeutic functions.

The recognition that the period of the 1950s and 1960s was one of political and cultural transition in Ireland is central to understanding the context within which psychiatric nursing developed in Ireland, and how this context impacted on the role of psychiatric nurses. The asylums established during the nineteenth century continued to constitute the mainstay of care provision throughout the decades in question and beyond. Consequently, in Ireland the systems of segregation, which had their origins in the eighteenth century and which prevailed throughout the nineteenth century, continued to exist and in some cases were consolidated throughout the first half of the twentieth century.

CHAPTER 12

Nurses as Managers: A History of Nursing Management in Ireland and England

Marie Carney

Until the late nineteenth century, religious women undertook the role of caring for the sick and infirm. In England, the development of modern nursing was directly influenced by women like Elizabeth Fry and Florence Nightingale, while in Ireland, their counterparts included the women who founded the Roman Catholic religious sisterhoods and the group of Protestant nursing leaders who were instrumental in the reform of hospital nursing. Although not having the title of nurse manager, Mary Aikenhead, who established the Irish Sisters of Charity in 1816, and Catherine McAuley, who founded the Order of the Sisters of Mercy in 1831, were among the first nurse managers in Ireland. Margaret Huxley and Annie McDonnell, who were active in their professional lives in the late nineteenth and early twentieth centuries, were among the later examples of the nurse manager in Ireland. Even though women in nursing were utilising many of the twenty-first century management principles and skills in their work, they were not recognised for their management skills and the managerial aspects of their work have remained largely unrecognised.

Early Management Principles and Practice

Florence Nightingale and the Sisters of Mercy

Established by Pastor Theodore Fliedner, the Deaconess Institute at Kaiserwerth in Germany (a Lutheran religious foundation for the care of the sick) was destined to make a lasting impression on all subsequent nursing development.[1] Elizabeth Fry founded a small society of nurses to work among the poor having visited the Deaconess Institute in 1840. Later in that decade, Florence Nightingale also visited Kaiserwerth and was reportedly influenced by the work going on there.[2] Nightingale, who was from a wealthy upper-middle-class family, was instrumental in the reform of nursing in England.[3] Prior to her era, nurses were drawn from the servant classes and their conditions of employment were reputed to have been very poor. Fry and Nightingale were among the early nursing reformers and, in their respective professional roles, they were also among the first nurse managers.

Nightingale was clear about the type of person whom she wanted to lead nursing through both the process of nursing reform and in the post-reform period. In Peter Ardern's words, the 'Nightingale matron' was 'a middle-class woman used to looking after and managing a household of servants ... [who] exercised moral authority ... [and] enforced discipline and respect for authority'.[4] In reforming the voluntary hospitals in England and Ireland, the Nightingale matrons would be trained as nurses but would act like managers and would be the pioneers of the new system of hospital nursing that was based on proper nurse training.[5] By insisting on the proper training of nurses, Nightingale had exercised one of the first identified management principles at a time when many viewed training to be an unnecessary extravagance.[6] Indeed, Nightingale was over half a century ahead of her time, since it was only in 1911 that Frederick Taylor, the recognised management theorist of his time, developed the principles of scientific management. Although Taylor's principles were hailed worldwide as the leading management theory, Nightingale had implemented one of his basic principles, the scientific selection and training of workers, some half a century earlier.

The first religious order associated with hospital nursing reform was the St John's House Order in London.[7] In 1848, nurses were sent from St John's House for nurse training to the voluntary hospitals in London, firstly to the Westminster and Middlesex hospitals and, later, to the King's Hospital in 1849, and to Charing Cross Hospital in 1866. In 1854, nurses from the Westminster, the Middlesex and the King's hospitals accompanied Nightingale to the Crimea. The leadership and organisational skills of Nightingale in the Crimea were acknowledged by the secretary of war, Sidney Herbert, who declared that Nightingale brought order out of chaos; Herbert was of the opinion that Nightingale was the only woman capable of organising and superintending the nursing.[8] In her *Notes on Nursing*, Nightingale remarked that few men or even women understood what it was to be 'in charge', but it is evident from her writings that she understood the concept of leadership.[9]

Other women in the Crimea have also been recognised for their efficiency in the organisation and delivery of nursing care, most notably Mother Francis Bridgeman, the head of the contingent of Irish Sisters of Mercy who travelled to the Crimea from the Mercy Convent in Kinsale in 1854. A lady volunteer who wrote about the efficiency of the nursing system of the Irish Sisters of Mercy in 1856, commented on Mother Bridgeman's work, stating that the Koulali Hospital in Constantinople 'from first to last was admirably managed … we used to call it "the model hospital of the East"'.[10] Mother Bridgeman also had the assertiveness and the gentle but resolute persuasiveness that allowed her and the sisters to operate independently of Nightingale's control in the field hospitals. Bridgeman's qualities of efficient coordination, management skills and obvious leadership ability in the organisation of her nurses and the hospital at Koulali would undoubtedly meet with the approval of modern-day management theorists and practitioners.

Mary Ellen Doona has described the 'careful nursing' system, which the Sisters of Mercy used in their work in the Crimea, as Ireland's legacy to nursing,[11] while Therese Meehan has noted that Nightingale herself requested details of the careful nursing system used by the Irish sisters in the Crimea. Evidence for this is found in an entry into Mother Bridgeman's Crimean War diary, which reads: 'Miss N. took notes on our manner of nursing'.[12] Meehan postulates that Bridgeman and the other sisters were capable of utilising the resources available to them in the Crimea, through efficient and effective care delivery systems that incorporated 'careful nursing'. Peter Druker, who is regarded as one of the most influential management experts of the twentieth century, has observed that 'rarely, if ever, has a new basic institution, a new leading group, emerged as fast as management since the turn of the [twentieth] century', but it appears that a century and a half ago, the Sisters of

Mercy in the Crimea practised these same management skills, although there is no reference to their achievements in the extant management literature.[13]

District Nursing: Mary Aikenhead and Catherine McAuley

In the late nineteenth century, a branch of nursing that was a particular cause of concern for the medical profession was district nursing. At that time, district nurses were permitted to call a doctor to the patient's home if they deemed such a measure necessary. Since it was the district nurse's prerogative to decide whether or not a doctor was needed, doctors believed that this aspect of the nurse's role would adversely affect their status among the poor in society, and some doctors argued that the decision-making power of the district nurse appeared to be a reversal of the natural order of things.[14] Nevertheless, in her role in assessing a patient, the district nurse was engaging in the sort of decision-making process that today is listed in the repertoire of skills required of a good manager. She was required to conduct an assessment of the situation that she found when entering the home of the sick, consider the alternatives available to her, and arrive at a decision as to the best course of action.

As early as 1833, 'best practice' principles and methods in management were evident in the preparations for the opening of St Vincent's Hospital in Dublin. In advance of the opening, three nursing sisters from the Sisters of Charity were sent by Mary Aikenhead to the Hospital of Notre Dame de la Pitié in France to learn hospital administration and the best methods of taking care of the sick.[15] When they returned to Ireland, these nurses applied best practice methods and, according to Agnes Pavey, the Irish Sisters of Charity were known for the excellent technique of their nursing.[16] Aside from her foresight in preparing in advance for the opening of her hospital, Mary Aikenhead is renowned for her organisational skills, her mastery of the whole system of the French hospital, and the attention to detail which enabled her to set up and successfully run an efficient hospital.[17]

Best practice in management, as it is currently defined, was also evident in the work of Catherine McAuley and the Sisters of Mercy. In describing her own work among the poor of Dublin, McAuley commented on the importance of relieving distress and endeavoring 'by every practicable means to promote the cleanliness, ease and comfort of the Patients'. The philosophy and values of both the Sisters of Mercy and the Irish Sisters of Charity continue to be apparent in modern healthcare management theory and practice, where attention to the comfort of patients, now more often referred to as 'meeting the needs of clients', is espoused in contemporary textbooks for nurse managers.

Catherine Jane Wood

Before the advent of 'management theory' in nursing, nurses had also introduced and practised management skills in other areas. The system of sick children's nursing provided by Catherine Jane Wood, lady superintendent of the Hospital for Sick Children in London from 1878 to 1888, is readily recognisable in modern paediatric nursing in the early twenty-first century. Management practices employed by Wood included open visiting, a non-restrictive ward environment, and play therapy and learning for children during hospitalisation.[18] In addition, the children were assigned to a named nurse, nurses were expected to provide intelligent accounts of their patients' progress during the doctors' rounds, and nurses reported directly to the ward sister. On the patient allocation system, Wood insisted that 'the nurse must get to know them [the children] and their ways, before she can be successful with them'.[19] In modern nursing, the 'named nurse' system is seen as an important part of good practice at the level of clinical management, since it promotes continuity of care and the development of a good nurse–patient relationship, which is at the heart of quality nursing care.

Modern Managers and Entrepreneurs

While the position of 'head nurse' and her supervisory role can be identified in the late eighteenth century at the House of Infirmary in Dublin, the forerunner of her modern counterpart is found in the voluntary hospitals in the nineteenth century. The majority of the voluntary hospitals that operated in Ireland were situated in areas with large populations. In Dublin, for example, the city had a large number of voluntary hospitals situated in and around the city centre, including the Charitable Infirmary at Jervis Street, the Adelaide Hospital at Peter's Street and the Meath Hospital at nearby Heytesbury Street. Up to the last quarter of the nineteenth century, the matrons of the voluntary hospitals were not formally trained as nurses and their duties were more concerned with the management of the hospital household and the control of female servants, including the untrained nurses and wardmaids, and less with the actual organisation and coordination of the nursing care. In this period, the overall administration of the voluntary hospitals was in the hands of lay hospital boards of management, which comprised members of the aristocracy, professionals, medical men and clergymen.[20] The voluntary hospitals opened by religious congregations, notably the Mater Misericordiae and St Vincent's hospitals, were administered by the religious sisters themselves. The mother superior (or superioress) was the de facto head of the hospital and was the forerunner of the lady superintendents and hospital matrons who were appointed in the voluntary hospitals later in the nineteenth century and following the reform of hospital nursing. In some respects, the superioress was also the forerunner of both the modern lay hospital administrator and the modern director of nursing.

Arising out of the nursing and sanitary reforms of the late nineteenth century, a tripartite system of hospital management emerged, whereby lay managers, medical managers, and nursing managers were each responsible for aspects of the running of the hospital. The nurse manager (the lady superintendent and/or the hospital matron) managed the nursing arrangements, including the recruitment and training of nurses; and the hospital household arrangements, including cooking, laundry and hospital sanitation. This was not an inconsiderable range of functions, which in today's modern hospital would require individual departmental heads. The tripartite system became the accepted management pattern for the National Health Service in Britain and it still exists today in some of the voluntary hospitals in Ireland. The system remained in place for much of the twentieth century, after which time hospitals became ever more complex organisations. However, the matrons and lady superintendents continued to maintain their many and varied management functions, such as their responsibility for the organisation and delivery of nursing care, leadership in the provision of nurse training, and the management of the hospital household.

The matrons and lady superintendents in the post-reform period possessed a range of management skills which included the keeping of accounts and managing hospital budgets. While these skills only became a formally recognised part of the role of the nurse manager in the 1960s, lady superintendents in the Irish and English voluntary hospitals had been undertaking this function since the 1880s. In this same connection, Pauline Scanlan points out that some of these early nurse managers were entrepreneurs involved in the establishment of nursing homes attached to the voluntary hospitals in which they worked.[21] The nursing homes generated much needed revenue for the hospitals, and the lady superintendents were adept at employing good financial management skills in order to ensure that their institutions could turn a profit. Aside from the social service that the nursing homes offered, their establishment as finance-generating institutions was a forerunner of the trends in modern organisations, including healthcare organisations, to generate money in one area, in order to stave off losses in another. Their entrepreneurship was also expressed in the arrangements for providing a private nursing service to the middle-classes, which the lady superintendents put in place after formal nurse training had been introduced. The nursing of 'private cases' was a significant source of income for the voluntary hospitals.

While nursing reform in Ireland was driven by doctors, by hospital governors and by members of the middle- and upper-classes, particularly in Dublin, it was the lady superintendents who implemented the reforms in practice.[22] Appointed as a key element of the reform process, the lady superintendents did not limit themselves to implementing changes in the hospitals' nursing arrangements alone, but were instrumental in a whole range of reforms in hospital management, including the proper organisation of ancillary services, such as portering, cleaning and cooking.[23] The first cadre of nurse managers oversaw the reform of hospital sanitation in the late nineteenth century, including the introduction of new methods of cleaning and waste disposal. They were also responsible for the recruitment of nurses and wardmaids and, as part of the reform process that they oversaw, they also took responsibility for a range of demotions and dismissals from service, including the forced retirements of the untrained hospital matrons.[24] Their responsibility for training the newly recruited nurses was a significant part of their management function and, in this connection, they were required to develop new policies in the area of curriculum and instruction and, later, in such diverse areas as uniform design and vaccinations.

Margaret Huxley

There were some notable women among the first hospital matrons in the late nineteenth century and a number of the first matrons in Dublin, including Margaret Huxley and Annie McDonnell, were recognised for demonstrating efficiency in superintendence.[25] Born in London in 1856 and appointed matron of Sir Patrick Dun's Hospital from 1883–1902, Margaret Huxley was perhaps the most prominent of the early Irish hospital matrons.[26] Huxley held the combined post of matron and lady superintendent of Sir Patrick Dun's Hospital for nineteen years and during her professional career she demonstrated a range of administrative, management and leadership skills that went well beyond the confines of the hospital in which she worked. As a nurse manager, Huxley introduced a range of nursing reforms and was held in such high esteem as a manager that she was appointed to the board of governors of Sir Patrick Dun's Hospital in 1912. Appointments to such a key hospital management position were rare for a hospital matron at that time. Aside from her role as a nursing manager and, later, as a hospital manager, Huxley was a prominent campaigner alongside Mrs Bedford Fenwick in the international campaign for state registration and was a founder of the first centralised nurse training school, the Dublin Metropolitan Technical School for Nurses.[27] In her role as the honorary secretary of the school, she established a standardised syllabus of training for nurses in 1904, some fifteen years before the *Nurses Registration (Ireland) Act* and the founding of the General Nursing Council for Ireland.[28] As a member of the General Nursing Council for Ireland, Huxley sat on a number of important council committees which developed the policies for the newly regulated nursing profession in Ireland, including the rules committee which drafted the first official syllabus of training for nurses.[29]

Huxley's skills as a manager included her grasp of financial management. In 1890, she established one of the first nursing homes in Ireland; attached to Sir Patrick Dun's Hospital, the home provided private patients with surgical and medical nursing care and its operation was an important source of much needed income for the hospital.[30] Her acumen as a financial manager was also evident in her ability to ensure the recruitment of students and thereby the financial viability of the Dublin Metropolitan Technical School for Nurses at a time when hospitals could little afford to pay tuition fees to an independent body for their probationers in training. Huxley had the reputation of being a 'brilliant organiser'.[31] During the Great War, she coordinated the nursing services of the Dublin University College Hospital for Wounded Soldiers.[32] While Huxley is best remembered as the first leader of modern nursing in Ireland and as a founder of the International Council of Nurses, her management skills across a wide range of roles and activities exemplify the multiple tasks that her latter-day counterparts in nursing management could expect to perform as a routine part of their work.

Annie McDonnell

One of Huxley's students at Sir Patrick Dun's Hospital was Annie McDonnell, who was the lady superintendent at the Dublin House of Industry Hospitals from 1894 to 1909. Annie McDonnell had the distinction of being 'the first lady nurse trained in Ireland who became a Hospital Superintendent'.[33] Like Huxley, McDonnell was a nurse manager who demonstrated a range of diverse skills, including the skills to implement organisational change by introducing the reform of the system of nursing at her hospital, and skills as a leader while acting as a military nurse during the Boer War.[34] Upon her retirement in 1909, McDonnell was co-opted as a member of the Board of Superintendence of Dublin Hospitals, an important body with an inspectorate function over the hospitals of Dublin.[35]

Emily McManus

Another notable nurse manager was Emily McManus, who was matron at the Bristol Royal Infirmary during the early 1920s and, from 1927 to

1946, was matron at Guy's Hospital in London.[36] Half Irish and half English, McManus was one of the leading matrons in the inter-war years and her duties at Guy's included managing a staff of 800 and a patient group of 700. In her role as matron of one of the leading hospitals in England, McManus balanced the weighty responsibilities of a hospital manager with the duties of the head of the nursing services. In this latter role, she made a special point of staying in touch with the day-to-day activities of clinical nursing and she paid regular visits to the wards of the hospital, where she would chat with the nurses and their patients.[37] This capacity to keep in direct contact with the people who work in a large organisation is a hallmark of a good manager and for this Emily McManus was highly regarded. As a leader of nursing in England, she held many important national appointments, including president of the Royal College of Nursing and membership of the General Nursing Council for England and Wales. Miss McManus, the 'charming Irish girl', retired to County Mayo in 1946 and died in 1978.[38]

The history of nursing in Ireland also provides examples of the ideas and principles of modern management in the work of early nursing organisations. Founded in 1904, the Irish Matron's Association campaigned alongside other pro-registration groups in seeking to achieve professional regulation of nursing and improved professional education for nurses. In this activity, the association was promoting standards of training and practice that could be readily equated with modern management notions of quality assurance and quality improvement. In 1916, a College of Nursing was established in London with the aims of promoting the science and art of nursing and the better education of nurses, and its governing body of thirty-six members included six representatives from Ireland.[39] In promoting the efficiency of trainee nurses in the profession of nursing and in granting certificates and diplomas for proper training, the college was likewise applying the modern principle of quality assurance in nursing. Later in 1922, the newly formed Irish Guild of Catholic Nurses promoted the idea of leadership skills in nursing, as they promulgated the right of Irish nurses to achieve leadership in their profession.[40]

Management Training for Nurses

Up until the 1850s, there was little or no mention of the terms 'nursing administration' or 'nursing management'. In 1857, in a report to the Royal Commission on the Health of the British Army, entitled 'Notes on Matters Affecting the Health, Efficiency and Hospital Administration of the British Army', Florence Nightingale wrote of the nursing administration required to meet the health needs of the British army.[41] Later, when establishing the Nightingale School for the training of nurses at St Thomas' Hospital in 1860, Nightingale saw training in management as one of the functions of nurse training and she saw that the nursing care of patients should be properly organised by placing it under the direction of a properly trained female head nurse, who would take responsibility for every task being carried out and would be responsible for internal management and discipline. Nightingale insisted that the management of nurses and the nursing care that they provided should remain in the hands of nurses.

In the nineteenth century, the role of the hospital matron varied, depending on the type of hospital in which she worked. At the time, no formal system of training for the role of the nurse manager existed and neither 'administration' nor 'management' were mentioned in nurse training syllabi. The nurse manager developed her skills through the performance of her role and her management skills resided implicitly in the way that she carried out her duties and responsibilities. It was not until the last quarter of the twentieth century that a marked and relatively sudden increase in management training for senior nurses occurred in Britain. This surge in interest in nurse management training contrasted sharply with the years of neglect, in which only short courses in management were available for some nurses and, for a chosen few, a one-year course in nursing administration.[42] In 1949, the King Edward's Hospital Fund for London was founded and staff colleges for ward sisters opened to provide ward management training for senior nurses.[43] In 1958, *Principles of Administration Applied to Nursing Service*, a manual on nursing administration, was first published.[44] By the early 1960s, the Royal College of Nursing had recommended that major changes be made in the traditional patterns of nursing administration[45] and, in 1966, the Salmon Report recommended that nurse managers should attend line management courses.[46] In 1967, the British Minister of Health established the National Nursing Staff committee and, in its report, the committee declared that 'management training is the most important supplement to the nurse's professional skills'.[47] By the late 1970s, the General Nursing Council for England and Wales had recognised management as an integral part of the nurse's role.

In Ireland, one of the first references to management subjects taught to nurses appears to have been in the *Syllabus for the Certificate of Psychiatric Nursing*, published in 1960. During the period 1961–62, ethics, psychology, professional duties and attitudes, and professional adjustments were introduced to the general nurse training syllabus, and legal and administrative aspects were added to the training syllabus of sick children's nursing. By 1978, management as a subject had been introduced into the nursing syllabus under the heading 'Affairs of Management'. By the 1990s, management as a distinct subject was being taught to all nurses undergoing basic training and also to nurses undertaking postgraduate studies at higher diploma and masters levels.[48] Today, it is possible for an experienced nurse or midwife to pursue a professional career in management that includes line management at clinical manager grade and service management at director of nursing or director of midwifery grade; new management grades have also been developed, including that of nurse practice development coordinator. A nurse or midwife may enter management by completing a preparatory course at degree and masters levels; these courses include a bachelor's degree in nursing management, a management option on a nursing or midwifery master's degree programme, and a master of business administration (MBA).

Conclusions

The skills that modern nurse managers possess were being utilised by their predecessors in Irish nursing long before terms like 'decision-making', 'enabling', 'change-management', and 'quality improvement' had entered the lexicon on modern management theory. Nurse managers throughout the nineteenth and twentieth centuries have practised the skills of leadership and management, and the attributes that the early nurse managers possessed have contributed, in large measure, to the success of organised healthcare in Ireland. Furthermore, the women who were the early managers of nursing have passed down much of their knowledge and skill to successive generations of nurse managers, even in the absence of formal recognition of their leadership and management skills or formal training in the theory of management. With the announcement in Britain in 2000 of the Department of Health NHS Plan that includes a commitment to reinstate the hospital matron as a strong clinical leader, it may be that nursing has come full circle, in terms of the place of the nurse manager in the modern hospital structure.[49]

NOTES

Chapter 1

1 *Report of the Steering Group on Local Authority Records and Archives* (Dublin: Department of the Environment, 1996).

2 S. Helferty and R. Refaussé (eds), *Directory of Irish Archives*, 4th ed. (Dublin: Four Courts Press, 2003).

3 K. Magee, *Report of the Archival Manager; The Adelaide and Meath Hospital, Dublin Incorporating the National Children's Hospital [at Tallaght, Co. Dublin]*, A3 leaflet; No. 1, December 1997; No 2, December 1998.

4 B. D. Kelly, 'Mental illness in 19th-century Ireland: a qualitative study of workhouse records', *Irish Journal of Medical Science*, 173 (1), 2004, pp. 53–55.

5 E. Donnellan, 'Health Supplement', *The Irish Times*, 29 June 2004, p. 1.

6 *Annual Report of the Information Commissioner for 2003* (available at http://www.oic.gov.ie [Case 030874]).

7 Donnellan, 'Health Supplement', p. 1.

8 Society of Archivists, Irish Region, *Standard for the Development of Archives Services in Ireland* (Dublin: Irish Academic Press, 1997).

9 Local Authority Archivists' Group, *Local Authority Archives in Ireland*, 2003. As if to emphasise how newly-developing this area is, the publication was launched just as this book was undergoing final editing.

10 M. Ó hÓgartaigh, 'Archival sources for the history of professional women in late-nineteenth and early-twentieth century Ireland', *Journal of the Irish Society for Archives*, 6 (1), 1999, pp. 23–25.

11 Susan McGann's account of 'the fate of many records' is apt in this regard. See S. McGann, 'Archival sources for research into the history of nursing', *Nurse Researcher*, 5 (2), 1997–8, pp. 19–29.

12 *Report of the Steering Group on Local Authority Records and Archives*, Dublin: Department of the Environment, 1996.

13 Helferty and Refaussé (eds.), *Directory of Irish Archives*, p. 7.

14 E. J. Freeman, 'Historical, biographical and bibliographical sources', in L. T. Morton and S. Godbolt (eds), *Information Sources in the Medical Sciences*, 4th ed. (London: Bowker-Saur, 1992), p. 571.

15 *Ibid.*

16 M. O'Doherty, 'Irish Medical Historiography', *Irish Journal of Medical Science*, 170 (4), 2001, pp. 256–60.

17 http://www.nationalarchives.ie

18 http://www.nationalarchives.ie/othersirish.html

19 www.rcsi.ie/library. This catalogue of published books under 'Rare Books and Archives' should not be confused with an archive.

20 See for example in the *Directory of Irish Archives* the entries for the Royal College of Surgeons in Ireland and the Royal College of Physicians of Ireland, which include Board of Directors' Minute Books, Royal City of Dublin Hospital (at RCSI Library); Board of Governors Proceedings, Sir Patrick Dun's Hospital (at RCPI Library).

21 For examples of British parliamentary papers, see: House of Commons, *Dublin Hospitals Commission: Report of the Committee of Inquiry together with Minutes of Evidence and Appendices* (Dublin: HMSO, 1887); House of Commons, *Select Committee on the Registration of Nurses, together with the Proceedings of the Committee, Minutes of Evidence,*

Appendix and Index, H.C. (Dublin: HMSO, 1904) (281) vi. 701 and 1905 (263) vii. 301. For examples of Dáil and Seanad papers, see, for example, Acts of the Oireachtas, *The Nurses' Act 1950*, No. 27 (Dublin: The Stationery Office, 1950); Acts of the Oireachtas, *The Nurses Act 1985*, Dublin: The Stationery Office, 1985.

22 See, for example, General Nursing Council for Ireland, *Regulations Made by the General Nursing Council for the Recognition of Hospitals as Training Schools for Nurses* (Dublin: John Falconer, 1923). For an example of An Bord Altranais archives, see An Bord Altranais, *Regulations and Guides, to the minimum conditions which must exist before a Hospital or Training Institution is approved by above Board* (Dublin: An Bord Altranais, 1955).

23 For example, council directive of 27 June 1977 concerning the co-ordination of provisions laid down by law, regulation or administrative action in respect of the activities of nurses responsible for general care (77/453.EEC), *Official Journal of the European Communities*, Vol. 20, No. L 176, 1977, pp. 1–13.

24 McGann, 'Archival sources', pp. 19–29. Lorentzon uses journal debate to support other evidence in her exploration of the characteristics of the 'modern' reformed nurse; see M. Lorentzon, 'Grooming nurses for the new century: analysis of nurses' registers in London voluntary hospitals before the First World War', *International History of Nursing Journal*, 6 (2), 2001, pp. 4–12.

25 The centre was initially established as a virtual centre at the Royal College of Nursing in Edinburgh.

26 The first edition of the journal was published in 1888 and in 1922 the name of the journal was changed to the *British Journal of Nursing*. The journal ceased publication in 1956. See http://www.qmuc.ac.uk/hn/history/index.htm. See also www.rcn.org.uk/historicalnursingjournals.

27 A. M. Rafferty, 'Writing researching and reflexivity in nursing history', *Nurse Researcher*, 5 (2), 1997, pp. 5-16.

28 *Ibid*. See E. H. Carr, *What is History?* 2nd ed. (London: Penguin Books, 1987); and G. R. Elton, *The Practice of History* (London: University Press, 1967). For a discussion on the writings of Elton and Carr, see K. Jenkins, *Rethinking History* (London: Routledge, 1991). See also C. Hallett, 'Historical texts: factors affecting their interpretation', *Nurse Researcher*, 5 (2), 1997, pp. 61–71; G. M. Fealy, 'Historical research: a legitimate methodology for nursing research in Ireland', *Nursing Review*, 17 (1 & 2), 1999, pp. 24–29.

29 Jenkins, *Rethinking History*, p. 55. Concerns are epistemological and methodological.

30 Rafferty, 'Writing', p 8.

31 J. E. Brooks, 'Ghost of the past: capturing history and the history of nursing', *International History of Nursing Journal*, 5 (2), 2000, pp. 36–41.

32 S. Drudy and K. Lynch, *Schools and Society in Ireland* (Dublin: Gill and Macmillan, 1993).

33 *Ibid*., p. 30.

34 C. A. Connolly, 'Beyond social history: new approaches to understanding the state of and the State in nursing history', *Nursing History Review*, 12, 2004, pp. 5–24.

35 *Ibid*., p. 11. In Connolly's view, the paradigm shift to 'social history' was so great that political history had become all but marginalised in historical scholarship by the 1980s.

36 *Ibid*., p. 13.

37 *Ibid*., p. 10.

38 A. M. Rafferty, 'Historical perspectives', in K. Robinson and B. Vaughan (eds), *Knowledge for Nursing Practice* (Oxford: Butterworth-Heinemann, 1992), pp. 25–41. See also Rafferty, 'Writing', pp. 5–16.

39 C. Maggs, 'A history of nursing: a history of caring?', *Journal of Advanced Nursing*, 23,

1996, pp. 630–35.

40 Rafferty, 'Historical perspectives', p. 28. See also C. Rosenberg, 'Clio and caring: an agenda for American historians and nursing', *Nursing Research*, 36 (1), 1987, pp. 67–68.

41 B. Abel-Smith, *A History of the Nursing Profession* (London: Heinemann, 1960); Rafferty, 'Historical perspectives', p. 36.

42 Rafferty, 'Historical perspectives'.

43 M. E. Baly, *Nursing and Social Change* (London: Croom Helm, 1973).

44 M. E. Baly, *Florence Nightingale and the Nursing Legacy* (London: Croom Helm, 1986).

45 C. Davies, *Rewriting Nursing History* (London: Croom Helm, 1980); Maggs, 'A history of nursing', p. 632.

46 Rafferty, 'Historical perspectives', p. 37.

47 C. Maggs, *The Origins of General Nursing* (London: Croom Helm, 1983).

48 P. Holden and J. Littlewood (eds), *Anthropology and Nursing* (London: Routledge, 1991); R. Dingwall, A. M. Rafferty and C. Webster, *An Introduction to the Social History of Nursing* (London: Routledge, 1993); A. M. Rafferty, J. Robinson and R. Elkan (eds), *Nursing History and the Politics of Welfare* (London: Routledge, 1997).

49 A. M. Rafferty, *The Politics of Nursing Knowledge* (London: Routledge, 1996); A. Bradshaw, *The Nurse Apprentice, 1860–1977* (Aldershot: Ashgate, 2001).

50 Carr, *What is History?*, p. 13.

51 K. Williams, 'From Sarah Gamp to Florence Nightingale: a critical study of hospital nursing systems from 1840-1897', in Davies (ed.), *Rewriting Nursing History*, pp. 41–75.

52 Connolly, 'Beyond social history', p. 9.

53 E. Malcolm and G. Jones, 'Introduction: an anatomy of Irish medical history', in E. Malcolm and G. Jones (eds), *Medicine, Disease and the State in Ireland 1650–1940* (Cork: Cork University Press, 1999), pp. 1–17.

54 *Ibid.*, p. 2.

55 *Ibid.*, p. 1.

56 A notable exception is the volume of essays on medical history edited by Elizabeth Malcolm and Greta Jones. See Malcolm and Jones (eds), *Medicine, Disease and the State*.

57 The term 'amateur' is used here not in any derogatory sense. Rather, it denotes the fact that the writers in the tradition are not *historians* but professionals who have written histories of their profession. Professional historians use this term when referring to writers in the tradition. See J. McGeachie, '"Normal" development in an "abnormal" place: Sir William Wilde and the Irish School of Medicine', In Malcolm and Jones (eds), *Medicine Disease and the State*, pp. 85–101.

58 T. C. P. Kirkpatrick, *History of Dr Steevens' Hospital Dublin: 1720–1920* (Dublin: University Press, 1924), p. 290.

59 As their primary source of materials, all of these histories draw on their respective hospital archives. Among the early examples of hospital histories are L. H. Ormsby, *Medical History of the Meath Hospital and County Dublin Infirmary* (Dublin: Meath Hospital, 1888); T. C. P. Kirkpatrick, *History of Dr Steevens' Hospital*; T. G. Moorhead, *A Short History of Sir Patrick Dun's Hospital* (Dublin: Hodges Figgis and Co., 1942). For a discussion on the writing of medical history and a comprehensive list of hospital histories, see Malcolm and Jones, 'Introduction', pp. 1–17.

60 G. M. Fealy 'A History of the Provision and Reform of General Nurse Education and Training in Ireland, 1879–1994, Volumes I and II', Unpublished PhD Thesis, UCD, 2002.

61 E. T. Freeman, *Mater Misericordiae Hospital Centenary 1861–1961* (Dublin: Congregation of Our Lady of Mercy, 1962); J. D. H. Widdess, *The Charitable Infirmary*,

Jervis Street, Dublin, 1718–1968 (Dublin: The Charitable Infirmary, Jervis Street, 1968); E. O'Brien (ed.), *The Charitable Infirmary, Jervis Street, 1781–1987: A Farewell Tribute* (Dublin: The Anniversary Press, 1987), pp. 135–52; E. O'Brien, L. Browne and K. O'Malley (eds), *The House of Industry Hospitals: 1772–1987: the Richmond, Whitworth and Hardwicke (St Laurence's Hospital): a Closing Memoir* (Dublin: The Anniversary Press, 1988).

62 B. Walsh, 'Nursing at the Charitable Infirmary', in O'Brien (ed.), *The Charitable Infirmary*, pp. 135–52.

63 M. Kenny, T. Power and G. Power, 'Nursing in the Richmond', in O'Brien, Browne and O'Malley (eds), *The House of Industry Hospitals*, pp. 201–09.

64 D. Mitchell, '*A 'Peculiar' Place: the Adelaide Hospital, Dublin: Its Times, Places and Personalities 1839–1989* (Dublin: Blackwater, 1989).

65 Sister M. E. Nolan, *One Hundred Years: a History of the School of Nursing and of Developments at the Mater Misericordiae Hospital 1891–1991* (Dublin: Congregation of the Sisters of Mercy, 1991).

66 J. B. Lyons, *The Quality of Mercer's: the Story of Mercer's Hospital, 1734-1991* (Dublin: Glendale, 1991); D. Coakley, *Baggot Street: a Short History of the Royal City of Dublin Hospital* (Dublin: Royal City of Dublin Hospital Board of Governors, 1995); F. O. C. Meenan, *St Vincent's Hospital 1834–1994: an Historical and Social Portrait* (Dublin: Gill and Macmillan, 1995); P. Gatenby, *Dublin's Meath Hospital 1753–1996* (Dublin: Town House, 1996).

67 H. Burke, *The Royal Hospital Donnybrook: a Heritage of Caring 1743–1993* (Dublin: the Royal Hospital Donnybrook and the Social Science Research Centre, UCD, 1993).

68 M. Preston, 'The good nurse: women philanthropists and the evolution of nursing in Dublin', *New Hibernia Review*, 2 (1), 1998, pp. 91–110; A. Wickham, 'A better scheme for nursing: the influence of the Dublin Hospital Sunday Fund on nursing and nurse training in Ireland in the nineteenth century', *International History of Nursing Journal*, 6 (2), 2001, pp. 26–34.

69 M. Ó hÓgartaigh, 'Flower power and "mental grooviness": nurses and midwives in Ireland in the early twentieth century', in B. Whelan (ed.), *Women and Paid Work in Ireland 1500–1930* (Dublin: Four Courts Press, 2000), pp. 133–47.

70 M. Luddy, '"Angels of Mercy": Nuns as Workhouse Nurses', in Malcolm and Jones (eds.), *Medicine Disease and the State*, pp. 102–17. For a discussion on the role of religious women as nurses, see S. Nelson, *Say Little, Do Much: Nursing, Nuns, and Hospitals in the Nineteenth Century* (Philadelphia: University of Pennsylvania Press, 2001); H. Burke, *The People and the Poor Law in 19th Century Ireland* (Dublin: The Women's Education Bureau, 1987).

71 S. McGann, *The Battle of the Nurses: a Study of Eight Women who Influenced the Development of Professional Nursing* (London: Scutari Press, 1992).

72 R. Barrington, *Health, Medicine and Politics in Ireland 1900–1970* (Dublin: Institute of Public Administration, 1987).

73 P. Scanlan, *The Irish Nurse: A Study of Nursing in Ireland, History and Education, 1718–1981* (Manorhamilton: Drumlin, 1991).

74 For further commentary on Scanlan's work, see Malcolm and Jones, 'Anatomy', p. 14. See also Fealy, 'History', 2002, Chapter 1.

75 M. E. Doona, 'Sister Mary Joseph Croke: another voice from the Crimean War, 1854-1856', *Nursing History Review*, 3, 1995, pp, 3–41; M. E. Doona, 'Isabelle Croke: A Nurse for the Catholic cause during the Crimean War', in M. Kelleher, and J. H. Murphy (eds), *Gender Perspectives in Nineteenth Century Ireland: Public and Private Spheres* (Dub-

lin: Irish Academic Press, 1997), pp. 148–56. For a detailed exploration of the role of the Sisters of Mercy in the Crimea, see E. Bolster, *The Sisters of Mercy in the Crimean War* (Dublin: The Mercier Press, 1964); T. C. Meehan, 'Careful nursing: a model for contemporary nursing practice', *Journal of Advanced Nursing*, 44 (1), 2003, pp. 99–107.

76 S. Nelson, 'Pastoral care and moral government: early nineteenth century nursing and solutions to the Irish question', *Journal of Advanced Nursing*, 26, 1997, pp. 6–14.

77 T. C. Meehan, 'Heading into the wind: a Jubilee-Dudley nurse-midwife in West Galway from 1937–1943', *All Ireland Journal of Nursing and Midwifery*, 1 (2), 2000, pp. 66–70; H. M. Henry, *A History of the Irish Guild of Catholic Nurses: Seventy-five Years of Service* (Dublin: Irish Guild of Catholic Nurses, 1998).

78 J. Robins (ed.), *Nursing and Midwifery in Ireland in the Twentieth Century* (Dublin: An Bord Altranais, 2000).

Chapter 2

1 R. Porter, *The Greatest Benefit to Mankind* (London: Harper Collins, 1997).

2 R. D. Putnam, *Bowling Alone* (London and New York: Simon & Schuster, 2000).

3 F. Furedi, *Therapy Culture* (London: Routledge, 2004).

4 *Ibid.*

5 T. Tiede, *Self-Help Nation* (New York: Atlantic Monthly Press, 2001).

6 *Ibid.*

7 J. O'Donohue, *Divine Beauty* (London: Bantam Press, 2003).

8 K. Armstrong, *A History of God* (London: Vintage, 1999).

9 C. Helman, *Culture, Health and Illness* (London: Arnold, 2001).

10 F. Nightingale, *Notes on Nursing: What it is and What it is Not* (London: Duckworth, 1970 facsimile reprint of 1859 edition).

11 Royal College of Nursing, *Defining Nursing* (London: RCN Publishing, 2003).

12 Department of Health, *Health and Social Care Act* (London: The Stationery Office, 2001).

13 World Health Organisation, *Health 2: Health for all in the 21st Century: the Health for all Policy Framework for the WHO European Region* (Copenhagen: WHO, 1999).

14 S. Peres, Inaugural Address to Resolution and Conflict Conference, held in San Georgio Hotel, Valetta, Malta, 10–12 June 2003.

15 P. Gatenby, *Dublin's Meath Hospital, 1753–1996* (Dublin: Town House, 1996).

16 G. Lynch, *After Religion* (London: Darton, Longman and Todd, 2003).

17 A. Massie, 'The great modern question: just what is it all about?', *The Daily Telegraph*, 26 December 2000, p. 27.

18 F. Fukuyama, *The End of History and the Last Man* (New York: Penguin, 1992).

19 P. Kramer, *Listening to Prozac* (New York: Penguin Books, 1997).

20 Tiede, *Self-Help Nation.*

21 C. McGeachy, *Spiritual Intelligence* (Dublin: Veritas, 2001).

22 P. Broughton, 'In the Wake of a Disaster', *The Daily Telegraph*, 15 September 2001, p. 5.

23 J. Magnet, 'Sickened by the nurses who don't care', *News Review*, *The Sunday Times*, 23 November 2004, p. 9.

24 G. Collins, 'Taoiseach calls for campaign to recruit nurses', *Irish Independent*, 26 February 2004, p. 9.

25 Magnet, 'Sickened'.

26 *Ibid.*

27 O'Donohue, *Divine Beauty*.
28 G. FitzGerald, *Reflections on the Irish State* (Dublin: Irish Academic Press, 2003).
29 V. Griffin, *Enough Religion to Make us Hate* (Dublin: The Columba Press, 2002).
30 A. Campbell, *Moderated Love* (London: SPCK, 1984).

Chapter 3

1 This chapter is based on the author's inaugural lecture as Professor of Nursing at UCD, delivered in March 2004.
2 S. Nelson, *Say Little, Do Much: Nurses, Nuns and Hospitals in the Nineteenth Century* (Philadelphia: University of Pennsylvania Press, 2001), p. 5.
3 *Ibid.*, p. 5.
4 T. Fahey, 'Nuns in the Catholic Church in Ireland in the nineteenth century', in M. Cullen (ed.), *Girls Don't Do Honours: Irish Women in Education in the 19th and 20th Centuries* (Dublin: Women's Education Bureau, 1987), pp. 7–30.
5 E. Bolster, *The Sisters of Mercy in the Crimean War* (Dublin: The Mercier Press, 1964).
6 M. E. Doona, 'Sister Mary Joseph Croke: another voice from the Crimean War, 1854-1856', *Nursing History Review*, 3, 1995, pp. 3–41; M. E. Doona, 'Isabelle Croke: A Nurse for the Catholic cause during the Crimean War', in M. Kelleher and J. H. Murphy (eds), *Gender Perspectives in Nineteenth Century Ireland: Public and Private Spheres* (Dublin: Irish Academic Press, 1997), pp. 148–56; T. C. Meehan, 'Careful nursing: a model for contemporary nursing practice', *Journal of Advanced Nursing*, 44 (1), 2003, pp. 99–107; S. Nelson, 'Pastoral care and moral government: early nineteenth century nursing and solutions to the Irish question', *Journal of Advanced Nursing*, 26, 1997, pp. 6–14; S. Nelson, *Say Little, Do Much.*
7 Cited in Doona, 'Isabelle Croke', p. 152.
8 *Ibid.*
9 Doona, 'Sister Mary Joseph Croke', p. 5.
10 M. E. Doona, 'The Confidential Report on Crimean Nursing' (Conference paper) *International Council of Nursing Centennial Conference: Celebrating Nursing's Past: Claiming the Future* (London, June 1999).
11 Meehan, 'Careful nursing', p. 100.
12 Cited in Doona, 'Sister Mary Joseph Croke', p. 26.
13 Cited in Doona, 'The Confidential Report', p. 4.
14 Nelson, Pastoral care, pp. 6–7.
15 C. Hart, *Nurses and Politics: the Impact of Power and Practice* (Basingstoke: Palgrave Macmillan, 2004), p. 37.
16 Doona, 'Sister Mary Joseph Croke', p. 6.
17 Aside from personal diaries and the Confidential Report, the only formal records that exist from the Crimea are Nightingale's writings, including her widely published *Notes on Nursing.*
18 J. Clark, 'Nursing: an intellectual activity', *British Medical Journal*, 303 (6799), 1991, pp. 376–77.
19 C. L. McWilliam and C. A. Wong, 'Keeping it secret: the costs and benefits of nursing's hidden work in discharging patients', *Journal of Advanced Nursing*, 19 (1), 1994, pp. 152–63.
20 G. M. Fealy 'A History of the Provision and Reform of General Nurse Education and Training in Ireland, 1879–1994, Vols I and II', Unpublished PhD Thesis, UCD, 2002.

21 *Ibid.*, Vol. I, Chapter 3.

22 *Ibid.*, Vol. I, p. 197. See also A. M. Rafferty, 'The anomaly of autonomy: space and status in early nursing reform', *International History of Nursing Journal*, 1 (1), 1995, pp. 43–56; C. Helmstadter, 'Old nurses for new: nursing in the London teaching hospitals before and after the mid-nineteenth century reforms', *Nursing History Review*, 1, 1993, pp. 43–70.

23 M. P. Treacy, 'Gender prescription in nurse training: its effects on healthcare provision', *Recent Advances in Nursing*, 25, 1989, pp. 70–91; M. P. Treacy, 'Some aspects of the hidden curriculum', in P. Allen and M. Jolly (eds), *The Curriculum in Nursing Education* (London: Croom Helm, 1987), pp. 164–75.

24 J. Deeny, *The Irish Nurses Magazine*, 16 (11), 1949, pp. 2–5; Department of Health, *Working Party on General Nursing* (Dublin: The Stationery Office, 1980); An Bord Altranais, *The Future of Nurse Education and Training in Ireland* (Dublin: An Bord Altranais, 1994); Government of Ireland, *Report of the Commission on Nursing: A Blueprint for the Future* (Dublin: The Stationery Office, 1998).

25 R. R. Elms, B. Tierney and P. A. Boylan, 'Irish nursing at the crossroads', *International Journal of Nursing Studies*, 11, 1974, pp. 163–72.

26 Department of Health, *Working Party Report*; An Bord Altranais, *The Future*.

27 Fealy, 'History', Vol. II, p. 168.

28 *Ibid.*

29 S. Condell, *Changes in the Professional Role of Nurses in Ireland: 1980–1997: A Report Prepared for the Commission on Nursing* (Dublin: The Stationery Office, 1998).

30 See for example, L. H. Aiken, S. P. Clarke, R. B. Cheung, D. M. Sloane and J. H. Silber, 'Educational levels of hospital nurses and surgical patient mortality', *Journal of the American Medical Association*, 290 (12), 2003, pp. 1617–23.

31 K. Lutzen, 'A global perspective on domestic and international tensions in knowledge development', *Journal of Nursing Scholarship*, 32 (4), 2000, pp. 335–37.

32 J. Parker, 'Nursing Practice and Scholarship: Approaches to Effective International Alliance' (Conference paper) *Conference of the International Network for Doctoral Education in Nursing: The Social Relevance of Nursing Scholarship and Doctoral Education*, Copenhagen, June 2001.

33 Department of Health and Children, *A Research Strategy for Nursing and Midwifery in Ireland: Final Report* (Dublin: The Stationery Office, 2003).

34 The National Institute for Nursing Research was established within the National Institute of Health in 1986 to support clinical and basic research on the broad spectrum of nursing in the United States.

35 American Association of Colleges of Nursing, 'Defining scholarship for the discipline of nursing', *Journal of Professional Nursing*, 15 (6), 1999, pp. 372–76. See also E. Boyer, *Scholarship Reconsidered: Priorities for the Professorate* (Princeton NJ: Carnegie Foundation for the Advancement of Teaching, 1990).

36 Boyer, *Scholarship Reconsidered*.

37 *Ibid.*

38 *Ibid.*, p. 1.

39 *Ibid.*

40 American Association of Colleges of Nursing, 'Defining scholarship', p. 374.

41 *Ibid.*, p. 375.

42 M. Treacy, and A. Hyde, 'Contextualising Irish nursing research', in M. Treacy and A. Hyde (eds), *Nursing Research: Design and Practice* (Dublin: UCD Press, 1999), pp. 3–15.

43 *Ibid.*

Chapter 4

1 A.M. Rafferty, 'Practice made perfect', *The Guardian*, 26 January 1999. Rafferty is here referring to nursing education in the United Kingdom.
2 Government of Ireland, *Report of the Commission on Nursing: A Blueprint for the Future* (Dublin: The Stationery Office, 1998). The relevant recommendations are 5.22 and 5.30, Chapter 5, pp. 80–81.
3 This perspective is representative of the work of the Bakhtinian circle, which has been one of the key influences shaping the critical approach to discourse analysis. See J. Maybin, 'Language, struggle and voice: the Bakhtin/Volosinov writings', in Wetherell, Taylor and Yates, *Discourse Theory and Practice*, 2001 (London: Sage Publications 2001), pp. 64–67.
4 A. E. Musson, 'Evolution and the nursing situation today', *Irish Nursing and Hospital World*, 1 (9), 1931, p. 33–35.
5 *Ibid*., p. 34.
6 *Ibid*., p.35.
7 *Ibid*.
8 A. E. Musson, 'Evolution and the nursing situation today', *Irish Nursing and Hospital World*, 1 (10), 1932, pp. 33–35.
9 *Ibid*., p. 35.
10 *Ibid*., p. 33.
11 Dr R. Davitt's address to the nurses at the Annual Meeting of the Irish Nurses' Union in 1936, published in *The Irish Nurses' Journal*, 1 (1), 1936, p. 8.
12 L. G. Duff Grant, 'Training and qualifications for nursing teachers: (1) matrons; (2) sister tutors; (3) ward sisters; (4) examiners', *Irish Nurses' Journal*, 3 (4), 1938, p. 7.
13 *Ibid*., p. 5.
14 M. Pfeil, 'The skills-teaching myth in nurse education: from Florence Nightingale to Project 2000', *International History of Nursing Journal*, 7 (3), 2003, pp. 32-40.
15 Editorial, *Irish Nurses' Magazine*, 12 (18), 1942, p. 1.
16 M. Tierney, 'The Nursing Profession and its Needs – Comment No. 2' *Studies*, 31, 1942, p. 279. Professor Michael Tierney was vice-chairman of Seanad Éireann at the time of writing.
17 *Ibid*., p. 280.
18 A. M. Smithson, 'The Nursing Profession and its Needs – Comment No. 6', *Studies*, 31, 1942, p. 289. Annie Smithson was secretary of the Irish Nurses' Organisation at the time of writing.
19 Rafferty, 'Practice made perfect.'
20 E. Grogan 'The Nursing Shortage', *The Irish Nurses' Magazine*, 13 (49), 1945, pp. 3–5. Eleanor Grogan was general secretary of the Irish Nurses' Organisation at the time of writing.
21 *Ibid*., pp. 4–5.
22 J. P. Shanley, 'The Nursing Profession and Its Needs – Comment No. 3', *Studies*, 31, 1942, p. 282. Shanley was president of the Medical Association of Ireland at the time of writing.
23 *Ibid*, p. 281.
24 *Ibid*.
25 *Ibid*.
26 J. Fleetwood, 'The noble art that is nursing', *Irish Medical News*, 21 January 2002.
27 *Ibid*.

28 J. K. Jamieson, 'The Nursing Profession and Its Needs – Comment No. 5', *Studies*, 31, 1942, p. 282. Jamieson was Professor of Anatomy at the University of Dublin at the time of writing.

29 *Ibid.*

30 *Ibid*, pp. 286–87.

31 M. Traynor and A. M. Rafferty, 'Nurse education in an international context: the contribution of contingency', *International Journal of Nursing Studies*, 36, 1999, pp. 85–91.

32 Jamieson, 'The Nursing Profession' pp. 286–87.

33 *Ibid.* List-slippers are slippers fashioned from 'lists' or strips of fabric.

34 *Ibid.*

35 E. Meerabeau, 'Be good, sweet maid, and let who can be clever: a counter reformation in English nursing education?', *International Journal of Nursing Studies*, 41, 2004, pp. 285–92; S. K. Templeton, 'Nurses are "too intelligent to care for the sick"', *The Sunday Times*, 25 April 2004, p. 13; C. Hall, 'Young nurses "are too posh to wash"', *Daily Telegraph*, 11 May 2004.

36 N. Lawson, 'Irrelevant academic qualifications an insult to nurses – and useless to their patients: Is it the end for nurses?', *The Times*, 26 December 1996.

37 M. Devlin, 'Should our nurses be clever or caring?', *Irish Independent*, 11 August 1997.

38 M. Philips, 'How the college girls destroyed nursing', *The Sunday Times*, 10 January 1999.

39 J. Magnet, 'What's wrong with nursing?', *Prospect Magazine*, December 2003, pp. 40–45. *Prospect Magazine* is published by the think tank Civitas.

40 J. Magnet, 'Sickened by the nurses who don't care', *The Sunday Times*, 23 November 2003. This is a shortened version of Magnet's *Prospect* article, which was also the basis for an interview between Magnet and Josie Irwin on BBC Radio 4's *Today* programme, broadcast on 17 November 2003. Magnet's views were also reported in the *Daily Mail*.

41 H. Sergeant, 'The truth about NHS hospitals: nurses – I would not trust my dog, let alone my mother, to many nurses', *The Daily Telegraph*, 29 November 2003. Sergeant wrote three articles for the *Daily Telegraph*, which were published between 29 November and 2 December 2003. These articles were based on her report for the Centre for Policy Studies, *Managing not to Manage*, published on 2 December 2003.

42 Lawson, 'Irrelevant academic qualifications.'

43 Devlin, 'Should our nurses be clever or caring?' The Diploma in Nursing programme was introduced in Ireland on a phased basis from 1994. The programme established the first links between pre-registration nursing and higher education in Ireland and the first academic award for students at the point of entry to practice.

44 *Ibid.*

45 K. Myers, 'An Irishman's Diary', *Irish Times*, 28 March 2002.

46 *Ibid.*

47 Magnet, 'What's wrong with nursing?'

48 In an interview with Marion Finucane on RTÉ Radio 1, 8 December 2003. The interview coincided with the publication of Tormey's book, entitled *A Cure for the Crisis: Irish Healthcare in Context* (Dublin: Blackwell Press, 2003). The pre-registration BSc (Nursing) degree commenced in 2002.

49 Myers, 'An Irishman's Diary'.

50 Meerabeau, 'Be good, sweet maid.'

51 E. Meerabeau, 'Back to the bedpans: the debates over pre-registration nursing education in England', *Journal of Advanced Nursing*, 34 (4), 2001, pp. 427–35.

52 I. Murray, 'Back to the bedpans for student nurses', *The Times*, 16 January 1999.

53 Magnet, 'What's wrong with nursing?'
54 H. Sergeant, *Managing not to Manage*, p. 63.
55 Davitt's address to the nurses.
56 P. J. Gannon, 'The Nursing Profession and Its Needs – Comment No. 8' *Studies*, 31, 1942, p. 292.
57 Rafferty, 'Practice made perfect.'
58 C. Fagin and D. Diers, 'Nursing as metaphor', *The New England Journal of Medicine*, 309 (2), 1983, pp. 116–17.
59 Rafferty, 'Practice made perfect'.
60 C. J. Ward, 'Risk management: does it work? The U.S. and Ireland experience', *Medico-Legal Journal of Ireland*, 8 (1), 2002, pp. 14–22. Ward is Clinical Professor at the Department of Gynaecology and Obstetrics, Emory University School of Medicine, Georgia.
61 *Ibid*., p. 22.
62 *Ibid*.
63 *Ibid*. (Original emphasis).
64 Anon. 'Academic skills emphasis a threat to standards in Irish nursing', *Irish Medical News*, 19 (34), 16 September 2002, p. 10.
65 C. Lally, 'Close Beaumont and start from scratch', *The Irish Times*, 19 November 2002, p. 7. The nursing degree to which Hickey is reported as referring to here commenced two months prior to the article's publication and would not produce its first graduates until mid-2006. Far from 'flooding' the healthcare system, nursing undergraduates had not even entered the clinical areas at the time.
66 P. Redlich, 'Heart baby's death not a once-off horror', *Sunday Independent*, 6 July 2003.
67 *Ibid*.
68 *Ibid*. Redlich ignored or appeared to be unaware of the fact that training places reached record numbers with the commencement of the degree programmes. Since 2002, all places for general nursing have been filled as demand has exceeded supply. Redlich also appears not to recognise that the 'in-service trainees' to whom she refers are unlikely to have contributed to the staffing levels in a paediatric intensive care unit. She contradicts herself when she states her belief that 'a plethora of nursing duties do not require a four-year academic nursing degree', a trained nursing grade for some aspects of patient care should have been introduced 'leaving the academic nurses for specialist tasks like intensive care for babies.' Redlich's point now appears to be that it was a shortage of the very 'academic nurses' to be produced by degree programmes that contributed to the tragedy.
69 Philips, 'How the college girls destroyed nursing.'
70 M. Baynham, 'Academic writing in new and emergent discipline areas', in R. Harrison, F. Reeve, A. Hanson and J. Clarke (eds), *Supporting Lifelong Learning: Vol. 1 – Perspectives on Learning* (London: Routledge/Falmer and The Open University, 2002), pp. 188–202.

Chapter 5

1 G. M. Fealy, 'A History of the Provision and Reform of General Nurse Education and Training in Ireland, 1879–1994', Volumes I and II, Unpublished PhD Thesis, University College Dublin, 2002.
2 Anon., 'The Nurses of the Irish Hospitals: No III: St Patrick's Home for supplying trained

nurses to the sick poor in their own homes', *The Lady of the House*, 15 February 1895, p. 5.

3 G. M. Fealy, '"The good nurse": visions and values in images of the nurse', *Journal of Advanced Nursing*, 64 (5), 2004, pp. 649–56.

4 S. E. Lederer and N. Rogers, 'Media' in R. Cooter and J. Pickstone (eds), *Companion to Medicine in the Twentieth Century* (London: Routledge, 2000), pp. 487–502.

5 For a discussion of what historians can learn from film, see K. R. M. Short, 'Introduction: feature films as history' in K. R. M. Short (ed.), *Feature Films as History* (London: Croom Helm, 1981), pp. 16–36.

6 As well as explaining approaches to film sources, Grenville also explains why historians were reluctant to take up this source in J. A. Grenville, *Film as History: the Nature of Film Evidence* (Birmingham: Birmingham University Publications, 1971). Other historians to deal with this were J. Richards and A. Aldgate, *British Cinema and Society 1930–70* (Oxford: Oxford University Press, 1983); P. Smith (ed.), *The Historian and Film* (Cambridge: Cambridge University Press, 1978); and P. Sorlin, *The Film in History: Restyling the Past* (Oxford: Blackwell, 1980).

7 P. A. Kalisch and B. J. Kalisch, *The Changing Image of the Nurse* (California: Addison-Wesley, 1987); J. Hallam, *Nursing the Image: Media, Culture and Professional Identity* (London: Routledge, 2000); M. Shortland, *Medicine and Film: A Checklist* (Survey and Research Resource, Oxford: Wellcome Unit for the History of Medicine, 1989); M. S. Newby, 'Overview of nursing films from 1900 and the source problems of such feature films', paper presented at 'Nursing at the Movies' (Workshop), RCN Nursing History Society, London, 5 May 1989; M. S. Newby, 'Nursing at the movies', *Nursing Standard* 32 (3), 1989, p. 13; M. S. Newby, 'Reel nurses: portrayal of British nurses in feature films, 1930s to 1990s', paper presented at 'Nursing, Women's History and Politics of Welfare Conference', Nottingham University, September 1996.

8 Lederer and Rogers, 'Media', pp. 489–90.

9 Cited in Lederer and Rogers, 'Media', p. 492.

10 J. Hallam, 'From angels to handmaidens: changing constructions of nursing's public image in post-war Britain', *Nursing Inquiry*, 5, 1998, pp. 32–42.

11 Lederer and Rogers, 'Media', p. 499.

12 *Ibid.*

13 Hallam, 'From angels to handmaidens', p. 36.

14 A. M. Rafferty, 'Nurses' in Cooter and Pickstone, *Companion to Medicine*, pp. 519–29.

15 J. Hallam 'From angels to handmaidens', p. 35.

16 P. A. Kalisch and B. J. Kalisch, 'Improving the image of nursing', *American Journal of Nursing*, 83 (1), 1983, pp. 48–51.

17 M. McLoone, 'Strumpet City: the urban working class on television' in M. McLoone and J. McMahon (eds), *Television and Irish Society: 21 Years of Irish Television* (Dublin: RTÉ and Irish Film Institute, 1984), pp. 53–88. For a brief account of the work of Sydney Olcott, see A. Flynn, *Irish Film 100 Years* (Bray: Kestrel Books, 1996). For an examination of romantic images of Ireland, see M. McLoone, *Irish Film: the Emergence of a Contemporary Cinema* (London: British Film Institute, 2000), pp. 33–59.

18 For a discussion on the 'first wave' of indigenous film in Ireland, see McLoone, *Irish Film*, pp. 131–50.

19 A. Kuhn and S. Radstone, *The Women's Companion to International Film* (London: Virago, 1990).

20 H. Byrne, '"Going to the pictures": the female audience and the pleasure of cinema' in M. J. Kelly and B. O'Connor (eds), *Media Audiences in Ireland: Power and Culture*

(Dublin: UCD Press, 1997), pp. 88–106.

21 McLoone, *Irish Film*, p. 150. For a critical analysis of nationalist, religious and feminist aspects of *Hush-a-Bye-Baby*, see E. B. Cullingford, 'Virgins, and mothers: Sinéad O'Connor, Neil Jordan and The Butcher Boy', *The Yale Journal of Criticism*, 15 (1), 2002, pp. 185–210.

22 T Ryall, 'The notion of genre', *Screen*, 11 (2), 1970, pp. 22–33; S. Neale, *Genres* (London: BFI, 1980). For a concise overview of the subject of film genres, see T. Ryall, 'Genre and Hollywood' in J. Hill and P. C. Gibson (eds), *The Oxford Guide To Film Studies* (Oxford: Oxford University Press, 1998), pp. 327–38. For debate on film genres, see K. Grant (ed.), *Film Genre Reader 2* (Austin: University of Texas, 1995). See also R. Altman, *Film /Genre* (London: BFI, 1999).

23 Available at www.imdb.com. The quotes are from an external review of *The Verdict*.

24 *Ibid.*

25 K. Rockett, '1930s Fictions' in K. Rockett, L. Gibbons and J. Hill (eds), *Cinema and Ireland* (New York: Syracuse University, 1988), p. 59.

26 According to Reilly, 'the roles of female Irish doctors, nurses, ambulance drivers, canteen workers and numerous other war occupations have not been studied at all'. See E. Reilly, 'Women and voluntary work' in A. Gregory and S. Paseta (eds), *Ireland and the Great War* (Manchester: Manchester University Press, 2003), p. 67.

27 Rockett, '1930s Fictions', pp. 58, 60–69; J. Hill, 'Images of violence' in Rockett *et al.*, *Cinema and Ireland*, pp. 147–93.

28 Actor and playwright Gerard Healy produced the drama-documentaries *Voyage of Discovery* on tuberculosis and *Stop Thief!* on diphtheria between 1948 and 1951. See Rockett *et al.* (eds), *Cinema and Ireland*, pp. 80, 92n.

29 McLoone, *Irish Film*, p. 38. See also Rockett *et al.* (eds), *Cinema and Ireland*, pp. 202–03.

30 Rockett *et al.*, *Cinema and Ireland*, p. 100.

31 M. Daniels, 'Exile or opportunity? Irish nurses and midwives', *Occasional Papers in Irish Studies*, 5 (Liverpool: Liverpool University, 1993), p. 5.

32 J. Clarke and C. O'Neill, 'An analysis of how the *Irish Times* portrayed Irish nursing during the 1999 strike', *Nursing Ethics*, 8 (4), 2001, pp. 350–59.

33 Anon., 'Nurse of the year', *World of Irish Nursing*, 3 (7), 1974, p. 118.

34 *Ibid.*

35 For an analysis of *The Late Late Show* and its social role in Irish public life, see M. Earls, 'The Late Late Show, controversy and context' in McLoone and McMahon, *Television and Irish Society*, pp. 107–23.

36 *Nurses*, Episodes 1 to 6 (Galway: Power Pictures for RTÉ, 2001), Series director Niamh Walsh.

37 For a discussion on the political context for the introduction of the Sweepstake, see M. E. Daly, '"An atmosphere of sturdy independence": the State and the Dublin hospitals in the 1930s' in E. Malcolm and G. Jones (eds), *Medicine, Disease and the State in Ireland 1650–1940* (Cork: Cork University Press, 1999), pp. 234–52.

38 M. Carney (Personal communication), March 2004.

39 For a discussion of the metaphors that underlie the concept of 'nurse', see C. Fagin and D. Diers, 'Nursing as metaphor', *The New England Journal of Medicine*, 309 (2), 1983, pp. 116–17.

40 Hallam, 'From angels to handmaidens', p. 40.

41 *Ibid.*

42 A. J. Davis, A. Hershberger, L. C. Ghan and J. Y. Lin, 'The good nurse: descriptions from the People's Republic of China', *Journal of Advanced Nursing*, 15, 1990, pp.

829–34; Fealy, 'The good nurse', p. 652.

43 S. Taylor, 'Locating and conducting discourse analytic research' in M. Wetherell, S. Taylor and S. J. Yates (eds), *Discourse as Data: a Guide for Analysis* (London: Sage Publications, 2001), pp. 5–21.

44 *Ibid.*, p. 6.

45 B. Crowther, 'Viewing what comes naturally: a feminist approach to television natural history', *Women's Studies International Forum*, 20 (2), 1997, pp. 289–300.

46 *Ibid.*, p. 299.

47 Lederer and Rogers, 'Media', p. 500.

48 *Ibid.*; Byrne, 'Going to the pictures', pp. 88–106.

49 M. J. Kelly and B. O'Connor, 'Introduction' in Kelly and O'Connor, *Media Audiences*, pp. 1–16.

50 N. Fairclough, 'The discourse of New Labour: critical discourse analysis' in Wetherell, Taylor and Yates, *Discourse as Data*, pp. 229–66.

51 Hallam, 'From angels to handmaidens', p. 32.

PART II

Chapter 6

PRO (Public Record Office); TNA (National Archives of the UK); WO (War Office)

1 The primary sources on which this chapter is based are as follows: The annual reports of the Board of Superintendence of the Dublin Hospitals for the period; Members of QAIMNS, Reminiscent Sketches 1914–19 (London: John Bale and Danielson, 1922); National Archives of Ireland (NAI): F 1487/Dublin (D)/A-B Nurses' Insurance Society of Ireland; Royal College of Surgeons in Ireland: Royal City of Dublin Hospital, Nursing Committee minutes; Report of Joint War Committee of British Red Cross Society and Order of St John (London: HMSO, 1921); The National Archives of the United Kingdom: Public Record Office, War Office files. In addition, contemporary journals of the period were used. These included *British Journal of Nursing, British Medical Journal, Nursing Times* and *Red Cross* (the magazine of the British Red Cross Society).

Secondary sources were: H. C. Burdett, *How to Succeed as a Trained Nurse* (London: Scientific Press, 1913); D. Fitzpatrick, *Ireland and the First World War* (Dublin: Trinity History Workshop, 1986); D. Fitzpatrick, 'The Overflow of the Deluge: Anglo-Irish relationships 1914–18', in O. MacDonagh and W. F. Mandle (eds), *Ireland and Irish Australia: Studies in Cultural and Political History* (London: Croom Helm, 1986); I. Hay, *One Hundred Years of Army Nursing: The Story of the British Army Nursing Services from the Time of Florence Nightingale to the Present Day* (London: Cassell, 1953); K. Jeffrey, *Ireland and the Great War* (Cambridge: Cambridge University Press, 2000); L. MacDonald, *The Roses of No Man's Land* (Penguin: London, 1993); J. Piggott, *Queen Alexandra's Royal Army Nursing Corps* (London: Lee Cooper, 1990).

2 *British Medical Journal*, 4 March 1905, p. 504.

3 *British Medical Journal*, 5 October 1901, p. 1030.

4 TNA: PRO WO 399/1630.

5 Memorial to Irish nurses who died in the Great War, St Anne's Cathedral, Belfast, Northern Ireland.

6 *Report of Joint War Committee of British Red Cross Society and Order of St John* (London: HMSO, 1921), p. 91.

7 *British Medical Journal*, 26 February 1916, p. 323.
8 *Nursing Times*, X, 502, 12 December 1914, p. 1547.
9 *Joint War Committee*, p. 727.
10 *Nursing Times*, X, 502, 12 December 1914, p. 1572; *British Journal of Nursing*, 53, 5 December 1914, p. 449.
11 Matron-in-chief, QAIMNS, 'Preface', in Members of HM QAIMNS, *Reminiscent Sketches 1914–19* (London: John Bale and Danielson, 1922), p. iii.
12 TNA: PRO WO 399/6334.
13 TNA: PRO WO 399/1220: Miss Beecher, matron-in-chief, QAIMNS to Miss Sidney Browne, matron-in-chief, Territorial Force Nursing Service, 4 September 1916.
14 Royal College of Surgeons in Ireland (RCSI): Royal City of Dublin Hospital (RCDH) Nursing Committee minutes, August 1914–December 1918; Board of Superintendence of the Dublin Hospitals, *Annual Report*, 1917–18.
15 TNA: PRO WO 399/3334; WO 399/1220; WO 399/1138; WO 399/1425; WO 399/3670; WO 399/3734; WO 399/8510.
16 TNA: PRO WO 399/1425; WO 399/1858.
17 TNA: PRO WO 399/3734.
18 Board of Superintendence of the Dublin Hospitals, *Annual Report*, 1915; *British Journal of Nursing*, 55, 24 July 1915, p. 69.
19 *British Medical Journal*, 28 August 1915, p. 344.
20 TNA: PRO WO 399/9177; WO 399/6334; WO 399/8723; WO 399/1858; WO 399/3734; WO 399/3670.
21 TNA: PRO WO 399/9177.
22 TNA: PRO WO 399/1220.
23 TNA: PRO WO 399/8510; WO 399/9177.
24 TNA: PRO WO 399/1425.
25 TNA: PRO WO 399/8510; WO 399/1630; WO 399/9177; WO 399/3734; WO 399/1858.
26 Hay, *One Hundred Years*, p. 117.
27 *British Medical Journal*, 22 January 1916, p. 141.
28 QAIMNS, *Reminiscent Sketches*, p. 56–59.
29 *British Medical Journal*, 30 September 1916, p. 467.
30 TNA: PRO WO 399/9177, WO 399/1858, WO 399/3734, WO 399/8510, WO 399/1630; WO 399/6931; WO 399/1138.
31 TNA: PRO WO 222/2134: Appendix P (13/7/1919).
32 TNA: PRO WO 399/9177; WO 399/1858; WO 399/3734; WO 399/8510; WO 399/1630.
33 QAIMNS, *Reminiscent Sketches*, p. 43.
34 TNA: PRO WO 222/2134: Appendix P (13/7/1919).
35 QAIMNS, *Reminiscent Sketches*, p. 45.
36 *Ibid.*, p. 46.
37 Piggott, *Queen Alexandra's*, p. 50.
38 TNA: PRO WO 399/1527; WO 399/9177; WO 399/1630.
39 TNA: PRO WO 399/9177.
40 TNA: PRO WO 399/8135.
41 Allowances for board, lodging and laundry applied to both groups and therefore do not skew the data.
42 TNA: PRO WO 399/2011: appendix to Army Form A2; RCSI: RCDH Nursing Committee minutes, 1908–18; Burdett, *How to Succeed*, p. 10.

43 TNA: PRO WO 399/3670; WO 399/8510; WO 399/8135.
44 *British Medical Journal*, 4 July 1908, p. 59.
45 TNA: PRO PMG 42/1: Disability Retired Pay, Gratuities &c, Ministry of Pensions.
46 TNA: PRO WO 399/1970.
47 Burdett, *How to Succeed*, p. 67; *Joint War Committee*, pp. 84–85.
48 TNA: PRO WO 399/1138; WO 399/1220.
49 TNA: PRO WO 399/9177.
50 TNA: PRO WO 399/3734.
51 TNA: PRO WO 399/3334; WO 399/1220.
52 Hay, *Army Nursing*, p. 111.
53 TNA: PRO WO 399/3734.
54 Burdett, *How to Succeed*, p. 66.
55 TNA: PRO PMG 42/1-42/2: Disability Retired Pay, Gratuities &c, Ministry of Pensions.
56 *British Medical Journal*, 1 April 1916, p. 498; *British Medical Journal*, 24 November 1917, p. 702.
57 TNA: PRO PMG 42/1 - 42/2.
58 TNA: PRO PMG 42/1: Disability Retired Pay, Gratuities &c, Ministry of Pensions.
59 TNA: PRO WO 399/7960; WO 399/8679; WO 399/2011; WO 222/2134: Army Nursing Services France 1914–18; *British Journal of Nursing*, 55, 9 October 1915, p. 292; *British Journal of Nursing*, 57, 23 September 1916, p. 258; *British Journal of Nursing*, 61, 9 November 1918, p. 283; *British Medical Journal*, 9 October 1915, p. 550.
60 TNA: WO 399/1970.
61 TNA: PRO WO 222/2134: Army Nursing Services France 1914–18.
62 TNA: PRO WO 399/1527.
63 TNA: PRO WO 399/2646.
64 TNA: PRO WO 399/1970; WO 399/7960.
65 TNA: PRO WO 399/1527; WO 399/1970; WO 399/8723.
66 TNA: PRO WO 399/1970; National Archives of Ireland (NAI): F 1487/Dublin (D)/A-B Nurses' Insurance Society of Ireland.
67 British Red Cross Society, *Red Cross*, VII, 2, 15 February 1920, p. 16.
68 TNA: PRO WO 399/3670.
69 TNA: PRO WO 399/1858.
70 TNA: PRO WO 222/2134: Appendix N. Summary of report of decorations awarded to nursing staff in the British Expeditionary Force.
71 TNA: PRO WO 222/2134: Appendix N.
72 RCSI, Royal City of Dublin Hospital (Baggot Street), Nursing Committee minutes, 1917-18.
73 TNA: PRO WO 399/1630.
74 TNA: PRO WO 399/1527.
75 *British Medical Journal*, 3 July 1915, p. 27; Commonwealth War Graves Commission 624622; TNA: PRO WO 399/1630; *British Journal of Nursing*, 57, 23 September 1916, p. 258.
76 TNA: PRO WO 399/3670.
77 TNA: PRO WO 399/8510.
78 TNA: PRO WO 399/1220.

Chapter 7

1 The chapter title is a quotation from M. Dunn, 'Lady Superintendent of Queen Victoria's Jubilee Nurses in Ireland', *The Lady of the House*, 1893, p. 12.
2 Many were absentee landlords.
3 For further details of the development of Dublin in this period and the associated problems see M. Daly, *Dublin: the Deposed Capital* (Cork: Cork University Press, 1984); J. Prunty, *Dublin Slums, 1800–1925* (Dublin: Irish Academic Press, 1998).
4 In Belfast, by contrast, there were extensive tracts of new working-class housing. See F. Aalen 'Health and Housing in Dublin c.1850 to 1921', in F. Aalen and K. Whelan (eds), *Dublin City and County* (Dublin: Geography Publications, 1992).
5 Prunty, *Slums*.
6 Daly, *Dublin*, p. 276.
7 J. Tuke, *The Condition of Donegal* (London: Ridgway, 1889), p. 25.
8 R. Barrington, *Health, Medicine and Politics in Ireland 1900–1970* (Dublin: Institute of Public Administration, 1987), p. 10.
9 This activity was regarded with some suspicion by fellow Catholics, as until then, female religious congregations had traditionally been enclosed orders.
10 It was this order that opened St Vincent's Hospital in Dublin as a hospital for the sick poor in 1834.
11 The Sisters of Mercy founded the Mater Misericordiae Hospital in Dublin in 1861.
12 M. Luddy, *Women and Philanthropy in Nineteenth-century Ireland* (Cambridge: Cambridge University Press, 1995), p. 196.
13 Although active in caring for the poor, neither the Sisters of Charity nor the Sisters of Mercy trained lay nurses when certified nurse training was introduced in the Dublin voluntary hospitals in the 1870s and 1880s. See A. Wickham, 'A better scheme for nursing: the influence of the Dublin Hospital Sunday Fund on nursing and nurse training in Ireland in the nineteenth century', *International History of Nursing Journal*, 6 (2), 2001, pp. 26–34.
14 M. A. Nutting and L. A. Dock, *A History of Nursing, Vol. III* (London: Putnams, 1912); *Dublin Journal of Medical Science*, Report of Homes 8th Annual Report.
15 *Ibid.*, p. 109.
16 The building was also occupied by a Protestant Servants Home; see *Thoms Directory*.
17 H. C. Burdett, *The Nursing Profession: How and Where to Train* (London: Scientific Press, 1899); M. Stocks, *A Hundred Years of District Nursing* (London: George Allen and Unwin, 1960).
18 M. Baly, *A History of the Queen's Nursing Institute* (London: Croom Helm, 1987).
19 M. Preston, 'Lay Women and Philanthropy in Dublin 1860–1880', *Eire/Ireland*, 28 (4), 1993.
20 In the case of Ireland, the sum at that time was £19,000.
21 The Dublin committee consisted of: Gerald Fitzgibbon, James Alyle, William Perrin, R. O'B Furlong, R. P. Carton, QC, Joseph Woodlock, Charles Kennedy, James Talbot Power and Jonathan Hogg.
22 Wellcome Institute for the History of Medicine, Contemporary Medical Archives Centre, The Queen's Nursing Institute, SA/QNI//S2/1/1. Letter from the chairman of the QVJIN council to J. Hogg, honorary secretary to the Dublin Committee.
23 The City of Dublin Nursing Institution had come into being during the earlier phase of nursing reform when certificated training had been introduced in the principal voluntary hospitals in Dublin. The institution was financed by some members of the board of governors of the City of Dublin Hospital, and although bearing a shared name

and providing probationers to that hospital, it operated separately from the City of Dublin Hospital.

24 Lay Catholic nurses were trained at Dr Steevens' Hospital under a scheme established in 1882 by Mrs Eliza Browne at 26 Usher's Quay. The nurses were referred to as 'Mrs Browne's Nurses'.

25 Stocks, *A Hundred Years*, p. 85.

26 Wellcome Institute, SA/QNI/c2/10.

27 Miss St Clair was Scottish and Miss Noble was English.

28 Jane Thompson was noted as being deeply involved in the running of the home. She was honorary secretary for many years, visited the home every day and collected funds for it until her death in 1894. See C. MacSorley, *St Patrick's Nurses Home* (Dublin: Ponsonby and Gibbs, 4 [no date]).

29 Wellcome Institute, SA/QNI/c2/10. Letter from Jane Thompson, 26 February 1892.

30 Wellcome Institute, SA/QNI/c2/10. Letter from Mary Dunn to Mr Rathbone, 25 February 1892.

31 Wellcome Institute, SA/QNI/s2/1/1/. Letter of 5 March 1804.

32 Wellcome Institute, SA/QNI/S2/1/1/.

33 The nurses were Broe, Filder, Walsh and Shaw.

34 Wellcome Institute, SA/QNI/c2/10. Letter of 25 February 1892.

35 This matter also constituted a continuing problem.

36 P. Scanlan, *The Irish Nurse: A Study of Nursing in Ireland: History and Education, 1718–1981* (Manorhamilton: Drumlin, 1991), p. 86. Scanlan uncovered these records while undertaking her doctoral research. It is known that there are some records remaining but they are the property of an individual and, to date, access has been refused to researchers.

37 *Ibid.*

38 M. Preston, 'The good nurse: women philanthropists and the evolution of nursing in Dublin', *New Hibernia Review*, 2 (1), 1998, pp. 91–110.

39 The ratio was sixty-four Protestants to thirty-nine Catholics (data derived from Queen's Nursing Institute records).

40 The numbers were 102 Catholics to 82 Protestants.

41 37.5 per cent of these were Catholic and 62.5 per cent were Protestant.

42 This has been compiled from the individual records of nurses as they registered as Queen's nurses. Their religious affiliation has been derived from their place of training.

43 These percentages are derived from the foregoing figures.

44 These figures are derived from the Queen's Nursing Institute Records.

45 This pattern revealed by the Queen's Nursing Institute Archives is also confirmed by the recollections of Annie Smithson. See A. Smithson, *Myself and Others* (Dublin: Talbot Press, 1944) p. 173.

46 West of Ireland Association, *First Annual Report*, p. 40.

47 *Ibid.*

48 See, for example, E. Lengel, 'A "Perverse and ill-fated people": English perceptions of the Irish 1845–52', *Essays in History*, 38, 1996.

49 There are many books recording Irish folk cures. See, for example, S. Henry, *Tales from the West of Ireland* (Cork: Mercier Press, 1999). For an account of beliefs in miraculous cures see L. Geary, 'Prince Hohenlohe, Signor Pastorini and Miraculous Healing in Early Nineteenth-Century Ireland', in E. Malcolm and G. Jones (eds), *Medicine Disease and the State in Ireland 1650–1940* (Cork: Cork University Press, 1999), pp. 40–58.

50 West of Ireland Association, *First Annual Report*, p. 40.

51 In 1901, the association requested the QVJIN to continue this grant, as the association's funds were so low. See West of Ireland Association, *First Annual Report*, p. 40.
52 *Ibid.*
53 The IAOS had been set up as an attempt to rebuild agriculture in Ireland, particularly through agricultural co-operation.
54 Presumably the same Ms Kenny acting as local secretary for the West of Ireland Association in Mayo.
55 *The Irish Homestead*, 23 February 1901.
56 Those present were the Reverend Peter Finlay, SJ, who became chairman, Lady Plunket, Miss FitzGerald Kenny, Mrs Egerton, Miss Synnott, Miss Purser, Miss Boland, Mr H. F. Norman, Mr Anderson, Mr Russell, Dr Cox. The group who were present suggested members for a committee, these included: Father Finlay, Father O'Donovan, Lady Anne Daly, Miss Boland, Mrs Egerton, Miss Synnot, Lady Margaret Domville, Dr Cox, Mr P. Hannon, Reverend T. A. Finlay, The Honorable Horace Plunkett, Mr George Russell, Mr Anderson, Mr Norman, Miss FitzGerald Kenny, Mrs Stafford, Lady Plunket, Miss Purser, Madame De Bunsen, and Lady Arnott.
57 *The Irish Homestead*, 21 December 1901.
58 Pamphlet on the *Queen's Commemoration Fund for Providing Jubilee Nurses for the Irish* (nd).
59 *Lady Dudley's Scheme for the Establishment of District Nurses in the Poorest Parts of Ireland, First Annual Report*, p. 16.
60 M. Martin, 'St Lawrence's Catholic Home', *The Irish Monthly*, Vol. XXI, 17 January 1893.
61 'The Nursing of the Poor', *The Irish Homestead*, 23 February 1901, p. 126.
62 A. Summers, 'A Home from home: women's philanthropic work in the nineteenth century', in S. Burman (ed.), *Fit Work for Women* (London: Croom Helm, 1979), p. 59.
63 Smithson, *Myself and Others*, p. 173.
64 The presidents of the associations tended to be women of the highest social status in the local community. For example, Lady Rathdonnel in Dundalk, see *Dundalk District Nursing Association, 8th Annual Report*, 1902; Lady Castletown in Doneraile, See *Doneraile District Nursing Association, First Annual Report*, 1907; the Marchioness of Dufferin and Ava, see *Bangor District Nursing Society, 8th Annual Report*, 1905.
65 Lady Dudley's Nursing Scheme: *Third Annual Report*, 1905–06.
66 *Ibid.*, *Sixth Annual Report*, 1908, p. 15.
67 *Ibid.*, *Seventh Annual Report*, 1909, p. 13.
68 *Ibid.*, *Sixth Annual Report*, 1908, p.12.
69 *Ibid.*, *Eighth Annual Report*, 1910, p. 14.
70 *Ibid.*, *Fourth Annual Report*, 1906–1907, p. 19. Details of the work and conditions experienced by those working as Lady Dudley nurses in the west can be gleaned from the reports from individual nurses that were published each year in the annual reports. Whilst the need to raise money to fund the nurses and to expand the system undoubtedly led to the publication of such reports and to the photographs of the nurses at work that often accompanied them, there can be little doubt that these reports accurately reflected conditions. The establishment of the Congested Districts Board and its foundation reports, which provide harrowing details of the poverty of the western counties, suggest that the conditions the nurses describe are accurate.
71 A useful outline of nursing conditions can be found in M. Ó hÓgartaigh, 'Flower power and "mental grooviness": Nurses and midwives in Ireland in the early twentieth century', in B. Whelan (ed.), *Women and Paid Work in Ireland 1500–1930* (Dublin: Four Courts Press, 2000), pp. 133–47.

Chapter 8

1 This chapter is adapted from a paper published in the *All-Ireland Journal of Nursing and Midwifery*, 1, 2000, pp. 66–70. Funding for this study was provided by the Faculty of Nursing and Midwifery, Royal College of Surgeons in Ireland. The author wishes to thank Ríonach Uí Ógáin, Department of Irish Folklore, UCD, for her thoughtful review of this manuscript.

2 M. Stocks, A *Hundred Years of District Nursing* (London: George Allen and Unwin, 1960), p. 75.

3 Lady Dudley's Nursing Scheme, *Lady Dudley's Scheme for the Establishment of District Nurses in the Poorest Parts of Ireland, Eighth Annual Report*, 1910.

4 J. Murray, *Galway: A Medico-Social History* (Galway: Kenny's Bookshop, 1995).

5 A. Birrell, *Things Past Redress* (London: Faber and Faber Limited, 1937), p. 209

6 M. Quain, 'A day in the life of a Jubilee nurse' *Irish Nursing News*, June–July, 6–7, 1955.

7 M. Grossman, 'History: a way of knowing', *Canadian Journal of Nursing Research*, 26 (2), 1994, pp. 9–10.

Chapter 9

1 *The Malleus Maleficarum* was first published in 1439. A contemporary translation of the text is M. Summers, *The Malleus Maleficarum of Heinrich Kramer and James Sprenger* (New York: Dover Publications, 1971).

2 See J. Gélis, *History of Childbirth* (Cambridge: Polity Press, 1991), pp. 105–07.

3 The reason for this urgency to baptise was related to the fear that the 'evil woman' would take away the soul of the child.

4 N. B. White, 'A licence from a Bishop of Ossory to a Midwife', in *Journal of Archeological Society Kilkenny and Southeast Ireland*, 1866, pp. 412–13.

5 D. Wertz and R. Wertz, *Lying In: A History of Childbirth in America* (New York: Free Press, 1977).

6 E. Essen-Möller, 'A rare old Irish medical book', *Irish Journal of Medical Science*, 1932, pp. 312-314.

7 *Ibid.*

8 J. Wolveridge, *Speculum Matricis Hybernicum; Or, the Irish Midwives Handmaid* (London: E. Okes, 1671).

9 An electronic copy of the text is held in the Bodleian Library available from Early English Books Online at http://eebo.chadwyck. com/home. All references to *Speculum Matricis Hybernicum* in this chapter are to this electronic edition.

10 E. Roeslin, *The Byrth of Mankynde, Newly Translated out of Laten into Englysshe* (London: T. Raynald, 1540). This text is based on a translation by Richard Jonas of Roeslin's *Der Swangern Frauwen und Hebammen Rosegarten* (The Rose Garden for Pregnant Women and Midwives), (Argentine: Martinus Flach Junior, 1513), published in Worms.

11 W. Harvey, *Exercitationes de Generatione Animalium (On the Generation of Animals)* (London: Du-Gardianis, 1651), p. 276. Although this text laid the foundations for modern embryology, Harvey is best known for his discovery of the circulation of the blood, which he formally published in 1628 as *Exercitatio Anatomica de Motu Cordis et Sangiunis in Animalibus* (*Anatomical Treatise on the Movement of the Heart and Blood in Animals*).

12 Louise Bourgeois' writings were originally published in 1609 as the *Observations Diverses*

Sur La Sterilite, Perte de Fruict, Foecondite, Accouchements, et Maladies des Femmes, & Enfants Nouveaux Naiz. This is regarded as the first book on childbirth written by a midwife. Bourgeois was in service to the French court and attended Marie de Medici, Queen of France (1573–1642) during her labours. The first edition of the *Compleat Midwifes Practice* is attributed to T.C., I.D., M.S., and T.B (London: Nathaniel Brooke, 1656), and is noted to contain 'instructions of the Queen of France's midwife to her Daughter'.

13 N. Culpeper, *A Directory for Midwives, or, A Guide for Women in their Conception, Bearing, and Suckling their Children* (London: Peter Cole, 1656).

14 Percival Willughby's manuscript *Observations in Midwifery, as Also the Country Midwife's Opusculum or Vade Mecum* appears not to have reached a printed edition until the nineteenth century, when an edition was published by H. T. Cooke in Warwick in 1863.

15 Jacob Rüff, *The Expert Midwife* (London: E. G[riffin] for S. B[urton], 1637).

16 E. Shorter, *A History of Women's Bodies* (London: Allen Lane, 1982), p. 38.

17 A. Rich, *Of Woman Born: Motherhood as Experience and Institution* (London: Virago, 1977), p. 138.

18 Cited in Shorter, *A History of Women's Bodies*, pp. 35–36.

19 Wolveridge, *Speculum*, pp. A4–A5.

20 Harvey, *Exercitationes de Generatione Animalium*, p. 276.

21 Wolveridge, *Speculum*, pp. A5–A6.

22 See R. F. Foster, *Modern Ireland, 1600–1972* (London: Allen Lane Press, 1988).

23 A. Eccles, *Obstetrics and Gynecology in Tudor and Stewart England* (London: Croom Helm, 1982), p. 86.

24 See Gélis, *History of Childbirth*, p. 180–81.

25 T. P. Kirkpatrick, 'A note on the Speculum Matricis of James Wolveridge M.D.', *Irish Journal of Medical Science*, 1938, pp. 577–78.

26 Wolveridge, *Speculum*, p. 26.

27 *Ibid.*, p. 110.

28 *Ibid.*, p. 2.

29 Henry Daventer, *The Art of Midwifery Improv'd* (London: E. Curll, J. Pemberton and W. Taylor, 1716), p. 11.

30 J. Maubray, *The Female Physician* (London: J. Holland, 1724), p. 169.

31 H. Crooke, *Mikrokosmographia: A Description of the Body of Man* (London: William Iaggard, 1615), p. 276.

32 The charter, issued in 1756, states that the teaching of midwifery to doctors is an essential aspect of the Rotunda 'that it may prevent such Gentlemen as intend to practice Midwifery in our said Kingdom, from going abroad for Instruction.' See *A Copy of His Majesty's Royal Charter for Incorporating the Governors and Guardians of the Hospital for the Relief of Poor Lying-in Women in Dublin, 2 December, 1756*.

33 F. Ould, *A Treatise of Midwifry in Three Parts* (Dublin: Nelson and Connor, 1742), pp. 71–72.

34 M. Foucault, *The Birth of the Clinic, an Archaeology of Medical Perception* (London: Tavistock, 1976).

35 J. Murphy-Lawless, *Women and Childbirth: Male Medical Discourse and the Invention of Female Incompetence*, Unpublished PhD thesis, 1987, University of Dublin, Trinity College, Chapter 3.

36 W. Smellie, *A Treatise on the Theory and Practice of Midwifery in 3 Volumes* (London: D. Wilson, 1752). Smellie's technique of delivery of the after-coming head in a breech presentation with the infant resting on the physician's forearm is eponymously titled

'the Smellie method'.

37 P. M. Dunn, 'Bartholomew Mosse (1712–59), Sir Fielding Ould (1710–89), and the Rotunda Hospital, Dublin', *Arch. Dis. Child. Fetal Neonatal Ed*, 81 (1), 1999, F74–76.

38 Ould, *Treatise*, pp. 29–30.

39 *Ibid.*, p. ix.

40 *Ibid.*, p. x.

41 L. Jordanova, *Sexual Visions: Images of Gender in Science and Medicine between the Eighteenth and Twentieth Centuries* (Hemel Hempstead: Harvester Wheatsheaf, 1989), pp. 58–59.

42 L. Schiebinger, *The Mind Has No Sex?: Women in the Origins of Modern Science* (Cambridge, Mass.: Harvard University Press, 1989).

43 Ould, *Treatise*, p. 3.

44 Wolveridge, *Speculum*, p. 27.

45 Daventer, *Art of Midwifery*, p. 14.

46 *Ibid.*

47 Smellie, *A Treatise on the Theory and Practice of Midwifery*, pp. 448–49.

48 *Ibid.*, p. 449.

49 Elizabeth Nihell, *A Treatise on the Art of Midwifery Setting Forth Various Abuses therein, Especially as to the Practice of Instruments* (London, 1760), p. 71.

50 Ould, *Treatise*, p. xix.

51 *Ibid.*

52 Wolveridge, *Speculum*, preface.

53 Maubray, *The Female Physician*, p. 169. (Original emphasis).

54 See Ould, *Treatise*, p. 5. See also Smellie, *A Treatise on the Theory and Practice of Midwifery*.

55 See for example the classic account by Barbara Ehrenreich and Deirdre English, *Witches, Midwives and Nurses, A History of Women Healers* (New York: Feminist Press, 1973).

56 Shorter, *A History of Women's Bodies*, pp. 35–43.

57 Gélis, *History of Childbirth*, pp. 133–38.

58 Ould, *Treatise*, p. 30.

59 *Ibid.*, p. 64.

60 *Ibid.*, p. 50.

61 *Ibid.*, p. 58.

62 I. D. Graham, *Episiotomy: Challenging Obstetric Intervention* (London: Blackwell Science, 1997).

63 Ould did not use the term 'episiotomy'; the term was attributed to a doctor named Braun who used it in 1857 and who considered the operation ill-advised and unnecessary. See S. Inch, *Birthrights: a Parents' Guide to Modern Childbirth, 2nd Ed.* (London: Green Press, 1989), p. 133. The term is coined from Greek *epision* ('pubic region') and 'tomy' via modern Latin, 'tomia', from, ultimately, the Greek 'tomos', meaning 'cutting'.

64 Ould, *Treatise*, p. 145–46.

65 See S. B. Thacker, 'Midline versus mediolateral episiotomy', *British Medical Journal*, 320, 2000, pp. 1615–16. See also Graham, *Episiotomy*.

66 For example, see F. Stahl, 'Concerning the principles and practice of episiotomy – Why central preferable to lateral', *Ann. Gynaecol. Paediatr*, 8, 1895, pp. 674–677 and J. B. DeLee, 'The prophylactic forceps operation', *American Journal of Obstetrics and Gynecology*, 1, 1920, p. 34.

67 Ould, *Treatise*, p. 61.

68 Wolveridge, *Speculum*, p. 28.

69 *Ibid.*, p. 30.

70 M. Myles, *Myles Textbook for Midwives*, 9th ed. (London: Churchill Livingstone, 1981), p. 311.

71 J. Brown, 'Professional Language: Words that Succeed', *Radical History Review*, 34, 1986, pp. 33–51.

72 *Ibid.*, p. 37.

73 Ould, *Treatise*, p. 50.

74 *Ibid.*, p. 51.

75 See J. Murphy-Lawless, *Reading Birth and Death: A History of Obstetric Thinking* (Cork: Cork University Press, 1998).

76 Wolveridge, *Speculum*, p. 35.

77 L. Jordanova, 'Reproduction in the Eighteenth Century', in F. Ginsburg and R. Rapp (eds), *Conceiving the New World Order: The Global Politics of Reproduction* (Berkeley: University of California Press, 1995), p. 377.

78 *Ibid.*, pp. 370–71.

79 Ould, *Treatise*, p. vii.

80 Brown, 'Professional Language', p. 47.

Chapter 10

PCRCPI (Parliamentary Committee, Royal College of Physicians in Ireland)

1 J. Fleetwood, *The History of Medicine in Ireland* (Dublin: Browne and Nolan, 1983).

2 Evidence of Dr Lombe Atthill to the Select Committee on Midwives' Registration, 27 May 1892, paragraph 819, in Report from the Select Committees on Midwives' Registration, *British Parliamentary Papers, Health, General 15* (Shannon, 1970). See also *Dublin Journal of Medical Science*, April 1890, p. 21.

3 H. Handford, 'Monthly nurse or midwife?', *Public Health: The Journal of the Society of Medical Officers of Health*, February, 1909, pp. 177–80.

4 M. A. Kelly, 'The development of midwifery at the Rotunda', In A. Browne (ed.), *Masters, Midwives and Ladies-in-Waiting: The Rotunda Hospital 1745–1995* (Dublin: A & A Farmar, 1995), pp. 77–117. See also *Dublin Journal of Medical Science*, April 1890, p. 21.

5 Minutes of PCRCPI, 22 December 1890, Royal College of Physicians of Ireland, Kildare Street, Dublin.

6 *Ibid.*

7 *Ibid.*

8 Minutes of PCRCPI, 11 February 1891.

9 *Ibid.*

10 *Ibid.* This illustrates the fact that the RCPI was an important and influential lobby group in parliament, and could muster support at high levels at very short notice. It also indicates the interest that the RCPI was taking in the issue of midwife registration.

11 J. Towler and J. Bramall, *Midwives in History and Society* (London: Croom Helm, 1986).

12 Jean Donnison has dealt with this issue in great detail. See J. Donnison, *Midwives and Medical Men: a History of the Struggle for the Control of Childbirth*, 2nd ed. (New Barnet: Historical Publications, 1988).

13 Evidence of Dr Lombe Atthill to the Select Committee on Midwives' Registration, 27 May 1892, paragraph 812, *British Parliamentary Papers, Health, General 15* (Shannon, 1970).

14 *Ibid.*, paragraph 858.

15 Report of the Select Committee on Midwives' Registration, 8 August 1893, *British Parliamentary Papers*.

16 *Ibid.*

17 Minutes of PCRCPI, 31 October 1900.

18 Minutes of PCRCPI, 7 April 1898.

19 Evidence of Dr Lombe Atthill to Select Committee, 27 May 1892, paragraph 820, *British Parliamentary Papers*.

20 R. Barrington, *Health, Medicine and Politics in Ireland 1900–1970* (Dublin: Institute of Public Administration, 1987). The dispensary system did not operate in Britain and a salaried midwifery service was not provided in Britain until the 1930s. See E. Fox, 'Powers of life and death: aspects of maternal welfare in England and Wales between the wars', *Medical History*, 35, pp. 328–52.

21 Minutes of PCRCPI, 11 May 1898.

22 Minutes of PCRCPI, 1 May 1899.

23 *Ibid.*

24 Minutes of PCRCPI, letter to Irish MPs and members of the Standing Committee at Law, 26 March 1900; see also Minutes of PCRCPI, letter to Mr Heywood Johnstone and Sir William Moore, Bt, members of the Midwives' Bill committee, House of Commons, 11 April 1900; Minutes of PCRCPI, letter to the Clerk of the Privy Council, House of Commons, 1 May 1900.

25 This assertion was not however quantified.

26 Minutes of PCRCPI, 6 March 1902. The reason for this new objection is not clear from the material available.

27 *Ibid.*

28 R. Dingwall, A. M. Rafferty and C. Webster, *An Introduction to the Social History of Nursing* (London: Routledge, 1993), pp. 145–72.

29 Minutes of PCRCPI, 6 March 1902.

30 Donnison, *Midwives and Medical Men*, p. 172.

31 *Ibid.*

32 The role of the Irish members of parliament in opposing proposed legislation over a period of years, particularly when it did not at this point extend to Ireland, is most intriguing. It is alluded to but not explored in Donnison's work. See Donnison, *Midwives and Medical Men*. In her account of the Irish suffrage movement, Ward describes the opposition of the Irish Parliamentary Party to suffrage, at a somewhat later period, 1910–1913, and she describes the Irish Party as 'anti-feminist'. See Margaret Ward, '"Suffrage first – above all else!": An account of the Irish suffrage movement', in A. Smyth (ed.), *Irish Women's Studies Reader* (Dublin: Attic Press, 1993), pp. 20–44. Although outside the scope of the present discussion, the role of the Irish Party in relation to its opposition to the midwives bills and to legislation relating to women generally, is worth further exploration.

33 Minutes of PCRCPI, letter from Dr T. J. Stafford, 27 October 1906.

34 Barrington, *Health, Medicine and Politics*, p. 18.

35 Minutes of PCRCPI, 27 October 1906.

36 Minutes of PCRCPI, 30 April 1900.

37 Minutes of PCRCPI, 27 October 1906.

38 Minutes of Special Business Meeting, RCPI, 14 December 1906, Vol. 24, p. 1.

39 *Ibid.*

40 Minutes of the Monthly Business Meeting, RCPI, 4 January 1907, Vol. 24, p. 15.

41 Minutes of the Monthly Business Meeting, RCPI, 1 February 1907, Vol. 24, p. 20.
42 Minutes of PCRCPI, February 1907.
43 'Parliamentary Intelligence', *The Lancet*, 9 April 1910, p. 1039.
44 'Editorial: The Departmental Committee on the Midwives Act', *Public Health: The Journal of the Society of Medical Officers of Health*, 22 (5), 13 February 1909, p. 13. See also 'Editorial: The Midwives Act Amendment Bill and the Incorporated Midwives' Institute', *The Lancet*, 18 June 1910, pp. 1699–700.
45 *The Lancet*, 7 May 1910, p. 1293.
46 'Editorial', *The Lancet*, 18 June 1910, p. 1699.
47 Minutes of PCRCPI, 3 May 1910.
48 *The Lancet*, 2 July 1910, p. 64.
49 *Ibid.*
50 *Ibid.*, 25 June 1910, p. 1790.
51 *Ibid.*, 23 July 1910, p. 273.
52 Minutes of the Special Business Meeting of the RCPI, letter from Dr Andrew Horne to the Right Honourable A. Birrell, MP, chief secretary for Ireland, 22 July 1910, Vol. 24, p. 350.
53 *The Lancet*, 23 July 1910, p. 273.
54 Minutes of the Special Business Meeting of the RCPI, 16 June 1916, Vol. 25, pp. 342–44.
55 Minutes of the Monthly Business Meeting, RCPI, 7 July 1916, Vol. 25, p. 348.
56 *Ibid.*
57 Ward, 'Suffrage'. See also R. C. Owens, *Smashing Times: The History of the Irish Women's Suffrage Movement, 1889–1922* (Dublin: Attic Press, 1995); C. Murphy, 'A problematic relationship: European women and nationalism, 1870–1915', in M. G. Valiulis and M. O'Dowd (eds), *Women and Irish History: Essays in Honour of Margaret McCurtin* (Dublin: Wolfhound Press, 1997), pp. 144–58; R. C. Owens, 'Women and pacifism in Ireland, 1915–1932', in Valiulis and O'Dowd (eds), *Women and Irish History*, pp. 220–38; M. Jones, *Those Obstreperous Lassies: A History of the Irish Women Workers' Union* (Dublin: Gill and Macmillan, 1988); M. E. Daly, 'Women in the Irish Free State, 1922–1939: the interaction between economics and ideology', *Journal of Women's History*, 6 (4)/7 (1) (Winter/Spring, 1995), pp. 98–116. The activities of women involved in the development of Irish nursing and midwifery have not yet been explored to see to what extent they participated, as is likely, in the broader political events of their time.
58 Minutes of PCRCPI, 23 November 1917.
59 *Ibid.*
60 *Ibid*
61 *Ibid.*
62 Committee Stage, Midwives (Ireland) Bill, 24 January 1918, *Official Report, Parliamentary Debates*, House of Commons, 1918, Fifth Series, Vol. 101, Twelfth Volume of Session 1917, Monday 14 January 1918 to Wednesday 6 February 1918, p. 1742.
63 'Notice from the Privy Council Office, 13 September 1918', *The Dublin Gazette*, 17 September 1918, p. 1494.
64 Minutes of PCRCPI, 27 November 1917.
65 Minutes of a special meeting of the Central Midwives' Board Ireland, 13 March 1950.
66 Minutes of the Monthly Business Meeting, RCPI, 1 February 1918, Vol. 25, p. 456.
67 'Midwives' Board for Ireland', *The Lancet*, 25 May 1918, p. 756.
68 Notice from the Office of the Privy Council, *The Dublin Gazette*, p. 1494.

Chapter 11

1 D. Healy, 'Irish Psychiatry in the Twentieth Century', in H. Freeman and G. Berrios (eds), *150 Years of British Psychiatry, Volume II, the Aftermath* (London: Athlone Press, 1996).

2 B. Hensey, *The Health Services of Ireland* (Dublin: Institute of Public Administration, 1988).

3 *Nurses Registration (Ireland) Act* (H.C., Dublin: HMSO, 1919), 9 &10, c. 96.

4 J. Robins (ed.) *Nursing and Midwifery in Ireland in the Twentieth Century* (Dublin: An Bord Altranais, 2000).

5 C. Webster, 'Psychiatry and the early National Health Service: the role of the Mental Health Standing Advisory Committee', in Freeman and Berrios (eds), *150 Years*.

6 R. Barton, *Institutional Neurosis* (Bristol: J Wright and Son, 1959).

7 A. Digby, 'The changing profile of a nineteenth-century asylum: the York Retreat', *Psychological Medicine*, 14, 1984, pp. 739–48.

8 K. Jones, 'The culture of the mental hospital', in Berrios and Freeman (eds), *150 Years*.

9 E. Goffman, *Asylums* (New York: Anchor, 1961).

10 World Health Organisation, 'Technical Report Series No. 105', *Expert Committee on Psychiatric Nursing, First Report* (Geneva: WHO, 1956).

11 Department of Health, *Report of the Commission of Inquiry on Mental Illness* (Dublin: Thc Stationary Office, 1966).

12 A. Sheridan, 'An analysis of the activity patterns of psychiatric nurses practising in Ireland 1950–2000', Unpublished PhD Thesis, University of Birmingham, 2003.

13 *Ibid.*

14 D. Towell, *Understanding Psychiatric Nursing* (London: RCN, 1975).

15 T. A. Murphy, J. Robins, M. Byrne (eds), *Tumbling Walls: the Evolution of a Community Institution over 150 Years* (Portlaoise: Midland Health Board, 1983).

16 H. Henry, *Our Lady's Psychiatric Hospital Cork* (Cork: Haven Books, 1989).

Chapter 12

1 L. R. Seymer, *A General History of Nursing* (London: Faber and Faber, 1932).

2 M. Jolley, 'Retrospective: Pre-1900' in P. Allan and M. Jolley (eds), *Nursing, Midwifery and Health Visiting Since 1900* (London: Faber and Faber, 1982), pp. 19–32.

3 M. E. Baly, *Nursing and Social Change, 3rd ed.* (London: Routledge, 1995).

4 P. Ardern, *When Matron Ruled* (London: Robert Hale, 2002), p. 43.

5 *Ibid.*

6 A. V. Cowie, 'Organised labour', in Allan and Jolley (eds), *Nursing, Midwifery and Health Visiting*, pp. 215–32.

7 Jolley, 'Retrospective', p. 26

8 *Ibid*, p. 27.

9 F. Nightingale, *Notes on Nursing: What it is and what it is Not* (Facsimile of the 1860 Edition), (New York: Dover Publications Inc., 1969).

10 Cited in M. E. Doona, 'Sister Mary Joseph Croke: another voice from the Crimean War, 1854–1856', *Nursing History Review*, 3, 1995, pp. 3–41.

11 M. E. Doona, 'Careful Nursing: Ireland's Legacy to Nursing', *Third Annual Public Lecture for Nurses* (UCD: School of Nursing and Midwifery, 2000).

12 T. C. Meehan, 'Careful nursing: a model for contemporary nursing practice', *Journal of*

Advanced Nursing, 44 (1), 2003, pp. 99–107.

13 P. Druker, *The Practice of Management* (Oxford: Heinemann Professional Publishing, 1989), p. 3.

14 M. Stocks, *A Hundred Years of District Nursing* (George Allen and Unwin, London, 1960).

15 P. Scanlan, '*The Irish Nurse: A Study of Nursing in Ireland: History and Education, 1718–1981* (Manorhamilton: Drumlin, 1991), p. 63.

16 A. Pavey, *The Story of the Growth of Nursing* (London: Faber and Faber, 1938), p. 241.

17 The administration and organisation skills of Mother Mary Aikenhead, founder of the Irish Sisters of Charity, are described in: A Member of the Congregation, *The Life and Work of Mary Aikenhead* (London: Longmans and Green Company, 1924).

18 D. M. Saunders, 'Sick Children's Nursing', in Allan and Jolley (eds), *Nursing, Midwifery and Health Visiting*, pp. 141–49.

19 Cited in Saunders, 'Sick Children's Nursing', p. 143.

20 G. M. Fealy, 'A History of the Provision and Reform of General Nurse Education and Training in Ireland, 1879–1994, Volumes I and II', Unpublished PhD Thesis, UCD, 2002, Chapter 4.

21 Scanlan, *The Irish Nurse*, pp. 30–31

22 Fealy, 'History', Vol. I, Chapter 4.

23 *Ibid.*

24 *Ibid.*, Vol. I, p. 181.

25 J. D. H. Widdess, 'The Dublin House of Industry, 1772–1838', in W. Doolin and O. Fitzgerald (eds), *What's Past is Prologue* (Dublin: The Monument Press, 1952).

26 S. McGann, *The Battle of the Nurses: a Study of Eight Women who Influenced the Development of Professional Nursing, 1880–1930* (London: Scutari Press, 1992), pp. 130–59.

27 *Ibid.*, pp. 135–43. See also Fealy, 'History', Vol. I, Chapter 4. For an account of the role of Huxley as general secretary of the Dublin Metropolitan Technical School for Nurses, see G. Fealy, '"A place for the better technical education of nurses": The Dublin Metropolitan Technical School for Nurses' *Nursing History Review*, 13, 2005, pp. 23–47.

28 Fealy, 'History', Vol. I, p. 63.

29 *Ibid*, Vol. II, p. 31.

30 McGann, *Battle*, p. 133.

31 Anon., 'Obituary, Margaret Huxley, M.A., R.G.N., F.B.C.N.', *The British Journal of Nursing*, 88, 1940, pp. 31.

32 A. Reeves, 'An appreciation of the late Miss Margaret Huxley, R.G.N., M.A.', *The British Journal of Nursing*, 88, 1940, pp. 27–28.

33 Anon., 'The first Lady Nurse trained in Ireland to become a Hospital Superintendent', *The Lady of the House*, April 15, 1909, p. 6.

34 Fealy, 'History', Vol. I, pp. 175–78.

35 J. D. H. Widdess, *The Richmond, Whitworth and Hardwicke Hospital, St Lawrence's Hospital, Dublin, 1772–1972* (Dublin: Beacon Printing, c. 1972), p. 163.

36 Ardern, *When Matron Ruled*, pp. 74–86.

37 *Ibid.*, p. 82.

38 *Ibid.*, pp. 84 and 86.

39 Scanlan, *The Irish Nurse*, pp. 88–89.

40 B. N. Blake, 'The Irish Guild of Catholic Nurses', *Irish Nursing News*, 21 (1), 1942, pp. 6–7.

41 Cited in E. Cook, *The Life of Florence Nightingale* (London: Macmillan and Company, 1914).

42 D. Blenkinsop, 'The preparation of nurse managers', in Allan and Jolley (eds), *Nursing, Midwifery and Health Visiting*, pp. 158–65.
43 *Ibid*, p. 158.
44 H. A. Goddard, *Principles of Administration Applied to Nursing Service* (Geneva: World Health Organisation, 1958).
45 Royal College of Nursing and National Council of Nurses of the United Kingdom, *Administering the Hospital Nursing Service* (London: Royal College of Nursing, 1964).
46 Blenkinsop, 'Preparation', p. 160.
47 National Nursing Staff Committee, *A Report of the National Nursing Staff Committee on Staff Appraisal in the Hospital Nursing Service* (London: Royal College of Nursing, 1970).
48 In this period, a diploma in management for nurses was introduced by the Faculty of Nursing, Royal College of Surgeons in Ireland and at the Dundalk Institute of Technology, and a bachelor's degree in nursing management was introduced at the School of Nursing and Midwifery, UCD.
49 A. Hewison, 'The modern matron: reborn or recycled', *Journal of Nursing Management*, 9, 2001, pp. 187–89.